Henry Parry Liddon

Passiontide Sermons

Henry Parry Liddon

Passiontide Sermons

ISBN/EAN: 9783337085445

Printed in Europe, USA, Canada, Australia, Japan

Cover: Foto ©Lupo / pixelio.de

More available books at **www.hansebooks.com**

Passiontide Sermons

By H. P. LIDDON, D.D., D.C.L., LL.D.

LATE CANON AND CHANCELLOR OF ST. PAUL'S

LONDON
LONGMANS, GREEN, AND CO.
AND NEW YORK: 15 EAST 16TH STREET
1891

ADVERTISEMENT

AMONG the papers left by Dr. Liddon was a collection of Passiontide Sermons, which he is known to have intended for publication. It has seemed to his literary executors that no time should be lost in carrying out his intention with regard to these Sermons. They have added to them two (IV. and XIV.) also preached in Passiontide, two others (XVI. and XVII.) preached in Lent, and four short Sermons (XVIII.-XXI.) on the first four Penitential Psalms, preached by Dr. Liddon on Wednesdays in Lent, in his turn as Chancellor of St. Paul's Cathedral. The Sermons are arranged according to their subjects; and it has been thought best to print them in their entirety, although some repetition of doctrinal statements is necessarily involved in this course.

St. Andrew's Eve,
1890.

CONTENTS

SERMON I.
THE SINLESSNESS OF JESUS CHRIST.
St. John viii. 46.

Which of you convinceth Me of sin? 1

Preached at the Chapel Royal, Whitehall, on Passion Sunday, March 26, 1871.

SERMON II.
THE HUMILIATION OF THE ETERNAL SON.
Phil. ii. 5-8.

Let this mind be in you, which was also in Christ Jesus: Who, being in the form of God, thought it not robbery to be equal with God: but made Himself of no reputation, and took upon Him the form of a servant, and was made in the likeness of men: and being found in fashion as a man, He humbled Himself, and became obedient unto death, even the death of the cross . 18

Preached at St. Paul's on Palm Sunday, April 2, 1871.

SERMON III.
THE PERSON OF THE CRUCIFIED.
1 Cor. i. 13.

Was Paul crucified for you? 34

Preached at St. Paul's on Palm Sunday, April 6, 1884.

SERMON IV.

THE ACCEPTED OFFERING.

Heb. x. 5, 6, 7.

Wherefore when He cometh into the world, He saith, Sacrifice and offering Thou wouldest not, but a body hast Thou prepared Me: in burnt-offerings and sacrifices for sin Thou hast had no pleasure. Then said I, Lo, I come to do Thy will . . . 50

Preached at the Chapel Royal, Whitehall, on Passion Sunday, March 30, 1873.

SERMON V.

THE CLEANSING BLOOD.

Heb. ix. 13, 14.

For if the blood of bulls and of goats, and the ashes of an heifer sprinkling the unclean, sanctifieth to the purifying of the flesh: how much more shall the Blood of Christ, Who through the Eternal Spirit offered Himself without spot to God, purge your conscience from dead works to serve the living God? . . . 69

Preached at St. Paul's on Passion Sunday, April 7, 1878.

SERMON VI.

THE CONQUEROR OF SATAN.

Heb. ii. 14.

That through death He might destroy him that had the power of death, that is, the devil 83

Preached at St. Paul's on Passion Sunday, April 2, 1876.

SERMON VII.
THE CORN OF WHEAT.
St. John xii. 24.

Verily, verily, I say unto you, Except a corn of wheat fall into the ground and die, it abideth alone ; but if it die, it bringeth forth much fruit 100

Preached at St. Paul's on Good Friday, April 11, 1873.

SERMON VIII.
THE APPEAL OF THE CRUCIFIED JESUS.
Rom. x. 21.

But to Israel He saith, All day long I have stretched forth My hands unto a disobedient and gainsaying people . . . 119

Preached at St. Paul's on Palm Sunday, April 9, 1876.

SERMON IX.
THE SOLITUDES OF THE PASSION.
Psalm xxii. 11.

O go not from Me, for trouble is hard at hand, and there is none to help Me 138

Preached at St. Paul's on Palm Sunday, April 14, 1878.

SERMON X.
THE SILENCE OF JESUS.
St. John xix. 9.

Pilate saith unto Jesus, Whence art Thou? But Jesus gave him no answer 153

Preached at St. Paul's on Passion Sunday, April 3, 1881.

SERMON XI.

THE ASS AND THE FOAL.

St. Matt. xxi. 3.

And if any man say ought unto you, ye shall say, The Lord hath need of them 167

Preached at St. Paul's on Passion Sunday, April 2, 1882.

SERMON XII.

POPULAR RELIGIOUS ENTHUSIASM.

St. John xii. 12, 13.

Much people that were come to the feast, when they heard that Jesus was coming to Jerusalem, took branches of palm trees, and went forth to meet Him, and cried, Hosanna: Blessed is the King of Israel That cometh in the Name of the Lord . . 182

Preached at St. Paul's on Passion Sunday, April 6, 1879.

SERMON XIII.

RELIGIOUS EMOTION.

St. Matt. xxi. 9.

And the multitudes that went before, and that followed, cried, saying, Hosanna to the Son of David: Blessed is He That cometh in the Name of the Lord; Hosanna in the Highest . . . 196

Preached at St. Paul's on Passion Sunday, April 11, 1881.

SERMON XIV.

THE TRAITOR-APOSTLE.

St. Matt. xxvi. 24.

It had been good for that man if he had not been born . . . 210

Preached at St. Paul's on Palm Sunday, April 16, 1889.

SERMON XV.

THE ECONOMY OF RELIGIOUS ART.

St. Matt. xxvi. 8, 9, 10.

But when His disciples saw it, they had indignation, saying, To what purpose is this waste? For this ointment might have been sold for much, and given to the poor. When Jesus understood it, He said unto them, Why trouble ye the woman? for she hath wrought a good work upon Me 227

Preached at St. Paul's on Palm Sunday, April 6, 1873.

SERMON XVI.

THE LIVING WATER.

St. John iv. 13, 14, 15.

Jesus answered and said unto her, Whosoever drinketh of this water shall thirst again: but whosoever drinketh of the water that I shall give him shall never thirst; but the water that I shall give him shall be in him a well of water springing up into everlasting life. The woman saith unto Him, Sir, give me this water, that I thirst not, neither come hither to draw . . 244

Preached at St. Paul's on the Fourth Sunday in Lent, March 19, 1871.

SERMON XVII.

THE TRUE LIFE OF MAN.

St. Luke xii. 15.

A man's life consisteth not in the abundance of the things which he possesseth 259

Preached at Christ Church on the Second Wednesday in Lent, Feb. 14, 1883.

SERMON XVIII.

THE DEATH OF THE SOUL.

Psalm vi. 5.

For in death no man remembereth Thee: and who will give Thee thanks in the pit? 276

Preached at St. Paul's on the Fifth Wednesday in Lent, March 23, 1887.

SERMON XIX.

GUIDANCE OF THE PENITENT.

PSALM xxxii. 9.

I will inform thee, and teach thee in the way wherein thou shalt go: and I will guide thee with Mine Eye 281

Preached at St. Paul's on the Fifth Wednesday in Lent, March 14, 1888.

SERMON XX.

DISAPPROVAL OF FRIENDS.

PSALM xxxviii. 11.

My lovers and my neighbours did stand looking upon my trouble: and my kinsmen stood afar off 287

Preached at St. Paul's on the Fifth Wednesday in Lent, April 3, 1889.

SERMON XXI.

THE IDEA OF SIN.

PSALM li. 4.

Against Thee, Thee only, have I sinned, and done this evil in Thy sight; that Thou mightest be justified when Thou speakest, and be clear when Thou judgest 294

Preached at St. Paul's on the Fifth Wednesday in Lent, March 19, 1890.

SERMON I.

THE SINLESSNESS OF JESUS CHRIST.

St. John viii. 46.

Which of you convinceth Me of sin ?

IT has sometimes been inferred from the context of these words that the word "sin" really means here intellectual rather than moral failure. "Which of you convinceth Me of error? And if I say the truth, why do ye not believe Me?" The second question is thus made to repeat its meaning into the translation of the first. But the word translated "sin" means moral failure throughout the New Testament; and our Lord is arguing—if we may dare to apply our classifications of human arguments to His profound and sacred words—from the genus to the species, from the absence of moral evil in Him generally to the absence of a specific form of moral evil, namely, falsehood. He is maintaining that as they cannot detect in Him any kind of sin, they ought not by their disbelief to credit Him practically with falsehood, or, at least, indifference to truth, and His own means of attaining and proclaiming it.

It has also been thought that our Lord here only challenges the detective power of His Jewish opponents, and that He does not literally imply His Sinlessness. As though He had said: "You at least cannot point to any sin against veracity or some other virtue on My part which ought to forfeit your confidence. And as you know no moral reason for disbelieving Me, you ought to believe

Me." But such a meaning would be strangely at variance with the general tenor of our Lord's teaching—with His repeated contrast between the deceptiveness of outward appearances and the inward truths and facts of human life. If indeed this had been His meaning, the Jews might have retorted that the Lord Himself taught them to distrust the outside appearance of goodness, and to account that only worth respect which is beyond the ken of human sight, and is known to the Father Which seeth in secret.[1]

Besides which the challenge would hardly have been offered unless the Speaker had been conscious of something more than guiltlessness of public acts which might be pointed to as in some sense sinful. Sin, like holiness, is not merely a series of facts which may be measured and dated: it is a particular condition of the will, it is a moral atmosphere. The presence of sin is perceptible where there is no act of sin: it is breathed, it is implied, it is felt, it is responded to by sympathetic instincts when there is almost no visible or audible sign of its presence.

"The Powers of Ill have mysteries of their own,
   Their Sacramental signs and prayers,
Their choral chants in many a winning tone,
Their watchwords, seals, processions, known
   Far off to friend and foe; their lights and perfum'd airs.

And even as men, where warring hosts abide,
   By faint and silent tokens learn
At distance whom to trust, from whom to hide,
So round us set on every side
   The aerial sentinels our good and ill discern.

The lawless wish, the unaverted eye,
   Are as a taint upon the breeze
To lure foul spirits: haughty brows and high
Are signals to invite him nigh,
   Whose onset ever Saints await on bended knees."[2]

Our Lord claims, then, to be sinless in a very different sense from that in which a man might defy an opponent

[1] St. Matt. vi. 1-18.   [2] *Lyr. Inn.* iv. 8.

to prove against him a specific form of wrongdoing in a court of law. We are here in the atmosphere not of law but of morality; and morality is a question not of external facts merely, but of internal motives, postures of will, dispositions of affection.

But the question arises whether sinlessness is abstractedly possible. It has been argued that our experience goes to deny its possibility. To be human, so far as we individually come in contact with human life, is to be sinful—in very varying degrees, yet at least in some degree, sinful. In one individual and class, sin is outrageous, shocking, gross; in another, it is refined, and more or less attractive. But the essence of the thing—the contradiction between the free moral will and that Will of God which is the moral rule or order of the universe—is the same. "There is none righteous, no, not one,"[1] is as true now as in the days of the Psalmist and of St. Paul. "If we say that we have no sin, we deceive ourselves, and the truth is not in us,"[2] applies as certainly to Christians of the nineteenth century as to Christians of the first. But this general experience is not really at variance with the existence of an exception to it: and our faith in humanity, in man's proved capacity for moral improvement, in his experienced power of passing from one level of moral attainment to another, leads us up to the idea of One Who has reached the summit, or Who has always occupied it. Faith in humanity here coincides with faith in God. That God should have given man the capacities which he actually possesses for almost indefinite improvement, points to a purpose in the Divine Mind of which we should expect to see some typical realisation. These lines of thought are only interrupted by moral scepticism, expressing itself in such cynical proverbs as that "Every man has his price, if you only know it," and that "No

---

[1] Ps. xiv. 3; Rom. iii. 10.   [2] 1 St. John i. 8.

man's character should be taken for granted until you have cross-questioned his valet." Moral scepticism, which claims to be a very far-sighted common-sense, which repudiates all untenable ideals, and sits in judgment on human nature in a spirit of lofty impartiality, is in reality based not on experience, but on mistrust. It begins with mistrust, it does not merely end with it; and such mistrust blights within us fatally all the generous impulses of faith and love,—all the power we have of making self-sacrificing efforts for God's glory and the welfare of our fellow-men. This mistrust once recognised and conquered, we shall not mistake either the nature or the wide dominion of evil, but we shall see in men, struggling with imperfection and against it, reasons for faith in humanity. We shall have, at the bottom of our thoughts, no insuperable bar to believing—upon sufficient evidence—that one Being has actually appeared upon the stage of history, in Whom evil found no place at all.

1.

All that we know about our Lord goes to show that He was Sinless. If certain portions of the text of the Gospels should be—for the sake of the argument, and in no other sense—admitted to be of inferior or no authority, whatever might remain, enough would remain to sustain the impression of the Sinlessness of Christ. This impression was produced most strongly on those who were brought into the closest contact with Him. Take St. Peter. After the miraculous draught of fishes, St. Peter's exclamation is noteworthy: "Depart from me, for I am a sinful man, O Lord."[1] St. Peter does not say, "I am a weak and failing," but "I am a sinful man, O Lord." He feels the interval that separates him from the wonder-working

[1] St. Luke v. 8.

Christ: but it is not his Lord's power over nature, but His sanctity, which awes and distresses St. Peter. In the same way, when St. Peter had denied our Lord, a look from Jesus sufficed to produce in the soul of the apostle the extremest anguish : he "went out, and wept bitterly."[1] Why should our Lord's "look" have had this power? Had St. Peter associated with the character of his Master any one trait of selfishness, or ambition, or unveracity, or heartlessness, he might have felt, in the tragic catastrophe which led to the Passion, the presence of something like a retributive justice. It was the absence of this, it was his conviction of the absolute purity of Christ's character, which filled him with remorse at the thought that he had borne a part in betraying Him. This impression of Christ's character is observable in the worldly judge who yielded to the wishes of Christ's enemies, while he admitted the innocence of their Victim;[2] in the restless anxiety of the wife of Pilate, haunted in her dreams by the thought that the blood of "that Just Person" might be visited on her husband;[3] in the lower sense of the pregnant declaration made by the centurion at the cross —"Truly this was the Son of God;"[4] above all, in the remorse of Judas. Judas, who had known Christ as Peter had known Him for three years of intimate companionship; Judas, who would gladly, had it been possible, have justified his treachery to himself by any flaw that he could dwell on in his Master's character, was forced to confess that the "blood" which he had betrayed was "innocent,"[5] and was so burdened with his sense of guilt that he sought refuge from the agonies of thought and shame, in that which only makes shame and guilty thought irreversible—in suicide. In the hatred of the Sanhedrists, as described particularly in St. John's Gospel,[6]

[1] St. Matt. xxvi. 75. [2] St. John xix. 4, 6, 16.
[3] St. Matt. xxvii. 19. [4] Ib. 54. [5] Ib. 4, 5.
[6] St. John xi. 47-57; xii. 10, 11; xviii. 3; xix. 6, 7.

the purity and force of Christ's character is not less discernible. It is the high prerogative of goodness, as of truth, in their loftier forms, that they can never be approached in a spirit of neutrality or indifference; they must perforce create a decided repulsion when they do not decidedly attract. The Pharisees would have treated an opposing teacher, in whom any moral flaw was really discernible, with contemptuous indifference: the sinless Jesus of Nazareth provoked their irreconcilable, implacable hostility.

The Sinlessness of Christ is dwelt upon in the writings of the Apostles as a very important feature of the message about Him which it was their business to deliver to the world. St. Peter's earliest sermons dwell on the subject. Addressing the wondering multitude which had run together to witness the miracle performed by the two Apostles at the Beautiful Gate of the Temple, St. Peter tells them that He Whom they had denied in the presence of Pilate was "the Holy One and the Just."[1] The climax of St. Stephen's indictment against his judges, which led to their violent interruption and his own immediate death, was that they had been the betrayers and murderers of "the Just One."[2] The title by which Ananias announces Christ as the future Master of his destiny to the converted but still blinded Saul of Tarsus, is "that Just One"— Whose will the convert should know, the voice of Whose mouth he should hearken to, Whom indeed, in inward spirit as in outward vision, he should see.[3] The absolute holiness of Christ is equally assumed in the Epistles of each of the three great Apostles. St. Paul is careful to say that God sent His Son in the likeness only of sinful flesh[4]—in true human nature, that is, without its sin. St. Peter dwells on our Lord's sinlessness in its bearing both on His example and His atoning Death: the precious blood of Christ with which Christians are redeemed is, he

---

[1] Acts iii. 14.   [2] Ib. vii. 52.   [3] Ib. xxii. 14.   [4] Rom. viii. 3.

says, the blood of a Lamb without blemish, and immaculate;[1] the suffering Christ Who left all Christians, but particularly ill-treated slaves, an example that they should follow His steps, Himself "did no sin, neither was guile found in His mouth."[2] In St. John, Christ's sinlessness is connected sometimes with His intercession: "We have an Advocate with the Father, Jesus Christ the righteous;"[3] —sometimes with His regenerating power: "If ye know that He is righteous, ye know that every one that doeth righteousness is born of Him;"[4]—sometimes with the real moral force of His example: "Let no man deceive you; he that doeth righteousness is righteous, even as He is righteous."[5] Especially is the spotless sanctity of Christ connected in the Epistle to the Hebrews with Christ's priestly office. Although the High Priest of Christendom was "tempted in all points like as we are," yet is He "without sin."[6] "Holy, harmless, undefiled, separate from sinners," in His moral elevation not less than in His actual ascension, He needeth not daily, as did the priests of the old covenant, to offer up sacrifice, first for His own sins and then for the people's;[7] and His unsoiled robe of sanctity it is which makes His offering of Himself so perfectly acceptable to the Eternal Father.

II.

The Sinlessness of our Lord has been supposed to be compromised, sometimes by the conditions of the development of His life as man, sometimes by particular acts and sayings which are recorded of Him. When, for instance, we are told in the Epistle to the Hebrews that our Lord "learned obedience by the things that He suffered,"[8] this, it is argued, means progress from moral deficiency to moral

---

[1] 1 St. Pet. i. 19. [2] *Ib.* ii. 21, 22. [3] 1 St. John ii. 1.
[4] 1 St. John ii. 29. [5] *Ib.* iii. 7. [6] Heb. iv. 15.
[7] Heb. vii. 26, 27. [8] *Ib.* v. 8.

sufficiency; and, as a consequence, it implies in Him a time when He was morally imperfect. But although the growth of our Lord's moral Nature as Man implies that as a truly human nature it was finite, it does not by any means follow that such a growth involved sin as its starting-point. A moral development may be perfectly pure and yet be a development; a progress from a less to a more expanded degree of perfection is not to be confounded with a progress from sin to holiness. In the latter case there is an element of antagonism within the will which is wholly wanting in the former.

Nor is there any reason for denying His moral Perfection on the ground that a change in His conception of His work is observable as having taken place between His earlier and His later ministry in consequence of disappointment. This theory makes Him the slave, not the master of circumstances, since it maintains that He only reached the idea of a purely spiritual kingdom of God when His earlier aims, which had, according to the hypothesis, a mere political element in them, had been proved to be impracticable by the national hostility which they aroused. Against this whole theory we have to set the broad fact that the earliest allusions which our Lord made to His kingdom were as entirely indicative of its spiritual, heavenly, non-political character as the latest; and that the whole idea of a change of plan imposed upon Christ by the force of events is imported on purely *a priori* grounds into the history of the Gospels, and finds no support in the Sacred Text.

A more formidable difficulty, it has been urged, is presented by the Temptation. A *bona fide* temptation implies, it has been contended, at least a minimum of sympathy with evil, which is incompatible with perfect sinlessness. Either Jesus was not really tempted, in which case He fails as our example; or the reality of

His temptation is fatal to His literal Sinlessness. That this dilemma would not have been admitted by the Apostolic writers is plain from the statement in the Epistle to the Hebrews, that "He was in all points tempted like as we are, yet without sin."[1] It will be asked how this is possible. What, my brethren, is temptation? It is an influence by which a personal being on probation may receive a momentum in the direction of evil. It may be an evil inclination in the man's own soul; it may be a motive presented from without. The former, a corrupt inward inclination, was, we are maintaining, impossible in the case of Jesus Christ; but the motive from without could only have become a real temptation by making a place for itself in thought or in imagination. How was this practicable while leaving the Sinlessness of Christ intact? The answer is that an impression upon thought or imagination or sense is very possible indeed in very varying degrees short of producing a distinct determination of the will towards evil, and it is only when such a determination is produced that sinlessness is compromised by the presence of temptation. So long as the will is not an accomplice, the impressions of the tempter upon our intellectual or sentient life do not touch the moral being itself; and whether we examine the temptations to which our Lord was exposed from without in the wilderness,[2] or the temptations to which He was exposed from within in the struggle in Gethsemane,[3] it is perfectly clear that deep as was the impression and reality of the trial in each case, in each case also the will maintained an attitude of resistance—here to external solicitations, there to internal shrinking from suffering. Nothing could be more certain than the reality of His trial, except the fact that He passed it unscathed.

Among particular acts which have been insisted on as

[1] Heb. iv. 15.   [2] St. Matt. iv. 1-11.   [3] St. Luke xxii. 40-46.

incompatible with perfect sinlessness is His cursing the barren fig-tree.[1] Here the idea that our Lord betrayed something like irritation could only be entertained when the nature of a prophetical act had been altogether lost sight of: the fig-tree was a symbol of the Jewish people, doomed, on account of its unfruitfulness, to a swift destruction. In driving the buyers and sellers from the Temple,[2] He was acting, not under the influence of any sudden personal passion, as has been imagined, but strictly in His prophetical character: the conscience of the traffickers ratified the strict justice of His act. When it is urged that His driving the devils into the swine in the country of the Gadarenes[3] involved an interference with the rights of property, it must here be admitted that the act seems indefensible, unless it be perceived that Jesus, as Man, is God's Plenipotentiary, and that the act must be explained not simply with reference to the ordinary rules of human conduct, but by the laws of God's government of the universe. In that government material interests are strictly subordinated to moral interests, because in the view of the Self-Existent Moral Being the material universe is of less account than the moral. God does indeed, for great and sufficient ends, inflict keen loss upon individuals and nations; the individual suffering can only be accounted for as forming part of a scheme of government which extends beyond our view. This applies no less to our Lord's relation to Judas. The supposition that He did not know what Judas was and would become is inconsistent with Christ's moral penetration, to say nothing of His higher Superhuman Knowledge. But, if our Lord had this Knowledge, why did He enrol Judas among the Apostles? No satisfactory answer can be given, except that here too He was acting as God acts in providence,—not only per-

---

[1] St. Matt. xxi. 18, 19.   [2] St. John ii. 13-17; St. Matt. xxi. 12, 13.
[3] St. Mark v. 1-16.

mitting evil, but overruling even its worst excesses for good—comprehending its whole destined range and history, yet making it serve His purposes of grace and mercy in the end.

Once indeed He used words which, taken at first sight, might seem to imply that He admitted moral imperfection in Himself. He rebuked the young man who addressed Him as "Good Master" on the ground that "there was none good save One, that is, God."[1] But if we examine the moral condition of the young man, we shall conclude that no inference of this kind can be drawn from our Lord's expression. The young man's question betrays the levity of a shallow self-complacency. He addressed our Lord as "good" in the way of off-hand compliment, without meaning his words. It was not to such a soul that Jesus would reveal Himself; and when He rebukes the young man for his use of the epithet "good," He is addressing Himself to the young man's views and grasp of truth, He is not describing truth as it was present to Himself. God alone is good; but the Divinity of Jesus is a truth too high, as even the moral perfection of His Manhood is too high, for mastery by one whose eyes are not yet turned away from beholding vanity.[2] Christ does not forget His own warning against casting pearls before swine.[3]

On one side, indeed, our Lord's language is inconsistent with human perfectness, unless He is something more than man. His reiterated self-assertion,—His insisting that all should come to Him, cling to Him, listen to Him, love Him,—would not be human virtue in you or me. It would not be virtue in a sinless man. It implies a claim to the love and homage of humanity which is unjustifiable, unless the Speaker stand in a higher relation to man than is possible for any who is merely human. But then,

---

[1] St. Matt. xix. 16, 17.   [2] Ps. cxix. 37.   [3] St. Matt. vii. 6.

granting this, the Life of Jesus as a sinless whole sustains the implication of this apparent exception to His general bearing. If we deny that He was more than man, we are likely to proceed, with an English deist, to accuse Him of "vanity and incipient sacerdotalism;"[1] but then, the absence of dependence in Him, the absence of localising and narrowing elements in His character, of any traceable conflict between flesh and spirit, between the intellectual and the moral life, above all, the purity and intensity of love in Him,—are, apart from His miracles and the mysteries of His Life, in perfect harmony with His statements about Himself.

His Life is a revelation of the Moral Life of God, completing all previous revelations, not merely teaching us what God is in formulæ addressed to our understanding, but showing us what He is in characters which may be read by sense, and take possession of the heart. "The Word was made flesh, and dwelt among us," cried an Apostle, "and we beheld His glory, the glory as of the Only Begotten of the Father, full of Grace and Truth."[2] "He that hath seen Me hath seen the Father."[3]

III.

1. The Sinless Christ satisfies a deep want of the soul of man—the want of an ideal. No artist can attempt a painting, a statue, a building, without some ideal in view; and an ideal is not more necessary in art than in conduct. If men have not worthy ideals before their mind's eye, they furnish themselves with unworthy ones. Few things are more piteous in the recent history of mankind than the consideration that a character such as that of the first Napoleon should have been the ideal of three generations of a race so generous, so impulsive, so capable beyond

---

[1] Mr. F. W. Newman, *Phases of Faith*, pp. 153, 154.
[2] St. John i. 14. [3] *Ib.* xiv. 9.

other peoples of the heights of heroic virtue and of the depths of self-abasement as the French. Only now, if now, is that false ideal displaying itself, in its true historic outlines, before the eyes of a population disenchanted by unexampled suffering; and it will be well if no new master of all the sublime atrocities of government and war appeals to the imagination which has just unlearnt the lesson of three quarters of a century. There is ground, too, for the apprehension lest Frederick the Great—the highest embodiment, perhaps, in modern Europe, of successful brutality—whose memory was for a while buried at Jena, but who has risen in his successors with greater splendour than before, should again become the ideal monarch of North Germany. As each nation has its ideals, so has each city, each family, each profession, each school of thought, and how powerfully these energetic phantoms of the past control and modify the present is obvious to all who observe and think. There is no truer test of a man's character than the ideals which excite his genuine enthusiasm: there is no surer measure of what he will become than a real knowledge of what he heartily admires. And like other societies, other families, other schools of thought, other centres of enthusiasm, Christendom has had its ideals, many and various,—some of them looked up to by a generation, some by centuries; some of them the inheritance of a village, a city, a country; some the common glories of all who acknowledge the Name of Jesus Christ. But these ideals, great as they are in their several ways, fall short of perfection in some particular, on some side, when we scan them closely, however reverently we scan them; there is One beyond them —only One—Who does not fail. They, standing beneath His throne, say each one of them to us, with St. Paul, "Be ye followers of me, even as I also am of Christ."[1]

[1] 1 Cor. xi. 1.

But He, above them all, asks each generation of worshippers, each generation of critics, that passes beneath His throne, "Which of you convinceth Me of sin?" It is true that here and there a voice is raised which for a moment seems to attempt to fix on Him some flaw or stain that shall forfeit the homage of Christendom: but it dies away, that voice, into the silence of neglect, or amid the murmurs of indignation, and Christ remains in Christian thought, as in actual fact, alone on His throne of unassailable Perfection. "Thou only art holy; Thou only art the Lord; Thou only, O Christ, with the Holy Ghost, art most high in the glory of God the Father."[1]

2. The Sinless Christ is also the true Reconciler between God and man. Our Lord did not leave it to His Apostles to insist upon the importance of His Death and Sufferings to the world. He spoke of His Death as an indispensable part of His work. The corn of wheat, He says, must fall into the earth and die, if it is not to abide alone, if it is to bring forth much fruit.[2] As of old Moses lifted up the serpent in the wilderness for the healing of the people, so must the Son of Man be lifted up upon the cross, and the effect of this will be that all who believe on Him will not perish, but have everlasting life.[3] The Good Shepherd, when the hireling flees from the invading wolf, will lay down His life for the sheep:[4] He will give His life a ransom for many.[5] His life-blood is the Blood of the New Covenant; by being shed it will procure remission of sins.[6] This language falls hallowed and familiar on Christian ears, and it introduces us to the more explicit statements of the Apostolic Epistles. But like these statements it presupposes the absolute Sinlessness of Christ, if it is to be even tolerable. Let us conceive (if we may

---

[1] The *Gloria in Excelsis* in the Holy Communion Service.
[2] St. John xii. 24.   [3] *Ib.* iii. 14, 15.   [4] *Ib.* x. 11-15.
[5] St. Matt. xx. 28.   [6] *Ib.* xxvi. 28.

without irreverence) that some one single sin, untruthfulness, or vanity, or cruelty, could be really charged on Him, and what becomes of the atoning character of His Death? I do not ask what becomes of its efficacy, but how is it conceivable that He should have willed to die for a guilty world? For while, if we look at it on one side, His Death appears to have been determined by circumstances, on the other, it was as certainly the result of His own liberty of action. "No man taketh My life from Me, but I lay it down of Myself: I have power to lay it down, and I have power to take it again."[1] At once Priest and Sacrifice, Christ is represented in the Epistle to the Hebrews as "offering Himself without spot to God."[2] It was the crowning act of a life which was throughout sacrificial; but had He been conscious of any inward stain, how could He have desired to offer Himself in sacrifice to free a world from sin? Had there been in Him any personal evil to purge away, His Death might have been endured on account of His own guilt: it is His absolute Sinlessness which makes it certain that He died for others.

3. Thus, as our Ideal and our Redeemer from sin and death, He is the heart and focus of the life of Christendom. Christendom is Christian so far as it lives consciously in companionship with Christ; not merely with Christ as a memory of the past depicted in its annals, but with Christ as a living Being—unseen, yet energetic—seeing all, comprehending all, forming a judgment upon all that passes in His Church at large day by day, and in each separate life that composes it. There is, alas! too much to wound Him—too much to compel those who know little or nothing of His real secret empire over souls to pronounce His work in the world at large a failure. Often, too, it happens that men who are one in their love and devotion to Him differ,

[1] St. John x. 18. [2] Heb. ix. 14.

inevitably it may be, as to the line of duty which, under a given set of circumstances, that devotion prescribes: so that their loyalty to Him is the very measure of their opposition to each other. The distracting controversies which agitate the Church, and in which some of us, it may be sorely against our wills, are forced to take part by circumstances which we can neither explain nor control, are at this moment only too present to the minds of most men who take any interest in such questions at all. Not that these controversies are peculiar to Anglicanism, distracted as it is said to be by divisions, which are pointed to as the logical consequence of its original separation from the See which claims to be the normal centre of unity. They exist no less within the Roman unity itself—equal in point of intensity, although differing in their direction and their form. Even at this moment, the one theologian on the Continent to whose every utterance Europe, whether Catholic or Protestant, listens with a respect that is granted to no other—the great and noble Döllinger,—has but a few days left him to decide whether, in accepting the equal infallibility of a long line of self-contradicting Popes, he will renounce the highest certainties of history—of that history which furnishes the Gospel itself with the fundamental evidence of its truth—or accept the alternative ecclesiastical suspension and disgrace. To attempt to close questions, whether of doctrine or practice, which are, and have been, at least, open for centuries, is to inflict upon the Church as fatal an injury as to open questions which Revelation has closed. No such enterprises can be really carried out with impunity; and whether the Vatican or Exeter Hall be bent upon its project of proscription—here in the interests of a usurping ecclesiastical autocracy, there of a narrow and illiterate theory—the result is necessarily and equally disastrous; since such proscription invites opposition, suffering, division, weakness—weakness in all that Christ's true servants would fain see united and strong. It may indeed be impossible to agree altogether as to questions of Church order or questions of duty—now and here—during our brief day of life, without some sacrifice of that perfect sincerity which is one of the soul's most precious jewels. Our controversies belong to an imperfect vision of truth: but they are likely to be tempered in such proportion as loyalty to our Sinless and Divine Lord, and not any one of the subtle forms of self-assertion which are so apt to beset us, is our real governing motive when we take part in them. In looking to Him, all Christians who merit the name meet and are one: just as men who are separated by seas and continents gaze on the same sun in the material heavens, and bask in his warmth and light. Whatever criticisms we may level at each other, or may deserve at each other's hands—and none of us can suppose that we are not open to some, nay, rather to much, just criticism—we turn our eyes upwards towards the heavens, and fix them on Him Whom none has yet convinced of sin, even of the slightest—in Whose life on earth there was seen, eighteen centuries ago, as now on His throne in heaven, a perfect harmony between a human will and the moral law of the universe. In His Light we shall see light.[1] The heaviness of our misunderstandings and our controversies may endure for a night: the joy of union will come with the eternal Morning.[2]

[1] Ps. xxxvi. 9.   [2] Ib. xxx. 5.

SERMON II.

THE HUMILIATION OF THE ETERNAL SON.

PHIL. ii. 5-8.

Let this mind be in you, which was also in Christ Jesus: Who, being in the form of God, thought it not robbery to be equal with God; but made Himself of no reputation, and took upon Him the form of a servant, and was made in the likeness of men: and being found in fashion as a man, He humbled Himself, and became obedient unto death, even the death of the cross.

IN no passage of his writings does St. Paul carry us more into the heights and depths of Christian doctrine than in these words. Yet his object is a moral and practical one. Human nature was, under the eyes of the Apostles, and within the Church, what it is now within the Church and under our eyes. Christian Philippi was distracted by divisions, not of a doctrinal or theological, but of a social and personal character. One feud, in particular, there was between two ladies of consideration, Euodias and Syntyche, which the Apostle was particularly anxious to heal;[1] but it was probably only one feud among many. Small as it was, the church of Philippi already contained within its borders representatives of each of the three great divisions in race of the Roman world. The purple-dealer from Thyatira;[2] the slave-girl, who was a Macedonian, and apparently born on the spot, and who was, on account of her powers of divination, so profitable a possession to her owner;[3] the Roman colonist, who had

[1] Phil. iv. 2.   [2] Acts xvi. 14, 15.   [3] *Ib.* 16-18.

charge of the public prison [1]—all became converts to the faith. Here we have an important branch of commerce represented; there the vast numbers of people, who in very various grades made their livelihood in official positions under government; while the divining-girl was a member of that vast and unhappy class to whom the Gospel brought more relief than to any other—in whose persons the rights of human nature were as completely ignored as if they had been altogether extinguished : the slave population of the Empire. He Who represented humanity as a whole spoke through His messengers to every class in the great human family; since "there was to be neither Jew nor Greek, neither male nor female, barbarian nor Scythian, bond nor free, but all were one in Christ Jesus." [2]

And yet, human nature being what it is, this very diversity of elements within the small community which believed on and worshipped Jesus Christ at Philippi, was likely, at least occasionally, to foster disagreements: the serpent of the old Pagan pride in human nature had been scotched rather than killed. Jealousies which were natural, and even admirable, in heathen eyes, were intolerable in Christendom, kneeling beneath the Redeemer's Cross. St. Paul insists upon the duties of social unity. He begs the Philippian Christians to "be steadfast in one spirit," [3] to "strive together with one mind for the faith of the Gospel," [4] to "do nothing through strife or vain-glory." [5]

For himself, he protests he has no partialities to indulge: he prays to God for all; he thanks God for graces bestowed on them all; he has bright hopes and anticipations about them all; they are *all* of them, he says, his companions in grace; his companions—though severed by seas and countries—in suffering; he yearns after them all

---

[1] Acts xvi. 25-34. [2] Col. iii. 11. [3] Phil. i. 27.
[4] Phil. i. 27. [5] *Ib.* ii. 3.

—it is a most beautiful and suggestive expression—in the Heart of Jesus Christ.[1]

It is to the Incarnation and Cross of Jesus Christ that St. Paul points in order to justify his advice and to explain his meaning. "Let this mind be in you, which was also in Christ Jesus." What mind? That question can only be answered by a somewhat close examination of the passage before us.

I.

1. In looking into these words we observe, first of all, that St. Paul clearly asserts Jesus Christ to have existed before His Birth into the world. You and I, my brethren, it is unnecessary to say, had no existence before our natural birth; our immaterial nature is no older than our bodily nature; it was brought into existence contemporaneously with our bodies, by a special act of God's creative power. Jesus Christ too had a Human Soul, which was created contemporaneously with His Human Body; but before He had either the body or soul of man, He already existed. "Let this mind be in you, which was also in Christ Jesus: Who, existing (so it should be rendered) in the form of God." The structure of the language here makes it certain that the Apostle is speaking of a point of time, not merely earlier than that at which our Lord commenced His ministry, but altogether antecedent to His taking human nature on Him. Being in the "form" of God. What is here meant by "form"? The word which is here translated "form,"[2] when applied to objects of sense, means all those sensible qualities which strike the eye of an observer, and so lead us to see that a thing is what it is. Our English word "form" is mainly restricted in its application to objects of sense, so that we know at once what is meant by the "form" of

---

[1] Phil. i. 3-8.   [2] μορφή.

a man or of a public building. But the Greek word was applied quite commonly to immaterial objects, in which there was nothing to strike the bodily eye; the Greeks spoke of the "form" of an abstract idea just as naturally as we speak of the "form" of a house; and thus, the original drift of the word being exactly retained when it is applied to an abstract idea, the "collective qualities" of the idea which is before the mind's eye of the speaker are termed the "form" of that idea. Thus the "form" of justice would mean those qualities and capacities in man which go to make up the complete idea of justice. God, we know, is a Pure Spirit, without body or parts,— without any qualities that address themselves to sense, —the King Eternal, Immortal, Invisible.[1] The "Form" of God would have meant, in St. Paul's mouth and St. Paul's thought, all those attributes which belong to the Reality and Perfection of the One Supreme Self-existent Being. By saying then that Jesus Christ existed in the Form of God, before "He took on Him the form of a slave," St. Paul would have been understood by any one who read him in his own language to mean that, when as yet Christ had no human body or human soul, He was properly and literally God, because He existed in the "Form," and so possessed all the proper attributes, of God.

2. St. Paul goes on to say that being God, Christ Jesus "thought it not robbery to be equal with God." This sentence would be more closely and clearly rendered, Christ "did not look on His equality with God as a prize to be jealously set store by." Men who are new to great positions are apt to think more of them than those who have always enjoyed them; a crown sits more naturally on hereditary monarchs than on soldiers or statesmen who have forced their way up the steps of the throne; and some thought of this kind, derived from the things of

[1] 1 Tim. i. 17.

earth, colours the Apostle's language in describing by contrast those mysteries of heaven. Christ, Who was God from everlasting, laid no stress on this His Eternal Greatness: He made Himself of no reputation, or rather He emptied Himself (that is the exact word) of His Divine prerogatives or glory. Of His Divine Nature He could not divest Himself; but He could shroud It altogether from the eyes of His creatures: He could become a "worm, and no man, a very scorn of men, and the outcast of the people."[1]

3. Of this self-humiliation St. Paul traces three distinct stages. The first consists in Christ's taking on Him the form—that is, here as before, the essential qualities which make up the reality—of a servant or slave. By this expression St. Paul means human nature. Without ceasing to be what He was, what He could not but be, He wrapped around Himself a created form, through which He would hold converse with men, in which He would suffer, in which He would die.

"The form of a servant." Service is the true business of human nature; man, as such, is God's slave. There are created natures higher than our own—who, like ourselves, are bound to yield a free service to their Maker, and who, unlike ourselves, yield it perfectly,—Intelligences far vaster and stronger than any among the sons of men; Hearts burning with the fire of a love which, in its purity and its glow, surpasses anything that man can feel; Wills which in their freedom and their determination are more majestic than any which rules among the sons of men. Cherubim and Seraphim, Angels and Archangels, Thrones, Virtues, Dominions, Powers, Principalities—Christ surveyed them all, and passed them all by: He refused the elder born, and the nobler, the stronger of creation, and chose the younger, and the meaner, and the weaker.

[1] Ps. xxii. 6.

the Eternal Son.

He took not on Him, St. Paul says, angels, but He took on Him the seed of Abraham.[1] He was made Man. By taking our nature upon Him, Christ deigned to forfeit His liberty of action : He placed Himself under restraints and obligations; He entered into human society, and at that end of it where obedience to the will of others is the law which all must obey. "Even Christ pleased not Himself:"[2] the Master of all became the Slave of all.

The second stage of this humiliation is that Christ did not merely take human nature on Him : He became obedient to death. St. Paul here implies that it might have been otherwise; that Christ might conceivably have taken on Him a human form, and have ascended into heaven in it, without dying on the Cross or rising from the grave. Death is the penalty of sin;[3] it is the brand of physical evil set upon the universal presence of moral evil. How then should the Sinless One die ? St. Paul implies that He was not subject to the law of death; and that He submitted to it, after becoming Man, by a distinct effort of His Free Will. "He became obedient unto death." This was indeed, it is distinctly stated as a matter of fact, His object in becoming Incarnate :—"Forasmuch then as the children are partakers of flesh and blood, He also Himself likewise took part of the same ; that through death He might destroy him that had the power of death, that is, the devil; and deliver them who through fear of death were all their lifetime subject to bondage."[4] It was for our sakes, then, that He died : we die because we cannot help it: "it is appointed unto all men once to die."

Death is a tyrant who sooner or later claims the homage of all of us : Christ alone might have defied him, yet He freely submitted to his sway. As He Himself said : "No man taketh My life from Me, but I lay it down of Myself:

[1] Heb. ii. 16.
[2] Rom. xv. 3.
[3] Rom. v. 12 ; vi. 23 ; St. James i. 15.
[4] Heb. ii. 14, 15.

I have power to lay it down, and I have power to take it again."[1]

The third stage in this humiliation is that when all modes of death were open to Him, He chose that which would bring with it the greatest share of pain and shame. "He became obedient unto death, even the death of the cross." The cross was the death of the slaves and malefactors. St. Paul himself no doubt reflected that in this he could not, if he would, rival the humiliation of his Master, as he could not, much more, rival his Master's glories. St. Paul knew that, as a Roman freeman, he would be beheaded if condemned to die. Upon this death upon the cross the Jewish law, as St. Paul reminded the Galatians, utters a curse;[2] and that Christ should thus have died seemed to present to each section of the ancient Eastern world especial difficulties. Christ crucified was to the Jews a stumbling-block, and to the Greeks foolishness.[3] And yet Christ "endured the cross, despising the shame."[4] He was bent upon drinking to the dregs the cup of self-humiliation; and God does not do what He does by halves: He is as Infinite in His condescensions as He is in His Majesty. He laid not stress on His Divine prerogatives. If He willed to die, why should He not embrace death in all the intensity of the idea, surrounded by everything that could protract the inevitable suffering and enhance the inevitable humiliation? If He willed to become Incarnate at all, why should He exempt Himself from any conditions of creaturely existence? why not in all things be made like unto His brethren,[5] sin only except? While on the cross of shame He endures "the sharpness of death," He is only completing that emptying Himself of His Glory which began when, "taking upon Himself to deliver man, He did not abhor the Virgin's womb."[6]

[1] St. John x. 18. [2] Gal. iii. 13. [3] 1 Cor. i. 23.
[4] Heb. xii. 2.   [5] Ib. ii. 17.   [6] *Te Deum Laudamus.*

Thus, as we read the passage over, we see the successive stages of the humiliation of the Eternal Son. Existing in the real Nature of God, He set not store upon His Equality with God, but emptied Himself of His Glory by taking on Him the real nature of a slave, and being made in the likeness of man—that is the first step in the descent—and being found in outward appearance as a man He humbled Himself among men, and became obedient unto death—that is the second; but when all forms of death were open to Him He chose to die in the manner which was most full of ignominy in the eyes of men—He became obedient to the death of the Cross—that is the third.

II.

Why may we suppose, my brethren, that God, by His providence acting in His Church, places before our eyes this most suggestive passage of Holy Scripture on this particular Sunday?[1] We may, I think, answer that question without much difficulty.

1. We stand to-day on the threshold of the Great Week, which in the thought of a well-instructed Christian, whose heart is in its right place, is beyond all comparison the most solemn week in the whole year. It is the Holy Week, so called because it is consecrated to the particular consideration of our Lord's Sufferings and Death. Day by day in the Gospels, which are specially appointed, and in the Proper Lessons, the whole story of Christ's bitter and tragical Passion is unfolded step by step before our eyes, first in the language of one Evangelist, then in that of another, until every recorded incident has been placed before us. Now, if we are to profit by this most solemn and instructive Narrative, it is of the first importance that we should answer clearly to ourselves this primary question:

[1] Phil. ii. 5-11 forms the *Epistle* for the "Sunday next before Easter."

"Who is the Sufferer?" and that we should keep the answer well in the forefront of our thoughts throughout the week. Even in everyday history we look upon exactly the same misfortunes in the case of different persons with very different eyes when we take into account the moral excellence or even the personal rank of the sufferers. Of the many persons in high rank who had their heads cut off in the Tudor period of English history, people like Sir Thomas More and Lady Jane Grey attract particular interest on account of the lustre of sincerity and goodness which attaches to their characters. Of the many innocent victims of the first French Revolution, Louis XVI. and his queen, Marie Antoinette, will always command a predominant share of sympathy and interest, from the mere fact that each was born of a race of kings, born to an inheritance of luxury and splendour which contrasts so tragically with the last hours and scenes in the prison and on the public scaffold. It will be said, perhaps, that, so far as suffering goes, a peasant may suffer as acutely as a king, and that one man's life is as good as the life of another. True. But, for all that, it is felt that the destiny to which the king was born of itself makes his tragical end more tragical than it could else have been; if the amount of physical agony be no greater than in the case of the peasant, at least there is room for a greater degree of mental agony. When we apply this principle to our Lord, and in the light of the great doctrine which St. Paul teaches the Philippians in the text about Christ's Person, how new and awful a meaning does it give to the whole story of our Lord's Betrayal and Trial,—of the insults, humiliations, and sufferings to which He was subjected,—of the various particulars of His Death upon the Cross! Had He been merely man, the story of His Death would have roused deep human fellow-feelings within us; it is said on one occasion to have moved a multitude of heathen savages to tears by the mere force of its pathetic beauty. What they felt was the innocence of the Sufferer; that He did no sin, neither was guile found in His mouth; that when He was reviled He reviled not again;[1] that the blood which He shed was precious, as being that, as St. Peter says, of a Lamb without blemish, and immaculate.[2] Doubtless the sinless innocence of Christ does pour a flood of moral meaning on the history of His Death. If He had no sins to expiate He could not have died for Himself; and we, as we look into our guilty consciences, can only exclaim with the Apostle, that "such an High Priest became us, holy, harmless, undefiled, separate from sinners."[3] But that which gives to the Passion and Death of our Lord its real value is the fact that the Sufferer is more than man; that, although He suffers in and through a created nature, He is Personally God. This fact was part of that hidden wisdom or philosophy of which St. Paul writes to the Corinthians, when he tells them that "if the princes of this world had known it, they would not have crucified the Lord of glory."[4] This fact is the key-note to a true Christian understanding of the story of the Passion; at each step the Christian asks himself, "Who is this that cometh from Edom, with dyed garments from Bozrah?"[5] Who is this betrayed, insulted, beaten, bound, reviled One? Who is this arrayed as a mock monarch, with fancy robe and fancy sceptre—Whose Brow is pressed with that crown of thorns—Whose Shoulders are laden with that sharp and heavy cross? Whom do they buffet— upon Whose Face do they spit—into Whose Hands do they drive the nails—to Whose parched Mouth do they lift the hyssop? St. Paul answers that question as the centurion answered it beneath the cross: it was not

[1] 1 St. Pet. ii. 22, 23.   [2] Ib. i. 19.   [3] Heb. vii. 26.
[4] 1 Cor. ii. 8.   [5] Isa. lxiii. 1.

one of the sons of men upon whom His fellows were thus venting their scorn and hate; it was He Who, "existing in the true nature or form of God, did not set store by His equality with God, but emptied Himself of His Divine prerogatives, and took on Him the form of a servant, and was made in the likeness of men."

And it is this consideration which enables us to enter into all that the Apostles, and especially St. Paul, teach us as to the effects of the Death of Jesus Christ. Their language seems very exaggerated to those who believe Him to have been only man, and such persons consistently endeavour to empty it of its force by resolving it all into metaphor. There can be no reason for supposing that the death of any mere man would have had the effects which the Apostles attribute to the Death of Jesus Christ. They tell us that Jesus dying is a propitiation for our sins;[1] that He is our redemption from sin;[2] that by His Blood we who were far off were made nigh to God;[3] that His Blood cleanseth from all sin.[4] They thus teach us that we are, apart from Christ, exiles from our Father's home, captives who have to be brought back from bondage, sinners whose guilt must be expiated before the justice of God; and that this restoration, this reconciliation, this expiation, is the work of our Lord and Saviour, more particularly in His Death.

If it be asked why His Death should have such effects, there are two questions to be separately considered. First, Why should His Death affect *us* at all? That a great act of self-sacrifice should be a blessing to a man himself, to those immediately in contact with him who have had opportunities of witnessing it, this we can understand. But how is its effect to be transferred to other persons, belonging to distant countries and distant times? The

---

[1] Rom. iii. 25; 1 St. John ii. 2. [2] Col. i. 14; Heb. ix. 15.
[3] Eph. ii. 13-16; 2 Cor. v. 18. [4] 1 St. John i. 7.

answer is that our Lord stands to the whole human race in the position of its Representative. We know what is meant by a representative man; a man who represents a country, a class, a line of thought, a political or social aspiration. England abounds in representative men in this lower sense of the term. But Christ represents human nature, as Adam represented it; He is, according to St. Paul, the Second Adam,[1] Who stands out from among all other members of the human family, as occupying a position corresponding to that of the first Adam,—a position which gives His Personality a relationship to all. In the first Adam the whole human family lived by inclusion; and his acts compromised all his descendants by the same law as that which at the present day makes the good or bad character of a father, or a father's bodily constitution, rendered healthy by sober living, or enfeebled by vice, as the case may be, the inheritance of his child. Between us and the first Adam the connection is natural and necessary : between us and the Second Adam it depends upon our being brought into real contact with Him by faith and love on our part, by the grace which comes from Him through the Sacrament of our New Birth and otherwise, on His. We have, in short, to claim from Him His representative relationship, and what it involves; but when this claim has been made, the acts of Christ become our acts, the sufferings of Christ our sufferings, the self-sacrifice of Christ ours. Thus He bears our sins in His own Body on the tree ;[2] thus as by one man's disobedience many were made sinners, so by the obedience of One many were made righteous ;[3] thus "as in Adam all die, even so in Christ" may "all be made alive."[4]

Christ's Death then does affect us,—not by any arbitrary or capricious arrangement, but because He

[1] 1 Cor. xv. 45.
[2] 1 St. Pet. ii. 24.
[3] Rom. v. 19.
[4] 1 Cor. xv. 22.

took on Himself that human nature in which we all claim a share. But what is it that gives His Death its power and significance? It is that He Who dies is more than man. The reason which makes the history of the Passion so interesting and so awful is the same reason which makes its effects of such unspeakable significance. It is the "priceless worth of the person of the Son of God" —to use Hooker's language—"which gives such force and effect to all that He does and suffers."[1] What that force and effect would be we could not guess beforehand without a revelation from Heaven. We could only be sure of this, that the Death as well as the Life of such an One as Jesus Christ must, from the nature of the case, be very different, in point of spiritual result, from that of any mere man. The Apostles tell us in what that difference consists, when they enumerate the several elements and consequences of what we call the Atonement; when they tell us that by it God and man are reconciled, that a propitiation for man's sin is offered to God, that man is brought back from captivity in the realm of death. The wonder is—if there be room for wonder—not that so much follows from such a cause, but that, so far as we are told, so little follows from it. Doubtless the Passion of the Son of God has had results in spheres of being of which we know nothing, and of which, since nothing has been told us, it would not profit us to know. But it is natural to ask with St. Paul, "If God spared not His own Son, but freely gave Him up for us all, how shall He not with Him also freely give us all things?"[2] The promise is more than equal to sustain any conclusion which the Apostles actually draw from it.

2. But besides this, it is well that we should take to heart the particular lesson which St. Paul draws for the benefit of the Philippians from the consideration of the Incarnation

[1] *Eccl. Pol.* v. 52. 3.   [2] Rom. viii. 32.

and Passion of the Son of God. It is a lesson which is as valuable to us as members of civil society as it is valuable to members of the Church of Christ. What is the main source of the dangers which threaten the wellbeing of civil society from very opposite directions? It is the assertion of individual self-interest, real or supposed, pushed to a point at which it becomes incompatible with the interests of the community. The real enemy of human society is individual self-assertion,—intolerant of wealth, reputation, power, in others,—intolerant of any supremacy except the supremacy of self, of any glory except the glory of self, of any aggrandisement except the aggrandisement of self. This assertion becomes sometimes a despotism, which sacrifices the liberties of an entire nation to the supremacy of a single man; sometimes, as we see in that beautiful and hapless city across the Channel, at this moment a revolutionary chaos, in which a thousand aspirants for power and wealth are talking of nothing more and thinking of nothing less than the real good of their country. And the source of this mischief lies in a false ideal of human excellence; in the notion that it consists in self-assertion rather than in self-repression; in making the most of life for self, rather than in spending it for others. Now here St. Paul teaches us that Christ Incarnate and Crucified is the true model for Christians—for mankind. If He did not set store on glory which was rightfully, inalienably His, why should we? If He shrouded it, buried it away out of sight, lived amongst men as if it had no existence, took on Him the form of a servant, why should we do otherwise? If when He might have humbled Himself without suffering, if, when two roads of sacrifice were open to Him, He chose the most exacting and the most painful, does this say nothing to us? Surely, brethren, we see here, perhaps more clearly than in any other place of Holy

Scripture, how closely the moral teaching of Christianity is bound up with its doctrine. As Doddridge says in his noble hymn—

> "When I survey the wondrous cross
> On which the Prince of Glory died,
> My chiefest gain I count but loss,
> And pour contempt on all my pride."

Humility is so beautiful in Christian eyes because Christ was humble: self-sacrifice—even to death—is so glorious, because He is its conspicuous Example. He has settled the question of what high excellence in life really consists in, for all time: and it can never be re-opened. Pagans might admire self-assertion; the making the most of a position for personal and selfish ends; the clinging anxiously to the poor shreds of reputation, or wealth, or power which it may confer on a possessor. Yet they too knew that all this ended with the grave: and they could only bid men make the best of the fleeting hour, and shut their eyes to its inevitable close. Christ has taught us Christians a better way, not by precept merely, but by example. He has taught us that the true force and glory of our human life consists not in self-advertisement, but in self-repression; not in enjoyment, but in sacrifice of self. The principle which was to heal the divisions of the little Christian society at Philippi is the only principle which can save society, imperilled as it is in so many ways in the Europe of our day. All who have lived for others rather than for themselves in His Church,—all who have, at the call of duty, laid aside wealth, honour, credit, and embraced ignominy and suffering, have been true to Him —true to the spirit of His Incarnation and His Death, true to what St. Paul calls "the mind that was in Christ Jesus." And the true saviours of society are the men who care more for labour than for honour, more for doing good to others than for high place and name, more for the inner peace which self-sacrifice brings with it than for the outward decorations which are the reward of self-assertion. Such there are in every generation; and they are in a line with, or rather they are pale reflections of the Saviour of the world. Still more certain is it that the Mind of Christ in saving us is the only mind which enables us individually to accept His salvation. St. Paul describes the Jews as "being ignorant of God's righteousness, and going about to establish their own righteousness, and so not submitting themselves to the righteousness of God."[1] The most fatal thing in religion, next to insincerity, is that confidence in self which makes much of what we are, and forgets what, by God's grace, we might have been,—which thinks much of the good opinion of friends and little of the accusing voice of conscience,—which is fully alive to personal excellencies, and blind to that vast mass of evil which the Holy God, and the pure beings who surround His throne, see in us. May He teach us, at least, to be true. The self-deceit which makes us think much of self is impossible when a man's eyes have been opened to see what God really Is in His Awful Sanctity: "Now mine eye seeth Thee," he cries, "wherefore I abhor myself, and repent in dust and ashes."[2] Only penitent and broken hearts have any rightful place at the foot of the Redeemer's Cross; but there is no reason why any or all of us should not, by God's grace, in this our brief day of life, and especially at this blessed season, learn true penitence and contrition. It is the moral rather than the intellectual eye which discerns the true majesty of the Humiliation of the Son of God; it is the man who has emptied Himself of self-complacency who finds in the Redeemer, disfigured with wounds and robed in shame upon His Cross, "an hiding-place from the winds of life, and a covert from the tempest; and a river of water in a dry place, and the shadow of a great rock in a weary land."[3]

[1] Rom. x. 3.   [2] Job xlii. 5, 6.   [3] Isa. xxxii. 2.

SERMON III.

THE PERSON OF THE CRUCIFIED.

1 Cor. i. 13.

Was Paul crucified for you?

WHEN a question is asked which can only be answered in one way, it is asked, not in order to extract information, but to set people thinking. And this is plainly the object of the question which the Apostle puts to the Corinthians. The Apostle knew, and the Corinthians knew, Who really had been crucified for them. Why then does the Apostle ask the question, to which one answer only was possible? Why does he ask them, "Was Paul crucified for you?" If they reflected, the Corinthians must have felt that they—or some of them—were acting as if Paul *had* been crucified for them. For what were they doing? They were breaking up the church of Christ at Corinth into divisions, which they named in three cases after human teachers; in one (but from a motive which was at least as bad as that of the rest) after our Lord Jesus Christ. One saith, I am of Paul; and another, I of Apollos, and I of Cephas, and I of Christ.[1] This was natural enough in the Greek schools of philosophy, where every teacher had his private speculation, and where nothing more solid and helpful than a speculation was, in the last resort, to be had at all. And

[1] 1 Cor. i. 12.

the Corinthians, who had all their lives been accustomed to the ways of the philosophers, were now bringing their old Pagan habits inside the Church. They could only be brought to reason by a question which should place the real import of their act in a startling light, by showing them that, in thus ranging themselves under a human teacher, they were forgetting what was due to the Author and Finisher of their faith.[1] And such a question was this: "Was Paul crucified for you?" Let us pause to observe that there is courage, and courage of a rare quality, in this question of the Apostle's. Many a man is physically courageous who is wholly lacking in moral courage; and many a man who has moral courage is incapable of that high exercise of it which is before us in the text. The Apostle does not begin by addressing himself to those who used in different senses the names of other teachers in rivalry to his own. He does not ask, Was Apollos, was Cephas crucified for you? No, his question is addressed to the very persons with whom an ordinary leader or teacher of men finds it most difficult to be perfectly frank and honest. It is addressed to his especial friends at Corinth, to those who generously took his part, who, with sincerity and enthusiasm made much of his name and his authority, and on whose sympathy and co-operation, humanly speaking, he had largely to rely.

My brethren, it is not difficult to find fault with those who oppose us: they are reputed fair game for criticism. Our self-love whispers to us that if they were not wrong they could not be our opponents; and our best and most serious convictions often reinforce what is thus whispered by our self-love. So they are told the hard truth, or what we take to be the hard truth, with an unshrinking frankness; and the operation costs us little effort, and it causes them no great surprise, since it is only what they

[1] Heb. xii. 2.

have to expect at our hands. So it is with human parties: we see it every day in this or that department of national and public life. But what we do not witness often is the spectacle of a leader of men who dares to tell the truth to his own friends. He may feel that there are truths which they ought to be told; that his silence may be misconstrued into an approval which he does not mean; that a true disinterestedness would risk much rather than be so misconstrued. But, notwithstanding, he reflects that he depends on them; he apprehends that plain speaking would breed divisions; that at least it would hinder hearty co-operation, and would tend to break up the party with which he acts. So he is silent, stifling regrets at that which he does not venture to criticise, and thus letting his friends take their erring or mischievous course, without interference or warning. So it was with Eli: he could not bear to be true with his own family, and thus, while his sons discredited the priesthood of Israel, he was silent.[1] So it was with some early Christian bishops, and more than one early Christian Emperor; the Emperor's assistance was too valuable to be endangered by plain speaking; it was not every bishop who, like St. Ambrose, would rebuke a Theodosius after the slaughter of Thessalonica. So it was with Luther. He could not afford to break with the Elector Frederick, and so he invented a sanction for bigamy which no man would have condemned more fiercely than he in a theological opponent. This is human weakness.

St. Paul was—God's grace had made him—strong and tender enough to begin his task of telling unwelcome truth, by telling it to his own devoted friends; to ask the men who showed such affection for him, but so mistakenly, "Was Paul crucified for you?" What, then, is the import of the question?

[1] 1 Sam. iii. 13.

It might seem to appeal, first of all, and on the surface of the words, to the sense of historic absurdity: "Was Paul crucified for you?"

Was not this Paul the very writer of the letter which asks the question? How, then, could he have died upon a cross for the benefit of those who were quietly reading his words at Corinth? The question is not whether what might have happened but did not happen, had happened. It is whether that which could not have happened, which could not be seriously thought of as having happened, had happened. Such a question was, of course, in a high degree provocative; it was deliberately calculated, as we have seen, to provoke self-questioning, self-distrust, self-reproach, self-correction, by asking that which could only be answered in one way, and impatiently, and which never would have been asked at all unless things had been very much amiss with those to whom it was addressed.

But this was not all. The question whether Paul was crucified suggests the thought, Who then was crucified? It suggests, first of all, the separateness, the deep impassable chasm, which yawns between any two personal existences. No one of us can possibly be another. Each personal being, whether created or Divine, whether man or angel, has his own niche to fill, his own work to do, his own particular destiny to accomplish. Other beings may nearly resemble,—they cannot be and do what he is and does. In the world of fact, and before the Divine Eye, each of us differs from all besides. The starting-point, the outset, the career, the characteristic acts, the efforts, the sufferings, the time and manner of the end, all are different. "Was Paul crucified for you?" Without for the moment going further, the question suggests, on the very threshold·

of the subject, the difference which parted the career of the Apostle from that of his Master. And in doing this it also pointed to a truth beyond: our Divine Master's isolation,—His awful, unapproachable isolation on the Cross. My brethren, we can understand something of the secret of this from what is passing just now before our eyes. At this moment the shadow of a great sorrow rests upon the Throne of this Empire. A life, still young, with energy and capacity and disposition such as would in any station have been held to promise a future of usefulness and success, and with opportunities such as can fall to a very few men in a century, has been suddenly cut short.[1] A widow with her orphan child—a mother mourning the loss of her youngest son: these are the figures on which the country is bending its profoundly sympathising gaze with a genuineness of anxious interest which provokes the wonder of foreigners. And it may here perhaps be asked whether such spectacles of human bereavement are not to be found by hundreds every day, in the streets of this Metropolis, and whether there is not something morbid in this lavish bestowal of consideration and sympathy on the sorrows of Royalty? Certainly, trouble is no monopoly of the great; the human heart is as tender and as exacting in the poorest hovels of the labouring man as in the palaces of kings. And yet it is a true human instinct which draws us with affectionate sympathy to the foot of the Throne at times like this, since we are really influenced, perhaps only half-consciously, by a sense of the isolation of the pathetic sufferer. Yes! that is one of the heaviest demands that are made upon earthly greatness: its owners inevitably live apart; they are denied all that human consolation and support which perfect reciprocity of thought and feeling ensures in the humbler walks of life, and which is ill replaced by the fixed proprieties of

[1] His Royal Highness the Duke of Albany died March 28, 1884.

courtly deference: they are like those loftiest peaks in a chain of mountains, which earn their elevation at the cost of solitary exposure to the icy blasts, which no rival summit intercepts, that it may rob them of some elements of their pitiless severity. The isolation of the Throne! Yes, that is one special reason why its occupant has, at all times, but especially at times like this, an especial claim on the prayers of the Church of Christ—a claim which, it may be feared, we Christians too often fail adequately to recognise. But we may not dwell longer on any merely human sorrow, however august the scene, on the Sunday in the year which, of all Sundays, is closest to the Passion of the Son of God,—to an anguish besides which any earthly anguish is but a passing sense of discomfort. In His case, the isolation of Gethsemane was only outdone by the isolation of Calvary: He too was the occupant of a throne, but His throne was a scaffold. He was alone with His load of sin and suffering at every step of the Passion, though He moved forward to His death amid the ostentatious noise and bustle of a multitude; "I have trodden the winepress alone, and of the people there was none beside Me,"[1] was the predestined and the actual language of His Soul: and with his eye upon this awful solitariness of his suffering Master, the Apostle asks the Corinthians, "Was Paul crucified for you?"

II.

" Was Paul crucified for you?"

The question implies, secondly, the unique efficacy of the Death of our Lord Jesus Christ.

Let us note that in this question the Apostle fixes on our Lord's Death in shame and torture as the most characteristic feature of His earthly career. Many a Christian,

[1] Isa. lxiii. 3.

ancient or modern, having the Apostle's object in view, would have asked a different question. Of old, men would perhaps have asked, Was Paul transfigured on the mount? Did Paul raise Lazarus from the dead? Did Paul rise from the dead the third day? And in modern times, too, many would have asked, Did Paul preach the Sermon on the Mount? In the Apostle's eyes our Lord's Teaching was of less account than His Death: nay, the glory with which His Manhood was invested, His power to raise the dead, and to rise from death, counted for less than the fact that He was crucified. Not in this passage only are these points thrust by comparison into the background, while His Death is treated as the prominent feature in His manifestation to the world. "O foolish Galatians," the Apostle cries, "before whose eyes Jesus Christ has been evidently set forth crucified."[1] "I determined not to know anything among you," he tells the Corinthians, "save Jesus Christ, and Him crucified."[2] "God forbid that I should glory," he writes again to the Galatians, "save in the Cross of our Lord Jesus Christ."[3] St. Paul plainly feels that the full meaning of Christ's work emerges in His Death; that His Death, and not His Teaching, is the climax of His self-manifestation to mankind; that the gift of Inspiration might conceivably have enabled an Apostle to teach side by side with the Master—that Divine Power might robe a purely human form with glory, might enable a mere man to raise the dead, or might Itself raise another Lazarus from death; but that no being of whom we know, no being, whether in earth or heaven, could possibly have taken the Redeemer's place upon the Cross of Calvary. For, indeed, the Corinthian Christians had been taught that when Jesus Christ was crucified, His Death had a virtue, was followed by results, which no other death had ever had since the world

[1] Gal. iii. 1.   [2] 1 Cor. ii. 2.   [3] Gal. vi. 14.

began. Christians were then taught that this Death was, first of all, a Propitiation for sin, a Propitiation, real and literal, offered on earth, accepted in heaven—a Propitiation of which the offerings on the Day of Atonement in the ancient Tabernacle were but a faint shadow and presentiment. Thus St. Paul says that Jesus Christ was set forth as a Propitiation, where the word means a propitiating victim,[1] through faith in His Blood: that is, He becomes this to us when we believe in the efficacy of this sacrifice of His Life; and St. John twice[2] calls our Lord Jesus Christ a Propitiation, using a word which means practically one who effects a propitiation for our sins, "and not for ours only, but also for the sins of the whole world." Again, Christians were taught that the Death of our Lord was a redemption from the guilt and penalty of sin; that it was an enfranchisement, purchased at a costly price, and that this price was none other than the Blood, that is, the symbol and also the essential element of the Life of Jesus Christ. Thus the Apostle tells the Ephesians that when members of Christ "we have redemption through His Blood, even the forgiveness of sins;"[3] and the Colossians, that in the Son of God's love we have our redemption, which is again explained to mean the forgiveness of our sins.[4] To this our Lord Himself referred when, on the occasion of the demand of the sons of Zebedee to sit on His right Hand and on His left in His kingdom, He told His disciples that the Son of Man had come not to be ministered unto, but to minister, and to give His Life a ransom, or price paid down, for many.[5] Once more, Christians were taught that the Death of our Lord, having this propitiatory and redemptive virtue, was thus a Reconciliation or Atonement between God and man. "We rejoice in God," he

---

[1] ἱλαστήριον, Rom. iii. 25.   [2] ἱλασμός, 1 St. John ii. 2; iv. 10.
[3] Eph. i. 7.   [4] Col. i. 14.   [5] St. Matt. xx. 28.

tells the Romans, "through our Lord Jesus Christ, through Whom we have now received the reconciliation."[1] God, he tells the Corinthians, "has reconciled us to Himself through Christ.... God was in Christ reconciling the world unto Himself, not imputing their trespasses unto them;" and this reconciliation was effected in the Garden of Gethsemane and on the Cross, when "Him Who knew no sin, He made to be sin on our behalf, that we might be made the Righteousness of God in Him."[2]

Thus the Death of our Lord is stated in the New Testament to be a Propitiation for sin, a Price paid to buy our freedom from sin's penalty, and an Act which reconciled sinful but penitent man with a holy God. It is open to people to say that they do not believe the Apostle's teaching; but what is hardly open to them, consistently with honest dealing with language, is to suggest that on so serious a subject the Apostle did not mean what he says, and was only using the phrases of poetry and metaphor. At this rate language ceases to be an instrument for the transmission of thought; if it has not become, as Talleyrand cynically put it, a means for concealing thought. The Death of our Lord is in the New Testament plainly credited with effects which are attributed to no other death in human history; and it is to this solitary efficacy of Christ's Death that St. Paul tacitly refers in the question, "Was Paul crucified for you?"

No doubt, already the Apostle himself had undergone much for the sake of that Faith by which he hoped to promote the highest happiness of mankind, and, in this sense, he too suffered for his converts. Not long after he could write: "Of the Jews five times received I forty stripes save one. Thrice was I beaten with rods, once was I stoned, thrice I suffered shipwreck, a night and a day I have been in the deep; in journeyings often,

[1] Rom. v. 11. [2] 2 Cor. v. 18-21.

in perils of waters, in perils of robbers, in perils from mine own countrymen, in perils from the heathen, in perils in the city, in perils in the wilderness, in perils in the sea, in perils among false brethren; in . . . hunger and thirst, in fastings often, in cold and nakedness."[1] And although in the end he was not crucified, yet the day came when, in his own words, he was ready to be offered, and the time of his departure was at hand,[2] and he was led out beyond the Ostian gate at Rome to die by the hand of the executioner.

And yet, what was the effect of the prolonged sufferings and final martyrdom of St. Paul? They were a proof of his devoted love of his Crucified Lord; they were a witness to his profound belief in the truth of Christianity, as a creed worth living for, worth dying for. They thus enriched the Church of his generation, the Church of all succeeding ages, with an example which goes on, even now, drawing, kindling, invigorating souls in the service of their Redeemer. But did St. Paul's death act as a propitiation before God? Did it buy men back from the guilt and penalties of sin? Did it reconcile God and man? Did it, in fact, establish new relations between earth and heaven? No! the Death of our Lord Jesus Christ was followed by consequences which differ, not in degree merely, but in kind, from those which have followed the death of any of His servants; and St. Paul suggests this to the Corinthians by asking them, "Was Paul crucified for you?"

III.

If it be asked, why this should be so, we have only to shift the accent, as we ask the question, and it will answer itself.

[1] 2 Cor. xi. 24-27.   [2] 2 Tim. iv. 6.

"Was *Paul* crucified for you?"

For it suggests, this question, thirdly, the unique dignity of the Divine Redeemer. It is because He is what He is, that His Redemptive Death has this efficacy that is all its own. Observe here, that even our Lord's Nature as Man was in two respects unique.

First of all, it was Sinless. That taint of evil, which we all of us inherit from our first parent, and which, though its stain and degradation is removed in Baptism, yet hangs about our life, like an atmosphere charged with the possibilities of moral mischief, had no place in Him. Alone of the children of Eve, His was truly an Immaculate Conception, cutting off the entail of inherited corruption, and making Him all that the first father of the race had been before his fall. Still more certainly was He preserved from actual sin: although the darts of the tempter lighted again and again on the surface of His Human Soul, on His life of thought and feeling, and, we may dare say, of passion, yet in Him they found no response, however faint; they glanced off as from a polished surface which afforded them no lodgment. Thus He could address to His contemporaries a challenge which no other in human form ever could utter with impunity: "Which of you convinceth Me of sin?"[1] And His Apostle could proclaim "that He was made to be sin for us, Who knew no sin, that we might be made the righteousness of God in Him."[2] It was this Sinless Nature which, representing a world of sinners, hung in death upon the Cross; and the Apostle's consciousness that he himself had been "sold under sin,"[3] and that he was parted by an immeasurable interval from the Sinless Redeemer, Who had bought him with the price of His Blood—this consciousness underlies his question, "Was Paul crucified for you?"

Next, our Lord's Human Nature, being thus Sinless, was

[1] St. John viii. 46.   [2] 2 Cor. v. 21.   [3] Rom. vii. 14.

also representative of the race. It has been said, with truth, that when the Eternal Word, or Son of God, was made flesh, He united Himself, not to a human person, but to human nature. His Humanity had nothing about it that was local, particular, appropriate only to a single historical epoch, to a country, to a race. He was born in Palestine, and of a Jewish mother, yet He was without the narrowing characteristics of the Jew; He was born a member of a down-trodden and conquered race, when the Roman empire had reached the zenith of its fortunes, yet in Mind and Character He might have belonged as well to the race of the conquerors, or to any other epoch in the history of mankind. All races, all countries, all ages had a share in Him, yet He could be claimed as an exclusive possession by none.

This representative character of our Lord's Manhood is insisted on by St. Paul, when he calls Jesus Christ the Second Adam.[1] As the first Adam represented the whole human family by being the common ancestor, from whom all human beings derived the gift of physical life, so that his blood flowed in their veins, and their several lives, whatever their individual characteristics may be, are traceable to and meet in him; so the Second Adam was to represent the human family, not as the common source of bodily life, but as the parent of a moral and spiritual existence, which those children of the first Adam who would, might receive from Him. The Second Adam was, says the Apostle, a Quickening Spirit:[2] He held towards the spiritual and higher life of mankind a relation as intimate, and, in its purpose, as universal as the first Adam had held to man's natural life.

Now, in this representative character of our Lord's Human Nature we see the explanation of that which often embarrasses thoughtful readers of the Bible and the early

---

[1] 1 Cor. xv. 45. [2] Ib.

Christian writers. Why, they ask, should the great men of the old Jewish history be constantly represented as types of Christ? Why should there be any traceable correspondence between Abraham, or Joseph, or Moses, or Joshua, or David, or Solomon, and the Lord Jesus? The whole idea seems at first sight arbitrary; as though anybody might be a type, in the hands of a fanciful writer, of anybody else. Yet, brethren, it is not so in reality. Because Christ's Manhood is representative of all that is excellent in man, therefore each excellence of the ancient saints foreshadowed something that was to have a place in Him: therefore Abraham, and Joseph, and Moses, and Joshua, and David, and Solomon, reappeared, all of them, but without their attendant weakness, in the Son of Mary. Nay, it well may be that whatever was pure, and lofty, and noble in the human family beyond the favoured families of the chosen race, in Greece or India—mere natural excellencies, imperfect, but struggling,—was a true anticipation of the Perfect and Representative Man. He belonged to each, He infinitely transcended each, He summarised and recapitulated in Himself all that was true and great in all that had preceded Him; and as His Nature was thus comprehensively representative, His Acts and Sufferings were representative too. If He died, human nature at its best died in Him; and those who have, by gifts from Him, and by the voluntary and moral association of faith, a share in this typically Perfect Nature are vitally associated with His Death, and, by no arbitrary fiction, but as a matter of justice, share in its deserts and in its vast and beneficial consequences. Thus "if any man be in Christ, he is the new creation: old things are passed away, behold, all things are become new."[1] Thus Christians are "accepted in the Beloved,"[2] by actually sharing that new and representative Nature

[1] 2 Cor. v. 17.   [2] Eph. i. 6.

which the Son of God made His own, that it might be "obedient unto death."[1] But what of the Apostle? Paul was by the grace of God an Apostle and a Saint; but he had no pretensions to represent the Jewish people, much less the human family. He was a man of his time, deeply indented with strong individual traits, a man of whom few would have said, "Here is a representative nature, in which I trace, along with much besides, the lineaments of my own being and character." No! One only has ever represented the race at large by the very constitution of His Nature; and, conscious of this, the Apostle asks the Corinthians, "Was Paul crucified for you?"

But our Lord, although His Manhood was thus Sinless and Representative, was much more than man. In truth, His Manhood was but a robe which He had folded around His Person when He condescended to come among us; in the true seat of His Being He was much more than man: He was, as His Apostle says, "God over all, Blessed for ever."[2] When His Passion was approaching, and the first drops of the great storm that broke upon Him had begun to fall, He partly lifted the veil, as, in the tremendous words of last Sunday's Gospel, "Before Abraham was, I am."[3] When they were nailing Him to the Cross, He hinted at the solemn truth in the prayer, "Father, forgive them, for they know not what they do."[4] When the poor thief turned to Him in the penitence and faith of his dying agonies, He replied, in words which would have been absurd or blasphemous had He not been the true Lord of souls, and Lord of the abode of souls in the land beyond the veil, "To-day shalt thou be with Me in Paradise."[5] When He gave up the ghost, nature around was visibly troubled; the earth did quake, and the rocks were rent, and many bodies of holy Jews which slept arose, and went into the holy city, and appeared unto

[1] Phil. ii. 8. [2] Rom. ix. 5. [3] St. John viii. 58.
[4] St. Luke xxiii. 34. [5] St. Luke xxiii. 43.

many.[1] When all was over, the centurion, Pagan as he was, could not but feel the radiation of the great truth which gives the Passion its most solemn meaning, "Truly this was the Son of God!"[2]

Yes, this is the point which we Christians must never for a moment lose sight of as year by year we traverse the history of the Sufferings which our Redeemer underwent on our behalf. The solemn truth which gives each separate event its astonishing elevation is the truth that the Sufferer is God, Who, that He might suffer, has taken a nature in which suffering becomes possible. The flesh which is scourged is the Flesh of God; the hands which are pierced are the Hands of God; the brow which is crowned with thorns, the face which is buffeted and spat upon,—these are the Brow and the Face of God. The Blood which flows from His Five Wounds is rightly credited with Its cleansing power; It is no mere physical humour that is draining away the life of a human body; as the Apostle told the presbyters of Ephesus on the beach at Miletus,—it is the Blood of God.[3]

Who could have said beforehand what the Death of such a Being would or would not effect? In such a sphere human reason is altogether at fault; it can neither anticipate nor can it criticise the truth. It can but listen for what Revelation may say; and when Revelation tells us that this tremendous event has been a Propitiation for human sin, and has brought men out of captivity to sin's penalties, into freedom and peace, and has reconciled a Holy God and His erring creatures, we can only listen and believe. Certainly this was the Crucifixion as St. Paul thought of it; He thought of it as the decisive moment of the world's Redemption, because the Redeemer was indisputably Divine.

What then must have been the feeling of the adoring Apostle, when his mind rested for an instant on the idea,

[1] St. Matt. xxvii. 51-53.   [2] Ib. 54.   [3] Acts xx. 17, 28.

that human souls had thrust him unwittingly on the throne of the Uncreated, when he asked the question, "Was Paul crucified for you?"

One point in conclusion. Surely our Crucified Saviour should have a first place in the thought and heart of the Church at large, and of each of His redeemed servants. No other, be he man or angel, has remotely comparable claims. No religious teacher, in past ages or in recent times, has been crucified for us; no friend, or parent, or wife, or child, has or can for us overcome the sharpness of death, with the effect of opening the kingdom of heaven to our faith and love. Only when we gaze upon the Crucified do we behold the fullest unveiling of the Heart of God, face to face with the sin and suffering of human life. Only when we gaze upon the Crucified do we behold the Fountain and Source from Which flow all the streams that refresh and invigorate the great garden of souls—the Christian Church. Only when we gaze upon the Crucified do we behold the Source of pardon for sinners—for each one of ourselves,—and the standard of obedience and love for saints. Here is the true article of a standing or falling Church,—not how much we make of the poor thin emotions of the sinful soul, but how much, forgetting ourselves, we can prize the transcendent Sufferings of the Divine Redeemer. Be this our work, during the coming Week of penitence and grace, to erect in each heart a throne for the Crucified, to expel all rival affections that would usurp what should belong only to Him, and thus by His Cross and Passion as our Hope and Refuge, to be brought to the Glory of His Resurrection.

> "O let my heart no further roam,
> 'Tis Thine by vows, and hopes, and fears,
>   Long since; O call Thy wanderer home
> To that dear home, safe in Thy wounded Side,
> Where only broken hearts their sin and shame may hide."[1]

[1] *The Christian Year.* Hymn for Good Friday.

SERMON IV.

THE ACCEPTED OFFERING.

HEB. X. 5, 6, 7.

Wherefore when He cometh into the world, He saith, Sacrifice and offering Thou wouldest not, but a body hast Thou prepared Me: in burnt-offerings and sacrifices for sin Thou hast had no pleasure. Then said I, Lo, I come to do Thy will.

IN the old Liturgies and in old English divines this Sunday, the fifth in Lent and the second before Easter, is often called Passion Sunday. The name has disappeared from the pages of our Prayer-Books, but enough, or more than enough, remains in them to justify it. The Service for the day looks onward to Good Friday. The Gospel[1] describes that climax of the struggle between our Lord and the adversaries at Jerusalem which made all that followed—humanly speaking—inevitable, and which revealed to His murderers, in language which they well understood, the awful claims of their Victim. The Epistle[2] looks at the result in the light of Christian experience and Christian history: it speaks of the power of an Atoning Blood, the Blood of One Who is both Priest and Victim, in contrast with the impotent and fruitless bloodshedding of bulls and goats slain at the altar of the Jewish temple. Thus we see the note of the Passion is already sounded; the subject is approached on its historical as well as on its practical and experimental side, and accordingly, under the guidance of the text, we do well,

[1] St. John viii. 46-59. [2] Heb. ix. 11-15.

though at a distance, to stand this afternoon in view of the Cross, and reflect upon one element of its awful meaning.

"When He cometh into the world He saith, Sacrifice and offering Thou wouldest not, but a body hast Thou prepared Me." Here is a Speaker and His utterance—a Speaker Who can be only One, and a quotation of some words very familiar, I should suppose, to most of us. Let us, for the sake of clearness, reverse the order of ideas in the text. Let us first of all examine the drift and meaning of the passage quoted, and then the use which is made of it by the speaker in the Epistle to the Hebrews.

I.

Now, the passage quoted occurs in the fortieth Psalm, which, no doubt, simply because it contains this very passage, is used on the morning of Good Friday. The fortieth Psalm is traceable, as both the language and the allusions would lead us to believe, to the age and hand of David. To argue that the reference to the "roll of the book"[1] is an indication of its having been written about the time of Josiah's reformation, is as prudent as it would be to argue that an old English writer, referring to the privileges of Parliament, could not have written before the reign of Charles I., on the ground that Parliamentary privilege was then undoubtedly a matter of very general discussion. The language is, in point of form and structure, suited to the age of David: the circumstances are those of the close of the sad and suffering years when David was still persecuted by Saul, but already knew that his rescue and his triumph could not be long deferred. Like two other Psalms of the period,[2] this is a Psalm at once of praise and of complaint—complaint that there was

[1] Ps. xl. 10. [2] Pss. xxxi. and lxix.

still much to apprehend, praise that so much had been done so mercifully. David can only compare the miseries of the past to a deep morass, where there was no resting-place for his feet, and in which he felt himself sinking, until God "brought him out of this horrible pit, out of the mire and clay, and set his feet upon a rock."[1] God had, moreover, put a new song in his mouth—had given him a heart and a tongue for praise, and for the encouragement of his brethren and dependants; and he sincerely feels that God's mercies to him have been so many and so vast, that if he "should declare them and speak of them they would be more than he is able to express."[2] How shall he express, if he can express, his gratitude, and the sorrow for past wrong, and the hearty self-devotion which true gratitude calls forth? It would be natural for him to think—and for a moment he does think—of the regular provisions for expressing the needs and moods of the human soul which were afforded by the Jewish ritual. There were sacrifices of slain beasts, and bloodless offerings of fine flour: the burnt-offering to obtain the Divine favour; the sin-offering to make propitiation for wrong. But no, it will not do; the Psalmist's mind rests upon these ancient rites only to set them aside. In his deep trouble, it seems, he has been permitted to catch sight of the outline of a higher Revelation than that of Moses, and to learn, that whatever might be their provisional use and import, these slaughtered bulls and goats, these burnt-offerings and sin-offerings, could not really affect man's relations with God.

> "Sacrifice and Minchah Thou wouldest not,
> But mine ears hast Thou pierced;
> Burnt-offering and sin-offering Thou requiredst not.
> Then said I: Behold, I come
> With the roll of the Book which is written concerning me,
> To do Thy will, O God."[3]

---

[1] Ps. xl. 2.   [2] Ib. 3-7.   [3] Ib. 8-10.

David will not, then, offer the old sacrifices; at any rate, he will not offer them as the best he has to give; he will bring to God's Footstool something else, something better. What is it? "Mine ears hast Thou pierced," says the Hebrew text of the Psalm. "A body hast Thou prepared me," says the passage as quoted in the Epistle from the Greek LXX. translation of the Psalm. How shall we reconcile the discrepancy? Not to detain you with explanations which I could only mention to set aside, let us observe that in many cases the old Greek translation of the Hebrew Scriptures, which the New Testament writers so frequently quote, is, like all good translations, not always a literal rendering, but a paraphrase, especially in places where to render literally would be to be unintelligible. The Greek reader would never have understood all that the Hebrew poet meant by "piercing the ears." David meant to express very vividly that God had given him a sense and power of obeying His recognised Will; and in order to make this full meaning obvious to his readers—obvious to the utmost range of its applicability—the Greek translator of David renders, "a body hast Thou prepared me:" a body wherewith to render Thee a perfect, unstinted service. The idea of entire willingness to acknowledge and obey the Will of God is expanded into the idea of a body prepared for absolute surrender to that Will. It is, no doubt, a very free paraphrase; yet, on that very account, it is an admirable translation of the thought, if not of the language; the thought, the meaning, is plain enough. Real self-surrender to the Will of God is surrender of the life, of the body, of that which is outward and belongs to sense, as well as of that which is inward and belongs to spirit; it is surrender of the life, as distinct from any of its accessories, to that Perfect Will Which rules the universe.

When David proposes to express his thankfulness in

this way, it is plain that he thinks of God as a Person. This would be a trite remark to make under ordinary circumstances; but it is not, perhaps, altogether superfluous just now, when a brilliant and light-hearted essayist, airily discussing the relations which he presumes to exist between the Bible considered as literature and the great truths of Christianity, has recently gone so far as to say that the God Whom Israel served was not a Person at all; that He was in the belief of Israel only "an abstract, an eternal Power, or only a stream of tendency, not ourselves, and making for righteousness."[1] By this novel and circuitous expression the writer hopes, when speaking of God, to escape the necessity of using a metaphysical term like Person. He has a great dread of what he calls metaphysics, and a corresponding impatience of all that side of Divine Revelation which belongs to the sphere of the supersensuous, and which can only be brought home to the human understanding in language which inspired writers like St. John and St. Paul, or great Church assemblies and teachers have borrowed from the philosophy of abstract being. He is acute enough to see, and honest enough to admit, that to profess belief in a Personal God is to be just as deeply committed to a metaphysical doctrine as to profess belief in the Holy Trinity, or in the Consubstantiality of the Son; he sees that St. John and St. Paul were not less really metaphysicians in their way of speaking about God and our Lord than were Councils and Fathers; and that to talk of a Person carries us at once into the very heart of metaphysics. So, to go to the root of the matter, and get rid of what he so much dislikes, he would call God a Power or a Tendency—as distinct from a Person,—and he even persuades himself that the early writers in the Bible thought of God in this way too. They were not, he says, metaphysicians; and when

---

[1] Matthew Arnold, *Literature and Dogma*, chap. i.

we talk of a Personal Cause and Ruler of the universe, we are using language which is strange to them. Now certainly, if it be meant that the idea of Personality, as it is elaborated, for instance, in Bishop Butler,[1] is not presented to us thus sharply and consciously in the Hebrew or Christian Scriptures, there is no room for controversy. But the point to observe is that although the idea of a Person is not philosophically drawn out in Scripture, it is irresistibly implied in the entire Scriptural account of God. If a person,—unless when used in a narrower, exceptional sense of the glorious Three Who co-exist everlastingly within the Unity of God,—if, I say, a person ordinarily means a separate consciousness, will, and character, these three things are found from the very first in the God revealed by the Hebrew Scriptures, whether the word which collects and implies them in later language be there or not. Who can go through the Psalter and seriously imagine that the Being to Whom all that praise, that penitence, those tender expostulations, those passionate assurances, those earnest deprecations and entreaties, are addressed, was conceived of by the hearts which sought Him in Israel as only " an abstract Eternal Power or stream of tendency, not ourselves, making for righteousness "? Put this definition in each of the places in the Psalter—in the fifty-first Psalm, or in this fortieth Psalm, where the word GOD occurs—and see what will be the moral and, I may add, the literary result. Certainly if I say, " Lo, I come to do Thy will, O God !" I do not, I cannot, conceive myself as addressing any mere Power or tendency;—who would protest his readiness to do its will to a magnetic current, or to a political enthusiasm, or to a force which it would be metaphysical, and therefore wrong, to think of as conscious, or as having a real will or character at all?

[1] Butler, Dissertation I. : Of Personal Identity.

Depend upon it, my brethren, in this matter the common sense of mankind at large may very fairly be trusted. A real God is necessarily a Personal God; to talk of God and deny His Personality is to play tricks with language; there is no real room beyond belief in a Personal God for anything but atheism.

Yes! it was in entire self-surrender to the Holy Will of the Personal God that David learnt a higher service than that of the mass of his countrymen. He learnt to think less highly of the material than of the moral, of the outward than of the inward, of the partial than of the complete. No doubt, to many an Israelite the series of Temple sacrifices appeared in the light of a regular tariff, by complying with which, under varying circumstances, His worshippers set themselves right with God in a business-like way. So much fine flour, so many heifers, bulls, or goats, such and such expenditure, and all would be settled. Doubtless there were numbers who rose far higher than this, who read in the Jewish ritual its inherent and intentional imperfection, and something perhaps of what was to succeed it. But when David sings, as in this fortieth Psalm, he is like one of those higher Alps which the beams of the rising sun have lit up while the valleys at its feet are still wellnigh in twilight. Yet he was not alone or the first in this his early illumination. Probably he was himself thinking of Samuel's remonstrance with Saul, when, after the conquest of Amalek, the latter would have compounded for moral disobedience by animal sacrifices. "Hath the Lord as great delight in burnt-offerings and sacrifices as in obeying the voice of the Lord? Behold, to obey is better than sacrifice."[1] Probably he had heard of that famous reply of Balaam to the king of Moab, which was referred to by Micah in a later age for the benefit of degenerate Israel. To the question—

[1] 1 Sam. xv. 22.

The Accepted Offering.

> "Wherewith shall I come before the Lord,
> And bow myself before the High God?
> Shall I come before Him with burnt-offerings,
> With calves of a year old?
> Will the Lord be pleased with thousands of rams,
> Or with ten thousands of rivers of oil?
> Shall I give my first-born for my transgression,
> The fruit of my body for the sin of my soul?"[1]

the reply ran thus :—

> "He hath showed thee, O man, what is good :
> And what doth the Lord require of thee,
> But to do justly, and to love mercy,
> And to walk humbly with thy God?"[2]

And in his later life, when in his deep repentance for his darkest sin, a flood of light had again broken upon his soul, David himself again cries, "Thou desirest no sacrifice, else would I give it Thee: but Thou delightest not in burnt-offerings. The sacrifice of God is a troubled spirit: a broken and contrite heart, O God, Thou wilt not despise."[3] It is in the same sense that Asaph, in his vision of God's judgment of Israel, hears Him say, "I will not reprove thee for the sacrifices of thy burnt-offerings, because they were not always before Me.... Thinkest thou that I will eat bulls' flesh, or drink the blood of goats?"[4] It is thus, too, that God expostulates with Judah by the mouth of Isaiah : "To what purpose is the multitude of your sacrifices? saith the Lord; I am full of the burnt-offerings of rams, and the fat of fed beasts: I delight not in the blood of bullocks, or of lambs, or of he-goats."[5] It is in this sense that He asks later by Jeremiah : "To what purpose cometh there to Me incense from Sheba? or the sweet cane from a far country? Your burnt-offerings are not acceptable, nor your sacrifices sweet unto Me."[6] "I desired mercy," He says by Hosea, "and not sacrifice, and the knowledge of God more than burnt-

---

[1] Micah vi. 7.   [2] Ib. 8.   [3] Ps. li. 16, 17.
[4] Ps. l. 8, 13.   [5] Isa. i. 11.   [6] Jer. vi. 20.

offerings."[1] The contrast runs in a deeper note in Amos: "I hate, I despise your feast days: I will not smell in your solemn assemblies. Though ye offer Me burnt-offerings and meat-offerings, I will not accept them; neither will I regard the peace-offerings of your fat beasts. Take away from Me the noise of thy songs: I will not hear the melody of thy viols. But let judgment run down as waters, and righteousness as a mighty stream."[2]

The common drift of all these passages is—not that the Old Testament sacrifices were worthless; God Himself had appointed them, and, as the Apostle says, they "sanctified to the purifying of the flesh";[3] that is to say, they did all that was necessary in an outward system to preserve the covenant relation between the Israelites and God. But these passages do assert with vivid energy, with tremendous force, that in the service of the Perfect Moral Being the material and outward is worthless, or worse, if it be not promoted, inspired, by the moral and the inward; that no sacrifice, however costly—which is after all only a tax upon property, or time, or strength—can take the place of that gift of itself by a conscious and immortal spirit, which is the one true homage it can yield to the Perfect Author and Sustainer of its being. What God will have is a broken heart, according to David; it is justice, mercy, humility, according to Balaam and Micah it is streams of judgment and of righteousness, according to Amos; it is the piercing of the ears to hear, the offering of the body to express obedience, the coming to do One Will—and only One; again, according to David, it is the gift of the inmost life by His sincere penitent, by His accepted servant.

It is easy enough to mis-state and pervert this, as well as all other truths. If the Jewish sacrifices had their uses, although they could not confer grace, much more

---
[1] Hos. vi. 6.   [2] Amos v. 21-24.   [3] Heb. ix. 13.

have Christian works of mercy, Christian offerings of time, money, work, devotion, their place in every true Christian life. Nay, they cannot be dispensed with; but they are useless if they do not proceed from that greater all-including gift of self to the Perfect Will which God really values. They can never be substituted for this gift of gifts: this gift of the personality, of the life, of the inmost being, to the Author of our existence.

God has made us free; He has endowed us with the majestic and awful distinction of a freedom which is independent of circumstances; He has given us, as a necessary element of that freedom, the power of setting Him, the Master of the universe, aside, and of choosing the service of His enemy.; and we can only use this His great gift aright in one way, viz., by deliberately giving ourselves to Him. To give income to any amount without this gift of self; time, trouble, health, without this gift of self; obedience to religious rules and scrupulous use of religious ordinances without this gift of self, is to give that which He will not accept. Our religion must begin from within; it must begin with the surrender of that which is most properly ours to give; it must begin with the gift which includes all else as opportunity or prudence shall dictate, or it is on a wrong tack, and will get us into trouble. Even of our spiritual nature we cannot safely offer fragments; faith, hope, feelings, aspirations, assurances, are not trustworthy if they do not involve and issue from a conscious self-abandonment to the claims of God; if they do not echo, with its Christian paraphrase, the language :—

> "Sacrifice and offering Thou wouldest not,
> But a body hast Thou prepared me.
> Burnt-offerings and sin-offerings Thou requiredst not—
> Then said I, Lo, I come to do Thy will!"

"I come to do Thy will, O God." There are times in

every earnest life when these words express—or seem to express—the deepest feeling of the heart. "It is for nothing outward, O my God; for nothing that passes; for no human heart, for no human will, that I will henceforth live: but only for Thee. There is nothing that I can offer Thee that is not Thine already; I offer Thee that which alone I can refuse—myself. The times past of life may suffice for the rebellious sins, for the formal sacrifices, for the double-mindedness which has made me hitherto unstable in all my ways. I seek Thee now with my *whole* heart; I come to do Thy will." Alas! who of us that has ever felt thus does not know, by a humbling experience, what has followed. Again and again, how the fervour has died away, and the old material sacrifices which would buy God off have been offered in place of the moral sacrifice which gives Him everything; how human wills, human jurisdictions, have disputed the supremacy of the Divine Will within the soul, till the protestation of our first devotion has become insincere and meaningless. Nay, let us each one think over what has passed within him this very day,—since we rose from our beds,—and see how far One Will has ruled words, actions, thoughts; how far, if this obedience of ours is all that we can trust to, we can hope for acceptance with the Eternal God. Surely this language, to be realised as well as used, to be expressed in undeviating obedience as well as on the lips, must belong to a stronger and more direct will than yours or mine,—to a Will which may encourage us to hope, if it humbles us when we attempt to imitate.

II.

And this brings me to the question: How is the passage applied in the Epistle to the Hebrews? It is taken out of its original, historical setting; and it is connected with a new set of circumstances. It is taken from David's self-consecration in view of the throne which awaited him, and is applied to Jesus Christ as the High Priest of humanity, "taking upon Him to deliver man"[1] by His Incarnation and Death. "When He cometh into the world, He saith, Sacrifice and offering Thou wouldest not, but a body hast Thou prepared Me: in burnt-offerings and sin-offerings Thou delightest not; then said I, Lo, I come to do Thy will." Thus it is a motto of the Divine Incarnation; an authoritative announcement of its spirit, its drift, its purpose; and it proclaims that repudiation of the sacrifices and priesthood of the Jewish Law which the Gospel involved, and which is explained and justified at length in this Epistle. Now, how can this transfer of language be accounted for? Does it rest only on a shadowy coincidence, such as may be found, if we look for it, between any two periods, any two sets of circumstances, any two lives? Is it a quotation like those quotations which eloquent speakers in Parliament make from Virgil and Horace,—the embellishment and decoration of an idea which would else have had to be expressed in a mere commonplace and prosaic way? Or is it something more serious than this, and altogether different? Does it depend, in a word, in any real sense upon a principle,—upon a principle which can be ascertained and stated?

Observe, then, my brethren, that the Apostle makes this quotation in the very heart of an argument, and with a view to making it good. He is showing that the High-Priestly Service offered by Jesus Christ is unspeakably greater and more real than that offered by the sons of Aaron. He makes the Old Testament,—here as elsewhere,—witness against itself, or rather against that false notion about its containing a final revelation and system

[1] *Te Deum Laudamus.*

of worship which the Jews claimed for it. If this quotation from David had been, I will not say inapplicable, but fanciful or arbitrary, an opponent would naturally have rejoined that the argument of the Epistle broke down at a critical point; that language which was David's, and appropriate only to David, could not be placed in the mouth of Jesus Christ so as to sustain a grave inference as to the drift and character of His Incarnation. The writer then, we may be sure, meant that the language of the quotation really belonged to Jesus Christ. But the question still remains—how?

Here we must dismiss the idea that the fortieth Psalm is Messianic in such a sense as the twenty-second; that is to say, that it has no original historical references, no ascertainable background in the history of Israel or of the Psalmist, and is throughout a prediction of the coming Person to Whom Israel looked forward. Nothing in Jewish history before the Passion of Christ our Lord corresponds with the description of the Ideal Sufferer of Psalm xxii.: but there is no difficulty in pointing to the circumstances in David's own life which correspond to the language of Psalm xl., while in this Psalm there are also expressions and thoughts which certainly are not Messianic. The Psalm was really David's: it describes a great crisis in David's life; how then does its language belong to the Christ coming into the world at His Incarnation? The answer to this must be found in the relation in which our Lord, as the Representative or Ideal Man, stands to the whole human family and to its noblest members. When St. Paul speaks of our Lord as the "Second Adam," or the "last Adam,"[1] he must mean that our Lord stood to the human race in a relation which corresponded, in some way, to that in which our first parent stood towards all his descendants. The text of the Book of Genesis implies that our first

[1] 1 Cor. xv. 45.

parent, as *the* man, was the antitypal head and representative of all later generations of men. And the Second Adam corresponded to the first in this: He too was to be the Type and Pattern of man, of renewed man, as the first Adam had been of the first creation. In a different manner, yet as really, He became representative of the race. He represented it, not as it was, but as it had been meant to be; He represented possible and ideal humanity, not actual, historical, fallen humanity. Therefore, in Him as "the First-born of every creature,"[1] the "Beginning of the creation of God,"[2] all that was noblest, truest, purest, best, in the thought and language of His predecessors, met and was realised. All the mysterious yearnings of poets and thinkers after an indefinable perfection, all the vague aspirations after an ideal which was ever floating indistinctly before the eyes of men in their higher moments, yet ever eluding them,—all the cravings for reconciliation between antagonistic elements and tendencies in our fallen nature were satisfied at last in this Unique Sample of Humanity, Which included all the perfections to which men had aspired, Which excluded all the weakness and wrong to which man was liable. Everything that was best in human history was an unconscious prophecy of the Perfect One; and the noblest things that could be said of man conceived of ideally, or as he had issued from the hand of his Maker, were said of the New Head of our race with literal exactness. Thus, when the Psalmist proclaims that God had "made man to have dominion over the works of His Hands, and had put all things under his feet,"[3] St. Paul, seeing how, as a matter of fact, this ideal description is checked by the facts of man's perpetual struggle with the forces of savage nature,—with the elements, with disease, with death,—refers it at once to the Second Adam triumphing over the whole world of

[1] Col. i. 15. [2] Rev. iii. 14. [3] Ps. viii. 6.

sense in His unrivalled moral elevation, as in His Resurrection and Ascension into heaven.[1] And so when in the text David says, "Lo, I come to do Thy Will," it is in David's mouth the language of hope and intention; but in the mouth of Christ it is the prediction of a Moral Career which could not be other or less perfect than this. David no doubt meant to be perfectly true; but he used language which, strictly pressed, was applicable only to a strictly Holy Being; just as pure and noble-minded children, in their enthusiasm, often say things with entire sincerity, which, as older persons see, involve more than they contemplate or bargain for. David said, "Lo, I come to do Thy Will,—mine ears hast Thou opened." Yet he lived to become the murderer of Uriah and the paramour of Bathsheba; he lived to rise out of the profound misery of his moral degradation, as the typical penitent of Psalm li. But his higher aspirations were not lost; they belonged, in all their literal force and beauty, to the Real King of humanity, Who was to come of the loins of David in a later age. "When He cometh into the world, He saith, Sacrifice and offering Thou wouldest not,—a body hast Thou prepared Me: I come to do Thy Will, O God."

And this is one of the many points of view under which our Lord's Death upon the Cross may and ought to be considered: it was the last and consummate expression of a perfectly obedient Will. In this He stood alone when all else had failed; He was faultless. We are told, indeed, that He, too, as Man, "learned obedience"[2] by the road of experience, although this does not imply that He ever was disobedient, but only that "the things which He suffered" led Him as Man from one to another stage of moral intensity. "I do always," He said, "such things as please Him."[3] "My meat is to do the will of Him That sent Me."[4]

[1] 1 Cor. xv. 27.
[2] Heb. v. 8.
[3] St. John viii. 29.
[4] Ib. iv. 34.

IV] *The Accepted Offering.* 65

Throughout His human Life—in childhood and in manhood; in privacy, and in public; among multitudes, or in the retreat of the desert; when speaking, or on His knees; when acting, or in repose; in hunger, or at the wedding feast; the idol of popular enthusiasm, or the scorn of men and the outcast of the people [1]—He was true to this one unchanging law. He obeyed it to the last extremity: He was, as St. Paul says, "obedient unto death, even the death of the Cross." [2] "Therefore," He said Himself, "doth My Father love Me, because I lay down My Life, that I may take it again. No man taketh it from Me; but I lay it down of Myself. I have power to lay it down: and I have power to take it again. This commandment have I received from My Father." [3] Not that the tearing of soul and body asunder by a violent death; not that the mental anguish which He embraced in its immediate prospect cost Him nothing: He was truly human. "What shall I say? Father, save Me from this hour: yet for this cause came I unto this hour." [4] "Remove this cup from Me: nevertheless, not My will, but Thine, be done." [5]

This is what gives to every incident of the Passion, as described by the Evangelists, such transcendent interest: each insult that is endured, each pang that is accepted, each hour, each minute, of the protracted agony, is the deliberate offering of a Perfect Will, which might conceivably have declined the trial. "Thinkest thou that I cannot now pray to My Father, and He will presently send Me more than twelve legions of angels?" [6] And so when the suffering was over, He said, "It is finished," [7] just as at the close of His ministerial life, and on the threshold of His Agony, He had said, "I have glorified Thee on the earth; I have finished the work which Thou gavest Me to do." [8] His Life

---

[1] Ps. xxii. 6.   [2] Phil. ii. 8.   [3] St. John x. 17, 18.
[4] St. John xii. 27.   [5] St. Luke xxii. 42.   [6] St. Matt. xxvi. 53.
[7] St. John xix. 30.   [8] *Ib.* xvii. 4.

and His Death were a long commentary upon the words, "Lo, I come to do Thy Will, O God;" and He might seem to be expanding those words in reference to Himself. "I came down from heaven, not to do Mine own will, but the will of Him That sent Me."[1]

It is true, indeed, that it is our Lord's Higher and Eternal Nature which sheds over His Passion, as over all that He did and underwent here below, such extraordinary and inappreciable meaning and power. It is His Divinity Which makes His Blood so much more than that of a mere man; which gives its full meaning to the question, "If God spared not His own Son, but freely gave Him up for us all, how shall He not with Him also freely give us all things?"[2] But that which was accepted in Christ, living and dying, acting and suffering, was Humanity—Humanity true to its Ideal—Humanity absolutely conformed to that Perfect Will Which rules the universe. Standing by the very terms of His Incarnation in the relation of a Representative to the human race, Christ dying in agony to express entire devotion to the Perfect Will, dies in intention for all of us, dies actually, and, if we will, effectively, for each of us.

"He loved me, and gave Himself for me."[3] His might be justly described as an arbitrary substitution of the innocent for the guilty, if our Lord had been only a common specimen of the race for which He died, or if He had died against His will. He was, in fact, as the Head of our race, as qualified by natural law to represent us, as a father is to act on behalf of his own children; since in Him manhood was set forth in its widest and most universal character. And He freely made the most—if we may reverently so speak—of this His representative relation to the race; He did the utmost and the best for it with a generosity and love that knew no bounds. Thus He is

[1] St. John vi. 38.   [2] Rom. viii. 32.   [3] Gal. ii. 20.

"the Propitiation for our sins, and not for ours only, but also for the sins of the whole world,"[1] because He was, by the very terms of His Being, qualified to represent a sinful race, He freely suffered what was due to its accumulated transgressions. As Isaiah says, "the chastisement of our peace was upon Him;"[2] and St. Paul, that He hath "redeemed us from the curse of the law," that is, the curse incurred by breaking it, "being made a curse for us;"[3] and that He has "made peace through the Blood of His Cross;"[4] and He Himself, that He "came to give His life a ransom instead of many."[5]

Brethren, if we know, indeed, how far above us it is to make the words "I come to do Thy Will" our own, we know the great life-business for a Christian is to see that ere he dies he is "sanctified through the offering of the Body of Jesus Christ once for all,"[6] that he is "sprinkled with the Blood of Atonement," that he is "accepted in the Beloved."[7] We do not need this priceless blessing less than did our fathers. The face of the world, its public buildings, its political parties, its social divisions and subdivisions, its science, its systems of thought, its literature, its very language, are perpetually changing, and with this perpetual change there is the fascination for active minds of interest—various, keen, absorbing interest. The face of the world changes from generation to generation, almost from year to year, with the ever quickening march of our modern civilisation; we live, it is often said, at a much faster rate than did our fathers. But human nature, with its splendid aspirations and its practical impotence; with its burden of needs and woes, of shortcomings and uncertainties: the human soul with its strong temptations, with its facile dispositions, with its terrible pollutions, with its awful capacities,

---

[1] 1 St. John ii. 2.   [2] Isa. liii. 5.   [3] Gal. iii. 13.   [4] Col. i. 20.
[5] St. Matt. xx. 28.   [6] Heb. x. 10.   [7] Eph. i. 6.

presentiments, destinies—these do not change. They are what they were when our rude forefathers struggled with nature on the soil of England, under Plantagenet or Saxon kings; they are what they were when the Eternal Christ, eighteen centuries ago, reddened the soil of Palestine with His precious Blood. Human nature does not change with the changes—social, intellectual, political, æsthetic —which take place around us : it remains a weak and defiled thing, nor can the tinsel of our life disguise its defilement or invigorate its weakness. It remains; and the eternal realities in which alone it can find purity and strength remain also. Think not that some of our modern philosophies have changed all that; as well might you suppose that the clouds and fogs of the past winter had annihilated the sun, as dream that Christ our Saviour, God and Man, is less than of yore our only Mediator, or we less than our predecessors entirely dependent upon His Redemptive work. To union with Him—with this one Perfect Life, this unfaltering obedience expressed in Death, with this accepted Head and Representative of our kind—all faith, all sacraments, all Christian instruction and Christian effort, must ever and increasingly tend; in the conviction that all sacrifices and offerings which are merely our own are worthless, but that His obedience unto Death, which we may share if we will, is the mighty earnest of our acceptance with the Father, and of our endless peace.

SERMON V.

THE CLEANSING BLOOD.

HEB. ix. 13, 14.

For if the blood of bulls and of goats, and the ashes of an heifer sprinkling the unclean, sanctifieth to the purifying of the flesh: how much more shall the Blood of Christ, Who through the Eternal Spirit offered Himself without spot to God, purge your conscience from dead works to serve the living God?

TO-DAY we pass the line which parts the first five weeks in Lent from that last fortnight which is especially devoted to contemplating the Sufferings and Death of our Lord Jesus Christ. And accordingly, the Gospel[1] tells us of the attempt of the Jews to stone Him in the Temple—one of the first drops (as it has been well termed) of that storm which burst in all its fury upon Calvary.

And the Epistle[2] teaches us how to think about Him in the whole course of these His sufferings. He is not only a good man weighed down by so much pain of body and mind; He is the High Priest of the human race, Who is offering a victim in expiation of human sin, and that victim is Himself; He is the one real Sacrificer, of whom all the Jewish priests had, for long centuries, been only shadows; and His sacrifice is the One Offering which throughout all ages has power in heaven. And so, as He passes within the veil of the Sanctuary above, He is opening a way for

---
[1] The *Gospel* for the Fifth Sunday in Lent is from St. John viii. 46-59. The *Epistle* is from Heb. ix. 11-15.

us, if we will only follow, to an eternal home in the very Heart of God. "Christ being come an High Priest of good things to come, ... by His Own blood entered in once into the Holy Place, having obtained eternal redemption for us."[1]

I.

That which must strike all careful readers of the Bible, in the passages which refer to the Sufferings and Death of Jesus Christ, is the stress which is laid upon His Blood. A long course of violent treatment, ending in such a death as that of crucifixion, must involve, we know from the nature of the case, the shedding the blood of the sufferer. But our modern feeling would probably have led us to treat this as an accidental or subordinate feature of His Death. We, if we had had with our human feelings to write the books which are the title-deeds of Christendom, should either not refer to it, or we should pass lightly and quickly over it; we should throw it into the background of our description. We should give the outline, and let the details be taken for granted. We should trust to the imaginations of our readers to fill up the blank; we should shrink from stimulating their sensibilities to pain, from harrowing their feelings by anything beyond. Does it not seem as if we carried into modern life that rule of the old Greek tragedians that if possible, nothing tragic or violent, that spoils and gives pain, should meet the eye? If a deed of violence takes place in our streets or homes, do we not remove all traces of it as quickly as may be? Has it not been urged as a reason for putting criminals to death by hanging, instead of adopting some more rapid and certain mode of destroying life, that it is desirable to spare the bystanders the sight of blood?

[1] Heb. ix. 11, 12.

This modern feeling is far from being mere unhealthy sentimentalism; it arises from that honourable sympathy with and respect for human nature which draws a veil over its miseries or its wounds. But the New Testament, in its treatment of the Passion of Christ, is, we cannot but observe, strangely and strongly in contrast with such a feeling. The four Evangelists, who differ so much in their accounts of our Lord's Birth and public Ministry, seem to meet around the foot of the Cross, and to agree, if not in relating the same incidents, yet certainly in the minuteness and detail of their narratives. In the shortest of the Gospels, when we reach the Passion, the occurrences of a day take up as much space as had previously been assigned to years. From the Last Supper to the Burial in the grave of Joseph of Arimathea, we have a very complete account of what took place; each incident that added to pain or shame, each bitter word, each insulting act, each outrage upon justice or mercy, of which the Divine Sufferer was a victim, is carefully recorded. But, especially, the Agony and Bloody Sweat, the public Scourging, the Crowning with thorns, the nailing to the wood of the Cross, the opening the Side with a spear, are described by the Evangelists,—incidents, each one of them, be it observed, which must have involved the shedding of Christ's Blood. And in the writings of the Apostles to their first converts more is said of the Blood of Christ than of anything else connected with His Death—more even than of the Cross. As we read them we might almost think that the shedding of His Blood was not so much an accompaniment of His Death as its main purpose. Thus St. Paul tells the Romans that Christ is set forth to be a "propitiation through faith in His Blood;"[1] that they are "justified" by Christ's Blood.[2] He writes to the Ephesians that they have "redemption through Christ's Blood;"[3]

[1] Rom. iii. 25.   [2] Ib. v. 9.   [3] Eph. i. 7.

to the Colossians that our Lord has "made peace through the Blood of His Cross;"[1] to the Corinthians that the Holy Sacrament is so solemn a rite because it is "the communion of the Blood of Christ."[2] Thus St. Peter contrasts the slaves whose freedom from captivity was purchased with corruptible things such as silver and gold with the case of Christians redeemed by "the precious Blood of Christ, as of a Lamb without blemish, and immaculate."[3] Thus St. John exclaims that "the Blood of Jesus Christ the Son of God cleanseth us from all sin."[4] In the Epistle to the Hebrews this Blood is referred to as "the Blood of the Covenant wherewith Christians are sanctified,"[5] as "the Blood of the Everlasting Covenant,"[6] as "the Blood of sprinkling" which pleads for mercy, and so is contrasted with the blood of Abel that cries for vengeance.[7] And in the last book of the New Testament the beloved Disciple gives at the very outset thanks and praise to "Him That has washed us from our sins in His own Blood;"[8] and the blessed in heaven sing that He has "redeemed them to God by His Blood;"[9] and the saints "have washed their robes and made them white in the Blood of the Lamb;"[10] and they have overcome their foe, not in their own might, but by "the Blood of the Lamb;"[11] and He Whose Name is called "the Word of God," and Who rides on a white horse, and on Whose head are many crowns, is "clothed in a vesture dipped in blood."[12]

Much more might be said on the subject; but enough has been said to show that, in the New Testament, the Blood of Christ is treated as no mere accident of His Death, but as a very important feature of it; nay, as having a substantive value, of whatever kind, which is

[1] Col. i. 20.   [2] 1 Cor. x. 16.   [3] 1 St. Pet. i. 19.
[4] 1 St. John i. 7.   [5] Heb. x. 29.   [6] Ib. xiii. 20.
[7] Heb. xii. 24.   [8] Rev. i. 5.   [9] Ib. v. 9.
[10] Rev. vii. 14.   [11] Ib. xii. 11.   [12] Ib. xix. 11-13.

all its own. And the question is, How are we to account for the prominence which is thus assigned to it?

II.

This question is sometimes answered by saying that the language of the Apostles about the Blood of Christ is, after all, only the language of metaphor and symbol. The Apostles, we are told, found in the Old Testament a stock of poetic illustration and imagery ready to their hands, and although it had reference to the ideas and usages of a dying system, they employed it freely for their own purposes, much as cultivated gentlemen of a past generation used to quote the Greek and Latin poets in Parliament or in society by way of decorating new ideas with the phrases of a literature which had passed away.

This is what has been urged by some modern writers. But any such account of the Apostolic language about the Preciousness and Power of the Blood of Jesus Christ, is unworthy at once of the seriousness of the men and of the seriousness of the subject. Unworthy of the seriousness of the men; for, after all, the Apostles and Apostolic writers were not mere retailers of splendid phrases, but teachers of a truth which they believed to have come from heaven, and for which they were prepared to die. And unworthy of the seriousness of the subject; for surely the deepest truths that can move the hearts and wills of men, are not fit subjects for mere antiquarian or literary display; they would be better avoided, if they are not set forth in the clearest and plainest language which those who profess to teach them can command. If the Apostles used the language of the Old Testament about the Jewish sacrifices in order to describe their own faith about the Atoning work of Christ, this was because, in the belief of the Apostles, a real relation already existed between the two things; the Jewish sacrifices were predestined types and shadows of the Sacrificed Son of God.

In the passage before us the Day of Atonement and its characteristic rites are throughout present to the mind of the sacred writer; and of those rites the sprinkling the blood of the victims was a prominent feature. But the question still remains, Why should this effusion of blood have been a prominent feature on the Jewish Day of Atonement? Why should it have been allowed so largely to colour the thought and words of the Apostles? Why should the Blood of the Redeemer, rather than His pierced Hands, or His thorn-crowned Head, or His bruised and mangled Body, or His Face with its Divine Radiance shining through the tears and the shame, be dwelt on in the Apostolic writings as the chosen symbol of His Passion and Death?

Certainly, in all the languages of the world, blood is the proof and warrant of affection and of sacrifice. To shed blood voluntarily for another is to give the best that man can give; it is to give a sensible proof of, almost a bodily form to, love. This one human instinct is common to all ages, to all civilisations, to all religions. The blood of the soldier who dies for duty, the blood of the martyr who dies for truth, the blood of the man who dies that another may live—blood like this is the embodiment of the highest moral powers in human life, and those powers were all represented in the Blood which flowed from the Wounds of Christ on Calvary. And yet in saying this we have not altogether accounted for the Apostolic sayings about the Blood of Christ. It involves something more than any of these moral triumphs; it is more than all of them taken together.

Observe, my brethren, the peculiar and deep significance which is ascribed to blood in the earliest books in the Bible—the Books of Moses. There we are taught that between the blood, whether of man or animal, and the life-principle or soul, there is a certain and intimate connection. In those primal laws which were given to Noah after the Flood, man was authorised to eat the flesh, but not the blood of the animals around him. Why was this? Because the blood is the life or soul of the animal. "Flesh, with the blood thereof, which is the life thereof, shall ye not eat."[1] The Laws of Moses go further: the man, whether Israelite or stranger, who eats any manner of blood, is to be destroyed; and the reason is repeated: "The soul of the flesh," *i.e.* of the nature living in the flesh, "is in the blood."[2] This is why the blood of the sacrificial animals is shed by way of atonement for sin; the blood atones—this is the strict import of the original language—by means of the soul that is in it. Once more, in the Fifth Book of Moses, permission is given to the Israelites to kill and eat the sacrificial animals just as freely as the roebuck or the hart, which were not used for sacrifice. But, again, there follows the caution: "Only be sure that thou eat not the blood;" and the reason for the caution: "the blood is the soul; and thou mayest not eat the soul with the flesh. Thou shalt not eat of it; thou shalt pour it upon the earth like water."[3]

The thrice-repeated precept—not to touch animal blood—has passed away, together with much else in the ancient Law. True; it was enforced by prophets, who insisted little or not at all on the ceremonial provisions of the Mosaic code; it was upheld for a while even by Apostles, as binding upon the first converts from heathendom; it was adhered to, not indeed universally, but with much tenacity in the primitive Christian Church. But it has gone the way of the ceremonial system, of which it formed a part, and which was only fulfilled to disappear. Yet the reason of the precept remains, as a matter of

---

[1] Gen. ix. 4-6.   [2] Lev. xvii. 11.   [3] Deut. xii. 23, 24.

lasting interest; the reason, namely, that blood is that element of our animal existence which is most closely associated with the principle of life.

What life is in itself—whether in tree or animal, whether in man or angel—who shall say? It is a mystery ever close to us, yet ever eluding our inquisitive research. We associate intelligence with the brain; we trace the unspoken language of the soul in the movements or motionlessness of the countenance, in the expression of the eye, in the gesture of the hand, even in the gait or sway of the body. Of this we find little in Scripture which, without denying the relation of the soul to other parts of our bodily frame, does, unquestionably, so far as the soul is the principle of life, feeling, and growth, associate it with the blood.

The question may be fairly asked, whether this Scripture doctrine of the intimate relation of the soul or life-power to the blood is borne out by independent inquiry. It is obvious, first of all, that the strength of the body depends on the quantity of the blood; that with the loss of blood, feeling, power of movement, all the bodily activities, are lost also. The blood, then, is the basis or support of bodily life. But it is more: it is also the material from which the body and its various secretions arise: it is the substance out of which the animal life in all its forms is developed. Whether the various kinds of material which make up the human body are contained in the blood in a state of actual diversity, or whether they exist in it only in potency, and are drawn out of it by the functional powers of the bodily organs, is a matter of controversy; but it is agreed, by high authorities on such subjects, that they do thus pre-exist in the blood, which is thus the principle, not merely of bodily life, but of bodily growth and formation.

This, then, is what is assumed when Scripture speaks of

the blood as the life or soul of a man or animal. But, as a Jewish writer has observed,[1] the soul in question is only the sensitive soul, which man possesses in common with animals: it is not the thinking, intelligent, self-conscious being—the spirit—which proceeds immediately from God, and is encased in the sensitive soul as the apple of an eye is in the eye. The spirit of man is only so far resident in the blood as it is resident in the sensitive soul, which is in the blood; the existence of the spirit of man is strictly independent of any element of his bodily life, and, as we know, will survive it.

But in Christ our Lord there was something more than body and soul and spirit; since in Him dwelt "all the fulness of the Godhead."[2] As man differs from the animals in possessing an undying spirit, as well as, and together with, a sensitive soul or life; so in Christ our Lord were joined, by an intimate and indissoluble union, not merely a human soul and spirit, but also, and above these, that Divine Nature which was "begotten of the Father before all worlds."[3] Nay, rather, it was this, His Eternal Person Which owned all else in Him, in Which all else centred, to Which all else attached itself. When He Who had already existed from all eternity vouchsafed to enter into the sphere of time, He wrapped around Him in its completeness, but without its stains, that human nature which then He made His own; He took it upon Him, not as a garment which He might lay aside, but as that which was from the moment of His Incarnation, and for ever, to form part of His Being. And therefore the Blood which flowed in His veins, and which He shed at His Circumcision and in His mental Agony, not less than in His Scourging, and on the Cross, was the Blood, not merely of the Son of Mary, but of the Infinite and Eternal Being thus condescendingly united to a created form;—it is an Apostle who

[1] Philo, *Op.* ed. Mangey, i. 206, 207.   [2] Col. ii. 9.   [3] Nicene Creed.

bids the pastors of the church of Ephesus "feed the Church of God, which He hath purchased with His own Blood."[1]

This, then, is what is meant in the text, when it conrasts the Atoning power of the Blood of Christ with that of the blood of bulls and goats. The blood of the sacrificed animal had a certain value, because, as we have seen, it was so intimately connected with the life or sensitive soul of the animal; as the Apostle puts it, it did, and by Divine appointment, sanctify to the purifying of the flesh. By the "flesh" is here meant the natural, outward, and earthly life of man; especially all that bore in the way of outward conduct and condition upon his membership of the commonwealth of Israel. The sacrifices on the Day of Atonement, and especially the sprinkling of the blood of the red heifer, towards the tabernacle, did signify the substitution of life for life, and were at any rate accepted as establishing the outward religious position of those for whom they were offered. That they could do more was impossible: the nature of things was opposed to it: "it was not possible that the blood of bulls and goats should take away sins."[2] The blood of these animals could not operate in the proper sphere of spiritual natures. But then it foreshadowed nothing less than the Blood of Christ. It was His Blood, Who through His Eternal Spiritual Being (it is not the Holy Ghost Who is here meant, but the Divine Nature of the Incarnate Christ) offered Himself without spot to God. The Eternal Spiritual Nature of Christ, vivifying the Blood of Christ, is contrasted in the Apostle's thought with the perishable life of the sacrificed animal resident in the blood of the animal; and so the value of the sacrifices, the power of the blood to cleanse or save, varies with the dignity of the life which it represents—in one case that of the creature, not even endowed with

[1] Acts xx. 28.   [2] Heb. x. 4.

reason or immortality; in the other that of the Infinite and Eternal Being Who for us men, and for our salvation, has come down from heaven.

"How much more shall the Blood of Christ!"

At length we see, then, what it is that the sacred writer really means. He says in effect to his readers, "You have no doubt that, under the old Jewish dispensation, the sacrifices on the Day of Atonement, the blood of the slaughtered goat and red heifer, could restore the Israelite who had done wrong to his place and his privileges in the sacred nation. It sanctified to the purifying of the flesh. But here is the Blood—not of a sacrificial animal, not of a mere man, not even of the best of men, but of One Who was God "manifest in the flesh."[1] Who shall calculate the effects of His self-sacrifice? Who shall limit the power of His voluntary death? Who shall say what His outpoured Blood may or may not achieve on earth or elsewhere? Plainly we are here in the presence of an agency which altogether distances and rebukes the speculations of reason; we can but listen for some voice that shall speak with authority, and from beyond the veil: we can but be sure of this, that the Blood of the eternal Christ must infinitely transcend in its efficacy that of the victims slain on the Temple altars; It must be much more than equal to redress the woes, to efface the transgressions, of a guilty world.

III.

This, indeed, is what the argument invites,—the absolutely limitless power of the Precious Blood. But the sacred writer puts, as it were, a restraint upon himself, and contents himself with pointing to a single result. "How much more shall the Blood of Christ purge your conscience from dead works to serve the living God?"

[1] 1 Tim. iii. 16.

"Dead works:" works that are not good, in that their motive is good, nor bad, in that their motive is bad, but dead in that they have no motive at all—in that they are merely outward and mechanical,—affairs of propriety, routine, and form, to which the heart and spirit contribute nothing. "Dead works:" to how much of our lives, ay, of the better and religious side of our lives, may not this vivid and stern expression justly apply! How many acts in the day are gone through without intention, without deliberation, without effort, to consecrate them to God, without any reflex effect upon the faith and love of the doer! How many prayers, and words, and deeds are of this character; and, if so, how are they wrapping our spirits round with bandages of insincere habit, on which already the avenging angels may have traced the motto, "Thou hast a name that thou livest, and art dead"![1] The Blood of Christ delivers from much else; but especially from those dead works. For as the blood of the slain animal means the life of the animal, so the Blood of Christ crucified means the Life of Christ,—His Life Who is eternal Truth and eternal Charity. And thus, when a Christian man feels Its Redemptive touch within him, he has a motive—varying in strength, but always powerful —for being genuine. He means his deeds, his words, his prayers. He knows that life is a solemn thing, and has tremendous issues; he measures these issues by the value of the Redeeming Blood. If Christ has shed His Blood, surely life is well worth living; it is worth saving. A new energy is thrown into everything; a new interest lights up all the surrounding circumstances—the incidents of life, its opportunities, its trials, its failures, its successes, —the character and disposition of friends, the public occurrences of the time, and the details of the home,—are looked at with eyes which see nothing that is indifferent;

[1] Rev. iii. 1.

and when all is meant for God's glory, though there may and must be much weakness and inconsistency, the conscience is practically purged from dead works to serve the living God.

The Blood of Christ! It was shed on Calvary eighteen hundred years ago: but It flows on throughout all time. It belongs now, not to the physical but to the spiritual world. It washes souls, not bodies; It is sprinkled not on altars but on consciences. But, although invisible, It is not for all that the less real and energetic; It is the secret power of all that purifies or that invigorates souls in Christendom. Do we believe in "one Baptism for the remission of sins"?[1] It is because Christ's Blood tinges the waters of the font to the eyes of faith. Do we believe that God "hath given power and commandment to His ministers to declare and pronounce to His people, being penitent, the Absolution and Remission of their sins"?[2] It is because the Blood of Christ, applied to the conscience by the Holy Spirit, makes this declaration an effective reality. Do we find in the Bible more than an ancient literature,—in Christian instruction more than a mental exercise,—in the life of thought about the unseen and the future more than food for speculation? This is because we know that the deepest of all questions is that which touches our moral state before God; and that, as sinners, we are above all things interested in the "Fountain opened for sin and for uncleanness" in the Blood of Christ.[3] Do we look to our successive Communions for the strengthening and refreshing of our souls? This is because the Blood of our Lord Jesus Christ, Which was shed for us of old, and is given us now, can "preserve our bodies and souls unto everlasting life."[4] Does even a single prayer, offered in entire sincerity of

[1] Nicene Creed.
[2] From the *Form of Absolution* in the Order for Morning Prayer.
[3] Zech. xiii. 1.
[4] Words of Administration in the Service of Holy Communion.

purpose, avail to save a despairing soul? It is because "we have boldness to enter into the holiest by the Blood of Jesus."[1] The Blood of Christ! Who of us does not need to be sprinkled with it? Christians as we are, what are our lives, our habits, our daily thoughts, the whole course of our existence, as they lie spread out before the Eyes of the All-seeing Judge? The works from which we need to be purged are, it may be, not merely soulless and dead, but actively evil! The prayer which befits us, kneeling before our Crucified Master, is not merely, "Purge my conscience from dead works to serve the living God," but, "Wash me throughly from my wickedness, and cleanse me from my sin."[2] Let one or both of these prayers, my brethren, be ours during this ensuing sacred season. If they are offered earnestly they will not be unheard; for the Eternal Spirit is here, to sprinkle all souls that seek purification or pardon with the Precious Blood. And the old promise made to Israel in Egypt still holds good, and may be claimed in a far higher sense by the Israel of God, whether in life or in death: "When I see the Blood I will pass over; and the plague shall not be upon you."[3]

[1] Heb. x. 19.   [2] Ps. li. 2.   [3] Exod. xii. 13.

SERMON VI.

THE CONQUEROR OF SATAN.

HEB. ii. 14.

That through death He might destroy him that had the power of death, that is, the devil.

IN his Rationale of the Book of Common Prayer, Bishop Sparrow tells us that the fifth Sunday in Lent is called Passion-Sunday; "For now," he says, "begins the commemoration of the Passion of our Lord."[1] And in truth, on this day, we pass a frontier-line in the sacred season of Lent; we enter upon the last and most solemn portion of it. In the Christian year, Easter answers to the Passover among the Jews much as the reality answers to the shadow. And as the Jews numbered fourteen days in the month before the Passover-feast came, so do we Christians in our reckoning of the days before Easter. To quote Bishop Sparrow again,—the Epistle and Gospel for to-day both speak of the Passion of our Lord. The Epistle[2] tells us how He gave His Life, both as Priest and Victim, for the sins of men. And the Gospel[3] describes the insult and violence to which He was exposed in the temple, when He told the Jews that before Abraham was born, He was Himself already existing—existing eternally. That scene was a first drop which announced the approach-

[1] Sparrow's *Rationale*, p. 98; ed. 1722.
[2] Heb. ix. 11-15.   [3] St. John viii. 46-59.

ing storm; and so from to-day onwards, throughout the next fortnight, and more particularly during the latter part of it, good Christians will try, as much as they can, to put all other thoughts aside, save those thoughts of their own sinfulness and misery which have hitherto occupied them from the beginning of Lent,—and to devote themselves, heart and soul, in such leisure time as they can command, to considering that wonderful proof of the Love and of the Holiness of God,—the Sufferings and Death of His Only-begotten Son.

And in the text we are reminded of one effect of this great event, which at all times, and especially at the present time, for reasons to which I need not more particularly refer, it is well to bear in mind. Through death, the Apostle says, Christ intended to destroy, that is, not to annihilate but to subdue and render ineffective, powerless, him that had the power of death, that is, the devil. This was one reason why the Son of God took on Him our nature. He took part in our flesh and blood,—so says the Apostle,—that He might put Himself into circumstances where death was possible; in order that thus, by dying, He might free us from our old enemy. He has won His victory; and now that He has died, it is our fault, not His, if we are not free. This is the plain meaning of the passage; and the subject is practical enough to deserve close attention.

I.

And here our thoughts turn towards the being who, the Apostle tells us, was to be reduced to impotence by the Death of Jesus Christ. Who and what is he? what do we really know about him, about his history, his character, his power of affecting ourselves and our destiny? There are two considerations among others which make a great many persons unwilling to approach this subject.

1. First, say they, it is an unpleasant subject. If the world and human life *are* haunted by such a being as the Evil One, we would rather, if we can, think of them without him. We like the bright side of religion, as we like the bright side of life. Tell us of heaven, of virtue, of Jesus Christ, of good men; if there is a dark side to the picture, we would rather not see it; if there is a devil, we would rather forget him, or think of him as seldom as we can.

Thus speaks the religion of feeling or of taste, as distinct from the religion of simple truth. True religion must base itself on truth; must desire to see truth all round; must welcome disagreeable truth not less than truth which brings consolation and strength; must desire, like the old Greek poet, if need be, to perish in the light,[1] but to know all that can be known, and at all costs. Nothing is gained and much is lost by shrinking from fact because it is disagreeable. There are some animals which close their eyes at the approach of the creature which preys upon them; but this precaution does nothing to avert their fate. Religion, beyond anything else, should have the courage to look truth in the face, from a conviction that whatever may be the anxiety or anguish of the moment, she can more than afford to do so, and that not to do so is to cease to be herself.

2. Secondly, some men suggest that the devil is an unprofitable subject for discussion: they do not think that much practically depends on our believing in him or not. If, they say, a man does what he knows to be good, so far as he can, and resists what he knows to be evil, so far as he can, it does not much concern him whether evil is or is not represented by a powerful invisible being, who makes it his business to administer and to promote it. The whole question, we are told in the phrase of the day, belongs to speculation rather than to practice; and specula-

[1] Homer, *Iliad* xvii. 647.

tion, however interesting to those who have time and taste for it, cannot touch the eternal weal of a being like man.

This kind of language appeals forcibly to our national character. We English are, before all things, practical. But is the question in hand so purely speculative, so remote from practical interests, as is here implied? Does it really make no difference whether a man believes only in a vague something, which he calls an "evil principle," or in an intelligent and working, *i.e.* a personal devil? Surely, in ordinary matters, it makes all the difference in the world to a man whether he supposes himself to be dealing with an abstract idea or tendency, or with a living will. We should cease to be human if it were not so; if we were not far more profoundly affected by feeling ourselves close to a living being than by feeling ourselves under the vaguer and more intangible influence, termed provisionally a principle, especially of an evil, that is to say, a negative principle. This, indeed, is true whether the principle be good or evil; and the reason is because we know that an abstract principle only affects us so far as we assent to it. It has not independent vital force in itself to propagate and enforce itself, and extend its sway, unless in the language of poetry and metaphor. Apart from human intelligences and human wills, it is an inert thing, not even having any independent existence, as a cloud or a gas has independent existence. It affects us just so far as it is apprehended; it has no real range or play beyond the intelligences which it sways. But let it be represented—let it be embodied—in a living intelligence, in a living will, and the case is very different. Then it may act upon us whether we are thinking of it or not; then it is dependent, not on our discretion, but on its own. An abstract evil principle, indeed! Why, any abstract principle, good or evil, without a living representative or embodiment, is like a philanthropic or political enterprise which has not yet found a good working secretary, and which as yet exists only upon paper. It may have much to say for itself in the way of argument; but it does not make much way to men's hearts and purses until somebody takes it up, and, as we say, pushes it. A doctrine in political economy, sound or mistaken, is of little account to the world, while it only exists in a treatise on the shelves of a library; but let a powerful finance minister adopt it, and set himself to give it practical expression, and it may save or ruin a great country. A vision of national unity or of national aggrandisement may for centuries haunt the imagination and inspire the poetry of a race; but until the man has appeared who gathers up into himself all this vague and floating sentiment, and gives it the dignity and force of ardent conviction and determined will—until the abstraction has become identified with the brain, the passion, the purpose, of a Napoleon or a Bismarck—there is before us only a patriotic or literary dream, which makes the fortune of a few publicists or poets, but leaves no trace upon the world. Do you suppose that goodness would still exert the strong attraction which it has for all good men if they believed in no Being Whose Nature it is—Who, as being what He is, embodies and represents it? Doubtless it is true that we fallen men have a bias or warp in the direction of evil; that, in order to assert its empire over us, evil does not require such energetic measures as goodness and truth. But the question here is whether a man's own sense of the power of evil, of the manner in which it is brought to bear on him, of the precautions which he must take against it, of the resistance which he must oppose to it, is unaffected by his belief in its propagation by a powerful, clever, and active being, who devotes himself unremittingly to the occupation? My brethren, if anything in the way of opinion is unpractical, it is the refusal to recognise the immense practical importance of the presence or absence of belief in the personal reality of the devil to the deepest interests of human life.

But further, when men discard the old teaching of the Bible and the Christian Church about the Evil One, and talk vaguely about an "evil principle," it is well to ask, What do they exactly mean by this imposing phrase? How can evil itself be, strictly speaking, a principle? The essence of evil is absence of principle, principle being something positive. Evil is contradiction to positive principle: every sin is in its essence a contradiction of one of those positive moral laws which are part of the necessary Nature of God, and by which He wills to rule the universe. Evil is a perverted, selfish quality of the will of an already existing, personal creature. Evil could not exist apart from such a creature, or unless the will of such a creature was free. Evil has no body or substance in itself: it is only that twist or warp in a created will which makes the creature refuse—not merely in opposition to God, but in opposition to the best instincts of its own being—to own God as its Lord, and to make itself conform to Him. But if this be the case, and it is, I believe, the substance of what the greatest Christian thinkers have always said on the subject, the phrase "an evil principle" melts away before our eyes as a mere mist of the imagination. On the other hand, it is plain that in some way or other evil does operate most disastrously; its desolating ravages are a mere matter of experience, and the alternative supposition is that this weird negation of good has found, at some time and somewhere, an invisible but energetic secretary,—that it is propagated in every possible manner by a person of the highest intelligence and of very resolute will.

But I am asked in turn, What do you mean by a

person? This question has been at least in part already answered; but it is of importance to be as clear as may be. Since it first entered into the speech of the Western world, the word "person" has had an eventful history. It meant at first the mask or disguise by which the face or figure of an historical character was represented on the stage; and in this sense men spoke of a great or of an insignificant person. But it was soon felt that that which marks off one man from another is not the countenance so much as the character; not the bodily form so much as the invisible soul or spirit. Accordingly the word "person" was transferred from the mask to the supposed bearer; from that which meets the eye to that which is beyond the ken of sense, and which belongs to spirit. And thus, in modern language, personality means the very central essential being of man; his conscious intelligence, his self-determining will. In this sense "person" is commonly opposed to "thing." The mineral, the vegetable, nay, the mere animal are "things." Man is a person; but man is not alone in personality. God, the All-surveying Intelligence, the absolutely Free, Who does what He ordains, and is bound by no law save His own Perfections,—God is the First of Persons, utterly distinct from the created things with which He has surrounded Himself, both in that they are created, and in that they lack personality. And good angels, whose existence and capacities are revealed to us, are persons,—possessing as they do, probably in very varying degrees of range and intensity, self-conscious intellect and self-determining will. If then we speak of the personality of Satan, we mean that he too is an Intelligence capable of reflecting on his own existence, and a Will which has had the power of determining its destiny; he possesses the very properties which are the essence of our manhood, only on a much larger scale than we.

II.

Now, whether an invisible person like Satan exists or not is one of those questions which cannot be really settled by the senses. Only the Author of this universe can tell us about portions of it which are so entirely beyond the reach of our observation; and Christians believe Him to have done so in Holy Scripture. When a modern writer compares Satan to Tisiphone, and says that "they are alike not real persons, but shadows thrown by man's guilt and terrors,"[1] he really assumes that the Bible is a mere reflex of human weakness and human passion instead of a Revelation of the Will of God. For all who believe the Bible to be a trustworthy source of information on such subjects, there is no real room for question as to the existence of a personal evil spirit. You must deliberately expunge a great many passages from the Bible if you would get rid of the belief. All that implies personality is attributed to Satan in Holy Scripture as distinctly as it is attributed to God. Read the description of Eve's temptation at the beginning of Genesis;[2] or the account of the origin of the trials of Job;[3] or the explanation of the pestilence which followed David's numbering the people as given in the Book of Chronicles;[4] or the still more vivid picture of Satan's resistance to Joshua in Zechariah.[5] In these histories you have before you a being who gives every evidence of self-conscious thought and determined purpose. And in the New Testament this representation is much fuller and more sustained. Not to dwell on what St. Paul teaches as to the various ranks of energetic evil spirits with whom Christians wrestle—as principalities, powers, rulers of the darkness of this world;[6] or on his description of their chief as "the prince of the

---

[1] M. Arnold, *God and the Bible*, pref. p. 25.   [2] Gen. iii. 1-6.
[3] Job i. 1-12.   [4] 1 Chr. xxi. 1-12.   [5] Zech. iii. 1, 2.   [6] Eph. vi. 12.

power of the air, the spirit that now worketh in the children of disobedience;"[1] or on his warning to the Ephesians against the "wiles" of Satan;[2] or to the Corinthians against his "devices;"[3] or to Timothy, three times, against his "snare;"[4] not to dwell on St. Peter's account of him as "a roaring lion, going about seeking whom he may devour;"[5] or on St. John's vision of his struggle with St. Michael and the good angels;[6] or on St. James's warrant, that if even *we* resist him, he will flee from us;[7]—let us consider what Jesus Christ, our Lord and Master, has said upon the subject. How significant is His warning in the parable of the Sower against the Evil One which takes away the Divine seed sown in the heart of man;[8] and in the parable of the Tares against the "enemy" who sows them along with the wheat:[9] thus representing him first as destroying good, and next as introducing evil within the range of his influence! How full of meaning is the announcement, "The prince of this world cometh, and hath nothing in Me;"[10] the declaration, "I beheld Satan as lightning fall from heaven;"[11] the warning to St. Peter, "Simon, Simon, Satan hath desired to have you that he may sift you as wheat;"[12] the saying about Judas, "One of you *is* a devil"[13]—a judgment which would be pointless enough if no such being existed to which Judas was already self-assimilated; the literal reality which is attributed to Beelzebub, the prince of the devils, associated historically with a form of neighbouring idolatry;[14] the tremendous denunciation to the Jews, "Ye are of your father the devil, and the works of your father will ye do. He was a murderer from the beginning. . . . When he speaketh of a lie, he speaketh of his own, for he is a liar,

[1] Eph. ii. 2.   [2] *Ib.* vi. 11.   [3] 2 Cor. ii. 11.
[4] 1 Tim. iii. 7; vi. 9: 2 Tim. ii. 26.   [5] 1 St. Pet. v. 8.
[6] Rev. xii. 7-9.   [7] St. James iv. 7.   [8] St. Matt. xiii. 3-8, 18, 19.
[9] St. Matt. xiii. 24, 25.   [10] St. John xiv. 30.   [11] St. Luke x. 18.
[12] St. Luke xxii. 31.   [13] St. John vi. 70.   [14] St. Matt. xii. 24-27.

and the father of it;"[1] the prayer bequeathed to Christians for all time, " Deliver us "—not from evil, but, as it should be rendered—" from the evil one."[2]

It has, I know, been said that this language of Jesus Christ must not be pressed closely, because He is only adapting Himself to the belief and intelligence of the men of His day. His own knowledge, it is patronisingly hinted, was in advance of such beliefs; but He accommodated Himself to them in the hope of doing such good as was possible among a superstitious people like the Jews.

It is difficult to understand how such a method of dealing with our Lord's teaching can possibly be adopted by any one who respects Him, I will not say as a Divine, but even as a human teacher. For what is the necessary inference as to Himself if the current faith about the Evil Spirit to which He so solemnly and so repeatedly set the seal of His approval is really false? He either knew it to be false, or He did not. If He did not, then in the eyes of those persons who now reject it He was Himself the victim of a stupid superstition. If He did know it to be false, and yet sanctioned and reaffirmed it, He was guilty of a much graver fault in a religious teacher than ignorance. Yes! it must be said, He encouraged acquiescence in known falsehood. What would you say, my brethren, of us, His ministers, if you had reason to suspect, that in order to uphold existing institutions, or to conciliate sympathies which would be otherwise irreconcilable, we were, not simply to connive at what we knew to be untrue, but, to reaffirm it—to enforce it with all the solemnity which belongs to an utterance in the Name of God? What is the condemnation which the human conscience has pronounced, in all countries and in all ages, on this crime against known truth, but the sternest that could be

[1] St. John viii. 44.   [2] St. Matt. vi. 13.

uttered? And how is it possible for any but His bitterest enemies to dare to impute even the shadow of such an offence to Him Who spake—the world itself being witness—as never man spake?[1]

No; our Lord Jesus Christ has identified the truth of this doctrine of a personal evil spirit with His own character as an honest Teacher of the highest truth. We cannot consistently deny the doctrine and continue to revere the Teacher Who reaffirmed it so solemnly; we cannot exculpate Him as if He were some Pagan philosopher, who had a secret truth for his chosen friends, while he patronised the current superstitions of the vulgar as being all that they were equal to. This contempt for humanity, blended with an equal contempt for truth, is utterly at variance with the Character and Mission of Him Who said on the eve of His death, "To this end was I born, and for this cause came I into the world, that I might bear witness unto the truth. Every one that is of the truth heareth My Voice."[1]

And do not the facts of human life, when we have once learnt to do them justice, bear out what we learn on this subject from the Christian Revelation? On the one hand we see great efforts for good produced upon men's characters and upon human society, at this or that period of the world's history; we see sudden and inexplicable conversions, like those of St. Paul or St. Augustine; we see immense efforts unaccountably made by bodies of men for such truth and virtue as they know of: and we say, "This is not only or simply human nature; here is another Agent at work; who is the real author of this momentum? we know what human nature is when left to its own resources; here is the Finger, the Spirit of God." But, on the other hand, when we see, as we do see, individuals and communities pursuing evil with deliberation, although

[1] St. John vii. 46.   [2] Ib. xviii. 37.

they know from experience, and without reference to a future state, that evil on the whole means misery; when we study characters and movements, ancient and modern, which have astonished even a bad world by their enthusiasm for pure unrighteousness; when we mark how much sin lies, so to speak, off the highway of nature, and is contradictory to nature; how the abandonment or murder of young children, cruelty to wives, dishonour and insult to parents, are matters of daily occurrence in the life of this vast hive of human beings; nay, when we who are in this Church look each and all of us within ourselves—all of us, of all classes, noble and humble, rich and poor, the aged and the young, clergy and laymen,—and find that we too have to repeat after the Apostle the paradoxical confession, "The good that I would I do not, but the evil that I would not that I do,"[1]—is it not reasonable to say, " Here, too, there is a personal agent at work of another kind; acting upon the propensities, the weaknesses, the passions of man; nature, we know, has a bad hereditary twist, but even depraved nature is ruled, when left to itself, in some degree by common sense"? And common sense, if it were alone and could have its way— common sense, gathering up man's accumulated experience of the results of moral evil—would surely counsel us to guard against evil as against an epidemic, to exterminate evil like a ferocious wild animal. This enthusiasm for evil as such which is to be observed in the actions, the conversation, the writings of no inconsiderable portion of mankind, is reasonably to be explained by the Christian doctrine, that in dealing with evil we have to do not with an impalpable abstraction, but with a living person of great experience and accomplishments; whose malignant action, within a smaller area, tells its own story as the action of a living person, just as truly as, on a larger scale, and in

[1] Rom. vii. 19.

an opposite direction, does the action of the Merciful and All-good God.

III.

There are two points in the Christian representation of the Evil One to which attention should especially be given.

1. The Satan or devil of Scripture was not always what he is now. He was once a glorious archangel: he became what he is by his own act and deed. Observe the importance of this, as sharply marking off the Christian belief from that Zoroastrian doctrine of an eternal evil principle, with which it is mistakenly confounded, and from which more mistakenly still, it is sometimes said to be derived. The difference is vital. The Oriental Ahriman is nothing less than an original anti-god; the existence of such a being is inconsistent with that of a Supreme and All-good God. It is inconsistent too with the fact that evil cannot be personal in any being in the sense in which good is personal in God. Evil cannot be personal in or of itself; it can only obtain the advantages of personal embodiment and action by being accepted by an already existing creature, endowed with will—a creature which freely determines implicitly to accept it by rejecting good. And therefore the Bible always represents Satan—not as a self-existing evil being—but as a fallen and apostate angel.

St. Peter speaks of the angels who sinned, and who were cast down to hell;[1] St. Jude of the "angels which kept not their first estate, but left their own habitation;"[2] St. Paul of the "condemnation of the devil," as resembling that of a novice among men "lifted up with pride."[3] In Satan evil has become dominant and fixed as in a previously existing personal being; there was no such thing in the universe of the Almighty and All-good God as a self-existing or originally created devil.

[1] 2 St. Pet. ii. 4. [2] Jude 6. [3] 1 Tim. iii. 6.

2. The Satan of Scripture has limited, although extensive, powers. It is necessary to remember that Milton's Satan is an audacious creation of poetry; invested with more than one false title to interest which the Satan of Scripture and of fact does not possess. It is a mistake to think of him as omnipresent; he is often enough in the way, but not always or everywhere. It is a still greater mistake to deem him omnipotent, or in any sense a rival, after the fashion of the Eastern Ahriman, to the All-good God. He is like a rebel chieftain who maintains a destructive warfare for a given period, but who might, and will eventually, be crushed.

"Why boastest thou thyself, thou tyrant, that thou canst do mischief?

"Whereas the goodness of God endureth yet daily. Thy tongue imagineth wickedness, and with lies thou cuttest like a sharp razor.

"Thou hast loved unrighteousness more than goodness, and to talk of lies more than righteousness. Thou hast loved to speak all words that may do hurt, O thou false tongue! Therefore shall God destroy thee for ever."[1]

The evil principle of the East is practically invincible; he defies the Goodness and the Empire of God. Satan is only tolerated; "the devil," says the Divine Book, "is come down having great wrath, because he knoweth that he hath but a short time."[2]

And if the question is asked, "How can you reconcile the continued toleration by God of such a being as the Evil One with God's attributes of Goodness and Almightiness?"—it must be answered that the full explanation must lie beyond our present range of vision. Only observe that the difficulty, if greater in degree, is the same in kind as that which we feel at the spectacle of a human being of the character and in the position of the

[1] Ps. lii. 1-6.   [2] Rev. xii. 12.

Roman Emperor Nero, who may be regarded, like all very bad men, as a serious approximation towards being a visible Satan. Here is a man invested with absolute power over millions of his fellow-creatures, and who employs that power after a fashion which entails the execration of the world, who contrives to do, within the range of his action, an amount of moral and physical mischief which it is appalling to contemplate. His reign comes to an end in time; but the question, why he is allowed to be where and what he is, during the few short years of empire, is the same question—different in scale, but the same in principle—as that about the toleration of the devil in the invisible world. Why are either of them, the devil, or Nero, tolerated even for a while, by such a Being as God? It is one department of that supreme mystery, the existence of evil, in a universe controlled by a Being who is All-powerful and All-good. We can only say that the Master of this Universe sees further than we do; and will one day, perhaps, enable us to understand in a measure those rules of His government which perplex us now. Meanwhile, experience comes here, as so often, to the aid of faith; and the facts and history of this visible world in which we live present exactly the same problems to our thoughts respecting the ways of God as that invisible world, the inhabitants of which are known to us only by Divine Revelation.

Above all, let us, as we take leave of the subject, fix in our minds the words and the lesson of the text. Christ came that He might render powerless him that had the power of death, that is, the devil. And He has done this: He has done it, when we might have least expected it, at that which, to the eye of sense, might have seemed the climax of His own humiliation and shame. Satan, the Apostle tells us, had the power of death. Like those brigand chiefs who ply their dark trade upon a mountain frontier or on a lonely road, so the Evil One had established a kind of recognised, though illegal, jurisdiction along the indistinct and mysterious boundary-line which parts the world of sense from the world of spirit. In addition to the physical anguish of dissolution there was present to the minds of generations of the dying the sense that in that dark hour something worse than bodily weakness or agony was to be apprehended: nothing less than the subtle and malignant onset of an invisible spirit, the soul's enemy and the enemy of God. Sin was the weapon by which he made death so terrible; "the sting of death is sin."[1] And it is from this apprehension that the faithful are freed by the Death of Jesus Christ. By dying, the Apostle tells us, our Lord, as Man, invaded this region of human experience and conquered for Himself and for us its old oppressor. When He seemed to the eye of sense to be Himself gradually sinking beneath the agony and exhaustion of the Cross, He was really, in the Apostle's enraptured vision, like one of those Roman generals whose victories were celebrated by the most splendid ceremonies known to the capital of the ancient world,— He was the spoiler of principalities and powers, making a show of them openly, triumphing over them in His Cross.[2] The Day of Calvary ranked in St. Paul's eyes, in virtue of this one out of its many results, far above the great battle-fields which a generation before had settled, for four centuries as it proved, the destinies of the world,—Pharsalia, Philippi, Actium. Satan was conquered by the Son of Man; because the sting of death—sin—had been extracted and pardoned; because it was henceforth possible, for all who would clasp the pierced Hands of the Crucified, to pass through that region of shadows as more than conqueror through Him That loved them.[3]

Here, brethren, we can only follow the guidance of

[1] 1 Cor. xv. 56.   [2] Col. ii. 14, 15.   [3] Rom. viii. 37.

faith. That there is an evil being who is at work in the world,—at work around, it may be upon or within ourselves,—is what we should naturally infer from what we see. Evil, like good, organises itself, propagates itself, forces its way, as if it could bring happiness and blessing to mankind, with a consistency and a vigour that, on its more limited scale, rivals the working and directing Providence of God, and betrays the scarcely concealed presence of a practised hand and an indomitable will. Do not let us refuse to recognise it; do not let us try to explain it or any other fact away; do not let us afford to our enemy a fresh proof of his practised genius and adroitness by ceasing, if we can cease, to believe in his existence. But, also, do not let us fear him; since for Christians he has ceased to be formidable. Such is the grace and mercy of our Lord, that all these evils which the craft and subtlety of the devil worketh against us will be brought to nought, and by the providence of Christ's goodness will be dispersed.[1] Such is Christ's grace, I say, that, in answer to prayer, it will please Him to beat down Satan under the feet[2] of the weakest of His true servants. When we are tempted to break any one of the known laws of God, to disown or contradict any portion of God's truth, we know who is near, luring us on, if he only can, to our failure or our ruin. But we know also Who is nearer still, his Ancient Conqueror and our own Best and Wisest Friend; and one aspiration to Jesus Christ from a believing soul will place all His grace and strength at our disposal. The results of Calvary do not really lessen with the lapse of time; and among these not the least blessed is the enfeeblement of Satan, and the deliverance of those who, through fear of death, would else be all their lifetime subject to bondage.

[1] Cf. Prayer in the Litany.   [2] *Ib.*

SERMON VII.

THE CORN OF WHEAT.

St. John xii. 24.

Verily, verily, I say unto you, Except a corn of wheat fall into the ground and die, it abideth alone; but if it die, it bringeth forth much fruit.

THIS is one of our Lord's own ways of speaking about His own Death. He had made His triumphal entry on Palm Sunday into Jerusalem, and certain Greeks, proselytes of the gate it would seem, asked an Apostle to let them see Him. There was no difficulty about this: the Greeks came to Jesus, and He told them that the hour for His glorification had come.[1] They were very likely to misunderstand this expression; they would probably think of some pageant of earthly splendour, or at least of some social or spiritual victory which would conquer all opposition at once and for good. Our Lord, as we Christians know, when He spoke of His being glorified, really meant that He would die in the course of four days upon a cross. He knew too that if the Greeks remained on in Jerusalem and saw Him die in this way, they would be greatly perplexed and shocked; and He, therefore, gives them a reason for His Death, couched in the language of parable: "Except a corn of wheat fall into the ground and die, it abideth alone; but if it die, it bringeth forth much fruit."

[1] St. John xii. 23.

I.

Here we learn from His own lips that it was necessary that our Lord Jesus Christ should die. We know that before His Death, and even after it, men who loved Him and who trusted Him had great difficulty in understanding this. Death to them seemed to have plainly stamped upon it the mark of weakness, failure, incapacity, or even guilt. Great saints of God in earlier ages had been exempted from submission to the law of death: if an Enoch was "taken,"[1] if an Elijah went up to heaven in a chariot of fire,[2] was He, of Whom these men were only shadows, in very deed to die? Was the one Perfect Human Life to which all the ages were pointing forward to be veiled at the last, like that of any sinner among us, in the humiliation and weakness which come in the train of death? Why call Him the Second Adam,[3] if He does not share the original immortality of the first Adam? How look to Him as the Saviour of men, if He must Himself pay tribute to man's last enemy?[4] These questions at first sight were natural enough. When the Jews saw Him nailed to the Cross—as it seemed, in the power of His enemies, and in the stern grip of death—they held that the question of His claims was practically settled. They that passed by, as they looked up and saw His Eyes closing in death, "reviled Him, wagging their heads and saying, He saved others, Himself He cannot save. If He be the King of Israel, let Him now come down from the cross, and we will believe Him."[5] And the feeling which prompted these sarcasms at the foot of the Cross was not altogether unshared, both before and after, by disciples of the Crucified. When our Lord predicted His Sufferings at Cæsarea-Philippi to St. Peter, the Apostle indignantly ex-

---

[1] Gen. v. 24.   [2] 2 Kings ii. 11.   [3] 1 Cor. xv. 45.
[4] 1 Cor. xv. 26.   [5] St. Matt. xxvii. 39-42.

claimed, "Be it far from Thee, Lord: this shall not happen unto Thee."[1] When the two disciples on the day of the Resurrection were joined on the Emmaus road by the Stranger Whom as yet they knew not, they confided to Him the bitterness of their disappointment. "We trusted that it had been He That should have redeemed Israel:"[2] His Death had shattered their hopes. When St. Paul would describe the effect of the preaching of the Crucifixion upon the two divisions of the ancient world among which he laboured, he says that it presented itself to the Jews as a scandal, that is, a stumbling-block in the way of their receiving faith, and to the Greeks as a folly, the exact reverse of everything they thought wisdom.[3] When the Epistle to the Hebrews was written, Christians were still raising difficulties about the Death of Christ; and Jews were taunting them with it, not without the effect of making them uncomfortable. Our Lord foresaw all this and much more, and He, therefore, sets His Death before the Greek visitors at Jerusalem, and before His disciples to the very end of time, in words which will be helpful to us, my brethren, I trust, on this evening of the most solemn day in the year to every believing Christian. "Except a corn of wheat fall into the ground and die, it abideth alone; but if it die, it bringth forth much fruit."

How then does He explain His approaching Death? Had He been speaking to born Jews, He would have said, as He did to the two disciples, that prophecy, properly understood, made it strictly necessary for any who claimed to be the true Messiah.[4] Had he been instructing Christians, like those addressed in the Epistle to the Hebrews, who believed that He was the true Representative of the Race, the Pattern or Ideal Man, He would have insisted, as did His Apostle, that as man He must submit to the law

---

[1] St. Matt. xvi. 22.
[2] St. Luke xxiv. 21.
[3] 1 Cor. i. 23.
[4] St. Luke xxiv. 25-27.

of Humanity; that, as it is appointed unto all men once to die, so Christ must once be offered,[1] though with results altogether transcending those of any ordinary human death. But speaking as He is to Greeks, who would have known little or nothing of prophecy or of His own relation to the race, but who were by taste and habit observers of the changes and forms of nature, He points to a great truth written on the face of nature by the Finger of God. Nature is one of God's two Books: the invisible things of God, says St. Paul, are seen in it by those who do not destroy their eyesight by disobedience to known Truth.[2] Nature, looked at superficially, seems to say that death is ruin, the ruin and end of all that is strong and beautiful in life: this mournful idea of death appears again and again in the poetry of the Greeks. Nature, scanned more penetratingly, more profoundly, shows that death is the precursor of new and vigorous life. The caterpillar forfeits its form to become the butterfly. The seed decomposes to become the plant. If the corn of wheat does not fall into the ground and die, it abides alone—intact, but dry, shrivelled, unproductive. If it dies, it forthwith becomes a principle of life: it bringeth forth much fruit.

The fruitfulness of death! Do we not see the truth of it every day of our lives in the world of thought and the world of action? God raises up some one man in a generation, the herald of a forgotten truth, or the apostle of a great discovery. He speaks; he writes; he warns; he entreats; but men shrug their shoulders, with a passing remark, at his well-meant enthusiasm, at his waste of energy. He perseveres, nevertheless, amid discouragement and coldness; he perseveres, it may be, in the teeth of interested opposition; he perseveres, until at last he feels that his strength is failing, and that his work will soon be done,—done, as it seems, to no purpose. He lies down to

[1] Heb. ix. 27, 28. [2] Rom. i. 20.

die, it may be, without any hopes for the future, it may be with a presentiment that the hour of his death will be that of his victory. And so in the event it is. When he is really gone; when the reiterated entreaties, appeals, warnings have ceased, men feel the silence, though they heeded not the voice, and are willing to believe a doctrine whose teacher is no more. The fact is, death makes his life more or less sublime; it refines our recollections of it; it puts the personal feelings, competitions, jealousies, which prevented justice to him, utterly and for ever aside; and as he speaks now, not in fact but in our memories, not in this, but, as it seems, from another world, we are willing, we are constrained to listen. Had he lived on, he would still have been impotent: his death has ennobled his work and made it fruitful. The grain of wheat would have done nothing for humanity, had it not fallen into the soil, and died.

Such is the law. Death, even when it comes only in the order of nature, has, not seldom, a fructifying power. The departed parent, the departed pastor, the true friend, whose voice was for so long unheeded, wields after death a power over hearts and wills which was denied him in life. But when death is freely accepted, as a sacrifice to truth or to duty, its fructifying power is enormously enhanced. And our Lord, of course, was contemplating His Death as an issue freely accepted by Himself, an issue which He might—as far as His power went—have declined. My brethren, if any one of the laws by which the moral world is governed is certain, this is certain: that to do real good in life is, sooner or later, costly and painful to the doer. It has ever been so. All the great truths which have illuminated human thought; all the lofty examples which have inspired and invigorated human effort—all have been more or less dearly paid for, by moral, or mental, or physical suffering. Each truth has had its martyr, unseen, it may be, and unsuspected, yet known to God. Here it is a violent death; there the gradual wasting away produced by exhausting labours: but the reality is the same. Here it is the soldier who saves a lost cause by his self-devotion; there it is a statesman who resigns power, influence, even personal safety, rather than retain them at the cost of his country. Elsewhere it is a teacher who throws his popularity to the winds, when, to keep it, he must echo some prejudice which he inwardly despises, or denounce some truth or creed which he heartily reveres. Like the legal impurities of the old tabernacle, the errors and miseries of the world are purged with blood:[1] everywhere in the great passages of human history we are on the track of sacrifice; and sacrifice, meet it where we may, is a moral power of incalculable force.

Do we think sometimes that Jesus Christ might have saved us in some less costly way than by shedding His Blood? Might He not have saved us, by putting forth His miraculous power, by showing among men His gracious presence, His severe purity, His inimitable tenderness? Might He not have sat, like the Greek teachers before Him, in some porch or garden, where the enterprise and intelligence of the world might have sought and found the Wisdom that would save it? So, perhaps, we think; and if Jesus had been only a Teacher of men, and had taught none but popular truths, so it might have been. As it was, to bring man close to God was a different task from any attempted by any old-world philosopher. Such deep work as Christ had to do—forcing the human conscience to stand face to face with the sternest and most unwelcome sides of truth ere He disclosed His Divine Remedy—could not be done without sacrifice, unless the existing conditions of human life were to be changed. And our Lord came, not to make a new world, but, at whatever cost, to redeem and invigorate an old one.

[1] Heb. ix. 22.

II.

Our Lord's Death, then, is fruitful. And, first, as a moral example of extraordinary power.

We all of us know the difference between precept and example. Precept is the easy part of teaching; example the difficult. Precept is the measure of the teacher's ability: example of his sincerity. Precept may lay burdens on others which the teacher does not touch with one of his fingers;[1] example gives precepts in the most persuasive way, and something into the bargain. Precept is the father who says to his boy, "Climb that mountain." Example is the father who says, "Follow me; see where I tread; put your foot where I put mine: lay hold on this rock, on that branch, just as I do; and we shall reach the top at last."

Now our Lord Jesus Christ taught men by precept. The Gospels are full of precepts which He gave. The Sermon on the Mount is a collection of them; there is no other code of precepts like it in the world. But His precepts—even His, we may dare to say,—would have died away upon the breeze, if they had not been enforced by His Example. And He gave that example in its fulness, when He became obedient unto death.[2]

The collect for Palm Sunday speaks of two forms of excellence, as taught us more especially by our Lord and Saviour. Of these the first is humility: He took on Him our flesh, and suffered death upon the cross that all mankind should follow the example of His great humility. Jesus had taught men by precept to be humble. They were to look on themselves as being what they are—nothing before God, or worse than nothing. They were to confess themselves unprofitable servants when they had done all that was required.[3] They were not to do their

---

[1] St. Luke xi. 46. [2] Phil. ii. 8. [3] St. Luke xvii. 10.

The Corn of Wheat.

alms before men;[1] they were not to be called Rabbi;[2] they must be converted, and become as little children, or they would not enter heaven; they must not be as the kings of the Gentiles, exercising authority for its own sake; the greatest must be first in service, lowliest in personal aim.[3] Knowing themselves to be sinners, they must rejoice if men thought of them, spoke of them, acted towards them, as being what they were. They must "rejoice," even if men said all manner of evil against them falsely;[4] if those particular charges were not deserved, others, they must know, were. The great thing was, never to forget what it is for a sinner to stand before the face of the Most Holy.

Such was the teaching of Jesus on this head. Our conscience tells us that it is true. Our wills tell us that it is very hard. Pride, we feel, in a coarser or more subtle form, has taken possession of the energies, poisoned the very springs, of our life.

Are we not constantly thinking of our good qualities; ranking ourselves higher than others; feeling annoyed when others are highly spoken of; defending our own opinion, even in indifferent matters, with obstinacy; assuming a quiet air of superiority in conversation, as if there could be no doubt about our right to assume it; desponding when our efforts do not succeed, as if we had a natural right to command success; rejoicing in showy work which attracts general admiration, rather than in quiet unostentatious work, known only to God and His angels; anxious that men should see and remark our good qualities; anxious perhaps to improve and become virtuous, not because God wills it and to promote His glory, but simply that in the contemplation of our attainments our vanity may have more to feed upon? It is hard, no doubt, to be really humble.

[1] St. Matt. vi. 1, 2.
[2] Ib. xxiii. 8.
[3] St. Matt. xx. 25-27.
[4] Ib. v. 11, 12.

This is what we feel: and Jesus, Who, as the Sinless One, cannot have the reasons for humility that we have, yet teaches us by example, what He has taught by precept. He was robed in humility from the first. The accessories of His birth, the employments of His youth and early Manhood, His relation to His parents, His choice of His disciples, His stern refusal of human praise and human honour: the silence which He enjoined about His miracles; the rebuke which He administered to the flatterer who, supposing Him to be only human, called Him "good"[1]—these, and much else, were His methods of teaching us humility.

But it was in His Passion that He taught this grace most persuasively. Then, of His own will, He was arraigned as an impostor, as a seducer of the people, as a blasphemer, as the enemy of God. He was arrested as if He were a thief, He was dressed in mockery by Herod as an idiot; He was buffeted as if He had been guilty of some gross insolence; He was scourged as a slave of the worst character; He was condemned to the shameful and cruel death reserved for the most desperate criminals; He was crucified between two thieves, as if He was the chief of them. He, the Uncreated Sanctity, the Eternal Wisdom, was, of His own free will, trodden down beneath the feet of His creatures as a sinner and a fool, that He might teach them at least one virtue—Humility.

And He has succeeded. It is not the precepts of Jesus: it is the figure of Jesus Incarnate and dying which has sunk deepest into the heart of Christendom. "Let this mind be in you which was also in Christ Jesus, Who, being in the Form of God, thought it not robbery to be equal with God, but made Himself of no reputation, and took upon Him the form of a slave, and was made in the likeness of man: and being found in fashion as a man,

[1] St. Matt. xix. 16, 17.

He humbled Himself, and became obedient unto death, even the death of the cross."[1] Wherever Christians have learned the greatness of humility, it has been by gazing on the Crucified. All the moral glories of self-renouncement in its higher and more splendid forms; all the noble ambitions to do great works for God, and to be misunderstood or undervalued or forgotten in doing them; all these passive virtues which really subdue the world, and which have their root in humility, show that the Corn of Wheat Which fell into the ground and died eighteen centuries ago has not died in vain.

Or take the other grace mentioned in the Collect, the grace of patience, the power of bearing resignedly and cheerfully the trials which come to us in the course of God's Providence, or at the hands of our fellow-creatures. Our Lord constantly insists on the need of this. If our Lord says that the mourners are blessed;[2] that the "persecuted for righteousness' sake" are blessed;[3] that His disciples are to account themselves blessed, when they are reviled, wronged, defamed;[4] why is this but because these are opportunities for the exercise of patience? "If any man strike thee on the right cheek, turn to him the other also."[5] "Do good to them that hate you, pray for them that despitefully use you: and ye shall be the children of your Father Which is in heaven."[6] The disciples who would call down fire from heaven know not "what spirit they are of."[7] The man who says to his brother "Thou fool" is guilty of hell fire.[8] The faithful will bring forth fruit with patience;[9] in the dark days that will come upon the world they will have the true mastery who in patience possess their souls.[10]

[1] Phil. ii. 5-8.   [2] St. Matt. v. 4.   [3] Ib. 10.
[4] St. Matt. v. 11.   [5] Ib. 39.   [6] Ib. 44, 45.
[7] St. Luke ix. 54, 55.   [8] St. Matt. v. 22.   [9] St. Luke viii. 15.
[10] St. Luke xxi. 8-19.

This is our Lord's teaching: these His very words. Our conscience—that deep ineradicable sense of right which He has given us—echoes this teaching. We see that it is right intuitively as soon as He utters it. But is it not hard to follow? we ask. We think, perhaps, that it is ideal only, impracticable, exaggerated.

"Very well, then," He says to us, "look at Me. Take up your crosses and follow Me." Forthwith He leads to Calvary. We follow Him from the Supper-room to the Garden; from the Garden to the Hall of Judgment; from the tribunal, along the Way of Sorrows, to the Cross. We note the delicacy, the exquisite sensitiveness, of His Body. If creatures are capable of pain in proportion to their place in the scale of being, what must have been the capacity of Jesus for suffering? We note the variety of pains to which He submitted. No one of His senses, no part of His Body, was exempt from its peculiar pain. We observe that some of the tortures, such as that produced by the crown of thorns, or by the scourging, or by the raising the Cross into the socket, must have been exceptionally painful; that His Sufferings were continuous; that there was no moment of reprieve throughout His Passion; and that, as when He refused the hyssop, He resolutely denied Himself any means of alleviation. Then we reflect that on the Cross as in the Garden His Human Soul is the scene of keener agony than that which afflicts His Body: the Agony produced not merely by the clear consciousness and detailed anticipation of physical suffering, but, in the case of the Sinless One, by the dreadful sight of the sins of a world which He had taken upon Himself, and which He was expiating. He says enough to show what He suffers: "My God, My God, why hast Thou forsaken Me?"[1] He does not say one word which impairs His patience. The prophet had

[1] St. Matt. xxvii. 46.

said of Him, "He is led as a sheep to the slaughter; and as a lamb before her shearers is dumb, so He openeth not His mouth."[1] The Apostle records of Him that "when He was reviled He reviled not again, when He suffered He threatened not."[2] The motto of the Passion is, "The cup which My Father hath given Me, shall I not drink it?"[3] And here, too, He has not died in vain. Think of the hundreds of thousands throughout Christendom who are lying in pain,—who are drawing nearer moment by moment to their last agony—or who are in the pains of death. If they can lie still; if they have the great grace to suffer uncomplainingly, brightly; if they irradiate the last sad scenes of our frail humanity with a radiance streaming from another world, what is the secret of their power? It is that they have been gazing steadily on Jesus Christ Crucified; that His patience has won them, and they have had an eye unto Him and have been lightened;[4] that they have said to themselves with one great sufferer, "If He could endure that for me, how little is this to suffer with Him!"

III.

Not, my brethren, that humility and patience were the only lessons taught us by our Lord from His Cross. They are but samples of that vast circle of teaching upon which from that day to this Christians have earnestly dwelt, and the full import of which they are as far as ever from having exhausted. But although Jesus Christ crucified teaches the world the truths and duties which it most needs to know, He does much more than this; and to limit the fruitfulness of His Death to this would be to do you and to do Him a grievous wrong. If in dying Jesus had only shown us His own teaching in practice,

[1] Isa. liii. 7.
[2] 1 St. Pet. ii. 23.
[3] St. John xviii. 11.
[4] Ps. xxxiv. 5.

He would have left us in despair. Like the Jewish law, but on a greater scale, He would have convinced us of sin and shortcoming, without providing a remedy. As it is, while He hung upon the Cross, He showed us that His Death would have results of quite a different kind from the death of the martyr to truth or to duty: effects which flow directly from His Representative relation to the human family, and from His Higher and Eternal Nature, and which are, in truth, all its own.

Three were crucified on Mount Calvary: the Most Holy in the midst, and a thief on either side. Two Evangelists tell us that the thieves joined with the mob in reviling their fellow-sufferer.[1] All classes, all interests, Herod and Pilate, Jews and Romans, nobles and the people, Pharisees and Sadducees, and even the victims with their executioners, were banded in one grand conspiracy against the Holiness of God revealed in Jesus. Why should they all hate Him, we ask? Ask why it is that the sunlight which gladdens nature, which invigorates healthy life, is torture to a diseased eyesight? It is not that the light is less beneficent, but the organ is diseased, and therefore the light brings irritation, discomfort, pain, and no effort is too great to escape it. The light of lofty sanctity is just as painful to diseased souls: in its highest and perfect form as manifested in Jesus, it goads them to madness: in its broken and imperfect forms, as we see it in Christians, it provokes dislike,— secret it may be, but strong, and only waiting its opportunity for speech or action.

It is easily explained, but, in the case of the dying thieves, the blasphemy of Jesus is especially dreadful. They know that life is ebbing from them, that all will soon be over; that this world has nothing more in reserve in the way of adventure or excitement, yet they blaspheme.

[1] St. Matt. xxvii. 44; St Mark xv. 32.

The Corn of Wheat.

Misfortune generally creates a certain sympathy between its victims; but for Jesus the thieves feel only hatred. Pain is God's own instrument for breaking hard hearts, for softening harsh characters, for teaching men to think tenderly of others, sternly of themselves. Alas! one of the most terrible spectacles in the moral world is the miscarriage and failure of this ministry of pain; most clergymen of any experience have seen it on deathbeds: and it was exhibited upon two out of the three crosses on Calvary. If pain does not soften, it scars; it burns up all that remains of tenderness, and almost of humanity; it scorches each finer sensibility of the soul, and leaves it hard, fierce, brutal, beyond any previous experience.

And yet, while that chorus of defiance and hate was being chanted around the dying Jesus, by the mob and by the thieves, one of the latter became silent. He had looked on the Face of the Divine Sufferer,—besmeared as it now was with tears and blood,—and he had seen traced beneath a Dignity, a Love, a Sanctity, which were utterly new to him. Probably his ear had caught the faint prayer, just as the Cross was being raised: "Father, forgive them, for they know not what they do."[1] It was a moment unlike any previous moment in his life: he felt a new movement in his soul, he was face to face with Truth, with Sanctity. The revelation of holiness is the revelation of sin. As he gazes on Jesus, he learns the truth about himself: he will make no excuses, such as we might make for him on the score of ignorance or lack of opportunity: he is not playing at penitence; his heart is broken. The Crucified Truth at his side has made all plain to him. "We indeed suffer justly," he cries; "for we receive the due reward of our deeds: but this Man hath done nothing amiss."[2] Nor is this all. His faith is even more striking than his repentance. By one of those rapid

---
[1] St. Luke xxiii. 34.   [2] *Ib.* 41.

glances into the depths of truth which are vouchsafed to souls in moments of exceptional illumination or agony, he sees that the Sufferer at his side, Who has revealed Himself to him, must be able to help him, even in his last terrible extremity. The life of souls, in these supreme moments, cannot be measured by the clock or the almanac; a lifetime may be compressed into a few minutes: there is no real relation between what passes and the lapse of time. And so the poor thief breathes a prayer which might have come at the end of a long life of labour from a martyred Apostle: "Lord, remember me —remember me when Thou comest into Thy kingdom."[1] It was enough: "To-day shalt thou be with Me in Paradise."[2] To-day: what readiness to receive him! With Me: what Companionship for a criminal! In Paradise: what a vision of repose!

He had yet to die in agony, it is true; but death was tolerable enough—it was even welcome—now. He had to linger on in agony; but pain, the worst pain, had been transfigured for him; he could more than bear it. He had to witness the last hour, to hear the last cry, "Into Thy hands I commend My spirit,"[3] uttered by His crucified Friend: he knows that that cry means for him the opening of the gates of Paradise. In these last hours of his agony he is a type of the dying Christian to the end of time; he is the first believer who enters the kingdom of heaven when the King had overcome the sharpness of death: he is the first sample of that mighty harvest of souls which was to be the fruit of the death of the Son of God.

IV.

Any man, my brethren, who seriously believes that Jesus Christ is the Eternal Son of God must feel that

[1] St. Luke xxiii. 42.   [2] Ib. 43.   [3] Ib. 46.

VII]   *The Corn of Wheat.*   115

such an event as His Death in human form must be attended by consequences altogether beyond those which would follow on the death of the best or wisest of the sons of men. What those consequences would be we could not reasonably conjecture: but here Revelation comes to our assistance. It sets the Death of Jesus Christ before us in three aspects: by It sin is atoned for; by It we are redeemed from the penalty of sin; by It sinful man and the All-holy God are reconciled. "Christ," says St. John, "is the propitiation for our sins; and not for ours only, but also for the sins of the whole world."[1] "Christ," says St. Paul, "hath redeemed us from the curse of the law; being made a curse for us."[2] "We have redemption through His Blood,"[3] and, as a consequence, "we are reconciled to God," says St. Paul, "by the death of His Son."[4] How, we ask, does His Death thus propitiate, redeem, reconcile? "Because," reply the Apostles, "He was made to be sin for us Who knew no sin, that we might be made the righteousness of God in Him;"[5] and so He "bare our sins in His own Body on the tree."[6] How, we ask again, could this transfer of guilt, of responsibility, have taken place? Is there not a contradiction here with our sense of natural justice; with the Divine rule that "no man can deliver his brother, or make agreement unto God for him"?[7] No; there is no contradiction; and for two reasons. First, Jesus is not merely a common or single specimen of the race. He is the Second Adam;[8] that is, like our first parent, He represents in some way all other men: He is human nature by Representation. So He loved to call Himself "the Son of Man,"[9] meaning, among other things, that He was the Representative, Ideal, Pattern Man, Who

---

[1] 1 St. John ii. 2.   [2] Gal. iii. 13.   [3] Eph. i. 7.
[4] Rom. v. 10.   [5] 2 Cor. v. 21.   [6] 1 St. Pet. ii. 24.
[7] Ps. xlix. 7.   [8] 1 Cor. xv. 45.
[9] St. Matt. x. 23; xii. 8, 32; xvi. 13; St. John v. 27; vi. 53, etc.

had relations to all others, and in Whom all others had a share, if they would. In Him the Eternal Father beheld not merely an individual, but the human race; the human race corresponding for once to the Ideal in the Divine Mind; the human race embodied in a Representative to Whom it was said from heaven, "This is My Beloved Son, in Whom I am well pleased."[1] Jesus represents the race, not as a member of parliament who is elected by his constituents, but as a parent represents his children. No one would deny the right of a parent to act for his young family on a critical occasion: and Jesus, dying on the Cross, is acting for those whom He already and naturally represents. And this leads me to the second reason for there being no injustice in the idea of the Atonement; namely, that Jesus, being thus by nature representative of us all, freely willed to die for us. We may dare to say it: His life was not taken from Him whether He would or not, like the lives of the victims slain at Jewish altars. "No one taketh My life from Me," He said, "but I lay it down of Myself; I have power to lay it down, and I have power to take it again."[2] He willed, in His love and in His pity,[3] to bear the burden which was really ours. He could bear it, because He already, by the terms of His Nature, represented us; and there was no injustice in accepting what was so generously, so freely offered. And if it be asked why Holy Scripture connects this salvation so particularly with the Death of Christ—why His Death has this Expiatory and Redemptive power—the answer is, that His Death is the highest expression of His perfect Obedience; it is His Obedience triumphing over the strongest motive which can urge men to disobey—the instinct of self-preservation. As St. Paul says emphatically, He was "obedient unto death."[4] And that which gave this obedience its literally

[1] St. Matt. iii. 17. [2] St. John x. 18. [3] Isa. liii. 9. [4] Phil. ii. 8.

infinite value was the Person of the Sufferer. "If God spared not His own Son, but delivered Him up for us all, how shall He not with Him also freely give us all things?"[1]

Yes! the Corn of seed has indeed brought forth much fruit by falling into the ground to die; like Samson, they whom Christ slew at His Death were more than they whom He slew in His life.[2] The power of death, the power of sin, the power of Satan,—these, if we will, are gone. All the agencies of restoration and grace which we find in the Church of God flow down from the Wounds of the Crucified. If Sacraments have power, if prayer prevails, if the Spirit is given to guide and to purify us, if consciences are clear, and hearts buoyant, and wills invigorated; if life's burdens are borne cheerfully, and death is looked forward to, not without awe, but without apprehension; this is because Jesus Christ has died. "If it die, it bringeth forth much fruit." Ever since His Ascension the store has been accumulating above; not a year, not a week, not a day passes without some addition to the company of the Redeemed who are gathered around the Throne of the Immaculate Lamb, to sing unweariedly, "Thou wast slain, and hast redeemed us unto God by Thy Blood, out of every kindred, and tongue, and people, and nation."[3]

My brethren, how utterly insignificant is any other question that we can ask ourselves compared with this: Shall I ever join that company? Will the Divine Redeemer own me as one of the fruits of His Death? Alas if any one of us should have hereafter to reflect, "He died, the Everlasting Son of God; but, as far as I am concerned, it was in vain." God's grace is not bound to great agencies or great occasions; the Eternal Spirit acts through the humblest means. A German nobleman was converted

---

[1] Rom. viii. 32.   [2] Judg. xvi. 30.   [3] Rev. v. 9.

from a life of careless indifference by seeing in a gallery a painting of our Saviour's Head crowned with thorns, with the words traced under,

> "This have I borne for thee;
> What willest thou for Me?"

God grant that the scenes of the Passion, which have passed before us this day[1] in the pages of the blessed Evangelists, may haunt us too, till we yield ourselves entirely and for good to God. There is no repentance in the grave, or pardon offered to the dead; and there is no name under heaven given among men whereby we may be saved,[2] but the Name of Jesus, our Crucified Saviour, and He, in His Love and in His Pity, is willing to save us to the uttermost.

[1] Good Friday.   [2] Acts iv. 12.

SERMON VIII.

THE APPEAL OF THE CRUCIFIED JESUS.

ROM. x. 21.

But to Israel He saith, All day long I have stretched forth My hands unto a disobedient and gainsaying people.

ST. PAUL is quoting the prophet Isaiah; and Isaiah is speaking to Israel in the name of God. "But unto Israel He saith, All day long have I stretched out Mine Hands unto a disobedient and gainsaying people." The Hebrew word compares Israel to a refractory animal; and St. Paul dissolves this expression, or the translation which he uses, into the two words "disobedient" and "gainsaying." To this people, which knew not how to obey God, and which continually criticised Him, God condescends to say that He stretched out His hands. As applied to a Being without body, parts, or passions,[1] this language cannot of course be explained by what it means in man. The gesture of stretching out the hands is everywhere understood by human beings; the phrase is natural to all human language. To stretch out the hands is to make appeal or entreaty with silent imploring earnestness; and this appeal God made to His disobedient and gainsaying people—so says the prophet in substance, so echoes the apostle—all the day long.

[1] Article I.

I.

All the day long! It is a pregnant expression, which may well have enlarged its scope with the lapse of time. It opens one vista to a Jewish prophet; and another to a Christian Apostle; and another, it may be, in practice to us of to-day.

(a) All the day long! It was a long day, which lasted from the work of the great lawgiver in the desert to the captivity in Babylon: some nine centuries at the least. They were centuries marked by vicissitudes of success and failure, of depression and buoyancy; and as they passed, one after another, they developed, with new circumstances, new features in the national character. The Jew of the later monarchy was in many respects a different man from his ancestor who had first crossed the Jordan. But so far as his resistance to God's will and contradiction of God's servants went, he was entirely unchanged. A later Psalmist could sing: "To-day if ye hear His voice, harden not your hearts, as in the provocation, and as in the day of temptation in the wilderness. When your fathers tempted Me, proved Me, and saw My work. Forty years long was I grieved with this generation, and said, It is a people that do err in their heart, and they have not known My ways."[1] Such was Israel in the desert, under the eye and guidance of the great lawgiver; fresh from the deliverance from the Egyptian bondage; fresh from the wonders of Sinai. Such too was Israel in the Land of Promise, first under the judges, and then under the kings. . The history of this people viewed from a moral, as distinct from a merely political standpoint, is a long paroxysm of rebellious folly. It frivolously threw aside its Divinely appointed

[1] Ps. xcv. 8-10.

government, in order to keep pace with the political fashions of the Pagan nations around. It drove for a while the greatest of its monarchs from his throne and capital: and ten tribes rose in successful insurrection against his son. It broke up the unity of the covenant race; and then it broke away, first in this direction and then in that, from the religion of the Covenant. No idolatry seemed to be unwelcome to a race which had learnt the awful Unity and Spirituality of God. The hateful nature-worship (for such it was) which Jezebel had imported from Tyre; the cruel rites of Moloch, the imposing falsehoods, half myths, half philosophies, which were popular among the ruling races on the Euphrates and the Tigris, were pressed to the heart of the people of revelation; and at last the end came. But during all those centuries the God of Israel had stretched out His Hands in loving entreaty to the nation which requited Him with disobedience and contradiction. Sometimes by prophets, sometimes by great rulers, sometimes by splendid successes, sometimes by tragical reverses, He bade them feel that He was there, behind the clouds which seemed to hide Him from them, —a Providence of unwearied, watchful compassion.

In later ages—when this first day of their history was over—Israel could bear to be told the truth about its own ancient perverseness, and the loving and repeated appeals of God. Read such a Psalm as the 106th, written probably by a psalmist of the date of the Captivity, who has learnt spiritual wisdom in a hard personal experience. It is little more than a catalogue of alternate sins and mercies—the sins of Israel, the mercies of God. After an exulting description of the great deliverance from Egypt, each offence of Israel in those early days shapes a separate stanza in the poem; each offence is graver than the preceding. They follow in a tragic series: the demand for quails, the rebellion of Korah, the worship of the golden calf, the contempt for the report of the land of promise, the degrading Baal-peor worship, the friendly relations with the accursed races of Canaan; ending in the guilt of even human sacrifices. And then the history is summarised :

> "Their enemies oppressed them:
> And had them in subjection;
> Many a time did He deliver them,
> But they rebelled against Him with their own inventions
> And were brought down in their wickedness.
> Nevertheless, when He saw their adversity,
> He heard their complaint.
> He thought upon His covenant, and pitied them
> According unto the multitude of His mercies:
> Yea, He made all those that led them away captive to pity them." [1]

And towards the close of the period the inexhaustible tenderness of God for Israel is nowhere more fully unveiled than in Hosea, the prophet who describes the sins of the ten tribes with such unsparing accuracy:

"How shall I give thee up, Ephraim? how shall I deliver thee, Israel? how shall I make thee as Admah? how shall I set thee as Zeboim? Mine heart is turned within me. My repentings are kindled together. I will not execute the firmness of Mine anger. I will not return to destroy Ephraim: for I am God, and not man; the Holy One of Israel in the midst of thee." [2]

So it was throughout: Israel's sin, followed by God's pleading love and pardoning mercy—not once or twice, but again and again, until at last the very flower of the nation was drafted away for a while into the dark prison of Babylon; and here once more, on a greater scale than ever, the same cycle of sin, warning, pardon, and deliverance was re-enacted. "All the day long have I stretched out My Hands unto a disobedient and gainsaying people."

(β) All the day long! The briefer dark day of the Captivity was perhaps more present to the thoughts of

[1] Ps. cvi. 41-44. [2] Hos. xi. 8, 9.

Isaiah than the long day of Israel's earlier history of mingled triumphs and reverses. If Isaiah is glancing backwards he is looking forward too. In the last twenty-seven chapters of his prophecy he has his eye upon all that will pass in Babylon long after he himself has been gathered to his fathers. Across the increasing degradation and final catastrophe of the intervening period, he sees the captives at home in the great heathen city. Some indeed may sit down and weep by its waters when they remember Zion; hanging up their harps upon the trees that are therein, and refusing to charm the ear of the conqueror with the songs of Zion,—the Lord's song, in a strange land.[1] Some may say, with that great captive who wrote Psalm cxix., "It is good for me that I have been in trouble, that I may learn Thy statutes."[2] But with a large majority it is otherwise. They are thoroughly at their ease in this metropolis of Pagan magnificence and crime; accommodating themselves with facile readiness to the habits and morals of their masters; forgetting Jerusalem; forgetting the faith of their forefathers. Isaiah, as he gazes into the future, descries

"A people that provoketh Me to anger continually to My face;
That sacrificeth in gardens,
And burneth incense upon altars of brick;
Which remain among the graves,
And lodge in the monuments;
Which eat swine's flesh,
And broth of abominable things is in their vessels:
Which say, Stand by thyself, come not near to me;
For I am holier than thou."[3]

God has been stretching out His Hands to these men, in judgments which, hard as they were, were an earnest of mercy; but suffering seems to have said as little to Israel as its brighter day of glory and success. God has other appeals in store; prophets like Daniel, statesmen

[1] Ps. cxxxvii. 1-4.   [2] Ib. cxix. 71.   [3] Isa. lxv. 3-5.

like Ezra, will speak in His Name: immense political catastrophes, like that which made the Persian kings masters of the East, will be a stretching out of the Hands of God to Israel. But Israel has retained or recovered little of its ancient self: nothing, it would almost seem, except its self-righteousness. It has no reverence for the Divine Law, no submissive silence with which to listen to the Divine Voice. The prophet exclaims, almost in despair, in his Master's Name, "All the day long have I stretched out My Hands to a disobedient and gainsaying people."

(γ) All the day long! St. Paul finds the expression ready to his hand in the page of Isaiah; and for St. Paul it means that new epoch which, when he writes, has already opened upon the world. "The day," in St. Paul's sense, is the day or age of the Messiah; the years which have passed since Christ and His Apostles have spoken to Israel. When St. Paul writes, indeed, a generation of Jews has already grown up to manhood since the Resurrection and Ascension of Jesus Christ: a generation of those lost sheep of the House of Israel, to whom alone our Lord proclaimed He was, in the first instance, sent.[1] What has become of this generation, or of their immediate predecessors—what, I ask, has become of it—as it listens to the Divine Message, as it gazes on the outstretched Hands of God? "There is a remnant," says the Apostle in reply, like that in Elijah's day, saved "according to the election of grace."[2] But of the great majority he adds: "The rest were blinded, or hardened;"[3] they repeat under new circumstances the obduracy of the Egyptian Pharaoh. They have seen or heard of the miracles of Christ; they have felt the force of His appeal to prophecy, to history, to conscience. That Loving Providence, Who has watched so forbearingly over centuries of disobedience and scorn,

[1] St. Matt. xv. 24.   [2] Rom. xi. 2-5.   [3] Ib. 7.

has at last taken Flesh and become visible, and exchanged the secret appeal of ages for the tones of a human Voice: "O Jerusalem, Jerusalem, that killest the prophets, and stonest them that are sent unto thee, how often would I have gathered thy children together, as a hen doth gather her chickens under her wings, but ye would not!" And then He adds: "Behold, your house is left unto you desolate."[1] He again comes to His own, and His own receive Him not.[2] Throughout the day of His ministerial life He stretches out the hands of compassion and entreaty to a disobedient and gainsaying people. They disobey and they malign Him; He is in league (they say) with Beelzebub;[3] He is a Samaritan, and has a devil.[4] And when He is gone it fares with the servants as it had fared with the Master. Stephen, before his Jewish judges, exclaims that Israel is at least true to its history: it is rebellious and gainsaying to the end. "Ye stiff-necked and uncircumcised in heart and ears, ye do always resist the Holy Ghost: as your fathers did, so do ye. Which of the prophets have not your fathers persecuted? and they have slain them which shewed before of the coming of the Just One; of Whom ye have been now the betrayers and murderers."[5] After His conversion, after those rude experiences of Jewish bitterness and violence which he encountered in almost every city where he preached the Faith of Christ—and which he describes so vividly in his first letter to the Thessalonian Church—St. Paul saw that Isaiah's words had not yet lost their force; that it was still true that God was stretching out His hands more earnestly, more persuasively, than ever before, and to a people which was fixed, as it seemed, for the most part, and fixed determinedly, in disobedience and contradiction.

---

[1] St. Matt. xxiii. 37, 38. [2] St. John i. 11. [3] St. Matt. xii. 24.
[4] St. John viii. 48. [5] Acts vii. 51, 52.

(δ) All the day long! There was one day, of twenty-four hours, within this last period, unlike any other before or since, and it is more than probable that St. Paul had this day in his mind when he quoted the words of Isaiah. You know, brethren, what I mean: the day of the Passion; the day of Calvary. From the first moment of our Lord Jesus Christ's mental Agony in the Garden on the preceding evening begins this supreme appeal to the heart and conscience of Israel and of the world; and it lasts until He has bowed His Head at three o'clock in the afternoon, and given up the Ghost. It lasts through the Agony and Bloody Sweat, through the treason of the false apostle, through the details of the arrest by the armed mob; it is eloquent for all who have ears to hear, as the Divine Prisoner is brought before Annas and Caiaphas; as He is spat upon and buffeted in the palace of the High Priest; as, denied by the first Apostle, He is led away to Pilate, and sent from Pilate to Herod, and mocked by Herod, as if He, the Eternal Wisdom, were a fool, and sent back to Pilate. This appeal, I say, becomes more and more urgent and impassioned, as He Who makes it is rejected in favour of the robber Barabbas, is publicly scourged by the Pagan magistrate, is crowned with thorns, robed in purple rags, and invested with a reed for His sceptre, and shown, already covered with wounds and blood, to the angry populace. Nor does it cease as He is condemned to die; as He carries His Cross along the Way of Sorrows to the place of death; as they nail Him to it, and lift Him up on it between earth and heaven. Nay, rather, as early teachers of His Church have felt—it may suffice to name Origen and Augustine—at that moment, and for the three hours which follow, Isaiah's words are fulfilled as never before. For now these Hands—the Hands of Providence and Compassion—are literally stretched forth upon the Cross; the Divine Attributes which have watched over Israel's destinies are become visible in the Incarnate Son. God's relations with the human history of fifteen hundred years, and of the centuries which are to follow, are epitomised into a short day. Now, as before, He stretches out His Hands; it is His own act, though others are empowered to carry it out. Others nail Him to the Cross, and yet He can say, "No man taketh My life from Me, but I lay it down of Myself. I have power to lay it down, and I have power to take it again."[1] Now, as before, His Hands, outstretched in anguish and death, appeal mutely to a people of disobedience and contradiction. True! there is the little group of faithful ones: the Mother in her agony, the beloved Disciple, the thief who prays for a remembrance at the gate of Paradise, the centurion who owns the Son of God. But the multitude rage around in coarse, visible, audible rebellion and blasphemy; alas! true to their ancestral spirit. The chief priests and the people vie with each other in the insults which they offer. "Thou that destroyest the temple, and buildest it in three days, save Thyself."[2] "He saved others, Himself He cannot save."[3] His dying Eye looked down upon a surging mass of rebellion and contradiction. Israel at the foot of the Cross was what Israel had been throughout the ages; in the wilderness, in Babylon: and over this unhappy race the Divine Sufferer must cry, "All day long have I stretched out My hands to a disobedient and gainsaying people."

II.

And we too, brethren, have our place, whatever it be, somewhere on Mount Calvary. As St. Paul told the Galatians, many years after the event, "Before your eyes Jesus Christ is evidently set forth crucified, among you."[4]

[1] St. John x. 18. [2] St. Mark xv. 29, 30.
[3] St. Mark xv. 31. [4] Gal. iii. 1.

Christ crucified belongs to no one age or place. For true Christian faith time and place are not of much account. Faith bridges over the intervening lands and seas, and lives on the holy sites where Jesus was born, and died, and rose, and ascended into Heaven. Faith leaps across the centuries at a bound; the modern period, the middle ages, the primitive times. Faith sees and experiences over again all that the Apostles saw and experienced. Then faith detaches Christ crucified, if I may so say, from geography and from chronology, and thrones Him in the Christian consciousness where He is independent of the local associations of space and of the sequence of time; where He hangs, as it were, for all time between earth and heaven on the Tree of shame, in awful but glorious isolation, the Lamb slain from the foundation of the world.[1] What then is the appeal which Jesus Christ makes, with His Hands stretched forth upon the Cross, to the hearts of us Christians? It is twofold.

(a) It is an appeal addressed to our moral sense on behalf of God's standard of holiness as against the laxity or sin of man. And He makes this appeal to us by the force of His own Example. Brethren, there are two methods of teaching duty: by word of mouth or precept, and by personal conduct or example.

The first is necessary, indispensable; but the second is more effective than the first. Teaching by precept is a method common to the saints and the philosophers. Teaching by example is a high prerogative of the saints. Teaching by precept begins with the understanding, and may or may not reach the heart. Teaching by example begins with the heart, and the understanding cannot fail to learn its lesson at a glance.

Now Jesus Christ our Lord used both methods. Between the Sermon on the Mount and the Last Discourse

[1] Rev. xiii. 8.

in the Supper-Room He was continually teaching by word of mouth; sometimes multitudes, sometimes single souls; sometimes His disciples, sometimes the Jews; now those who listened, and again those who refused to listen. "Line upon line, precept upon precept, here a little, and there a little,"[1] as men could bear the light of Heaven—this was His method. But side by side with the method of precept He employed the method of example. All through His life He reinforced His precepts by the eloquence of His conduct; but He gathered up all these lessons, or the most difficult of them, into one supreme appeal to the dormant moral sense in man, when He raised Himself on the Cross and stretched out His Arms to die.

And what are the excellencies upon which this Crucified Teacher lays most stress? They are chiefly, brethren, what we call the passive virtues. Not that He would depreciate the active virtues which Pagans admired and practised; temperance, justice, courage, generosity. But there were other virtues which the old heathen world did not deem virtues at all, but only half-vices, only poor-spiritedness and weakness, and of the beauty of which the Jews themselves made small account. Such are the two which the Collect of to-day mentions as especially taught us by the Passion of Christ, humility and patience. Yes, humility, so hard for us to learn, is taught us by Him Who, being in the Form of God, did not claim other than His own in claiming equality with God, "yet made Himself of no reputation, and took on Him the form of a slave, and was made in the likeness of man, and being found in fashion as a man, He humbled Himself, and became obedient unto death, even the death of the cross."[2] And patience—so necessary, sooner or later, for all of us, if we would be "perfect and entire, wanting nothing"[3]—

[1] Isa. xxviii. 11.   [2] Phil. ii. 6-8.   [3] St. James i. 4.

when He Who might have prayed to His Father, and presently been sent more than twelve legions of angels,[1] "was led as a sheep to the slaughter, and as a lamb before his shearers is dumb, so He opened not His mouth:"[2] when He, the alone Immaculate, when He was reviled, reviled not again, when He suffered, threatened not, but committed Himself to Him that judgeth righteously.[3] And, closely akin to this, resignation to the Divine Will. The words in the garden, "Not My will but Thine be done,"[4] answer to the words of prophecy: "In the volume of the book it is written of Me, that I should fulfil Thy Will, O my God; I am content to do it;"[5] and thus all is surrendered without reserve—reputation, friends, comfort, life. Not, as I have hinted, that Christ on the Cross teaches only passive virtue. Of the Seven last Words, one teaches us to work and pray for our enemies;[6] a second, to be considerate towards those who go wrong;[7] a third, to be dutiful to our parents;[8] a fourth, to thirst for the salvation of others;[9] a fifth, to pray fervently when under a sense of desolation;[10] a sixth, to persevere till we have finished what God has given us to do in life;[11] and the last, to commit ourselves, by a conscious act, both in life and death, into the Hands of God.[12]

(β) Secondly, Jesus Christ, with His Hands stretched forth upon the Cross, makes an appeal to our sense of what He has done for us.

Why is He there? Not for any demerit of His own; not only, or chiefly, to teach us virtue. He is there because otherwise we are lost; because we must be "reconciled to God by the Death of His Son."[13] He is there because He has first, by taking our nature, made Himself our

---

[1] St. Matt. xxvi. 53. [2] Isa. liii. 7. [3] 1 St. Pet. ii. 23.
[4] St. Luke xxii. 42. [5] Ps. xl. 10. [6] St. Luke xxiii. 34.
[7] St. Luke xxiii. 43. [8] St. John xix. 26, 27. [9] Ib. 28.
[10] St. Mark xv. 34. [11] St. John xix. 30.
[12] St. Luke xxiii. 46. [13] Rom. v. 10.

Representative, and then, in this capacity, is bearing a penalty which, in virtue of those moral laws whereby the universe is governed, is due to our sins. It is no arbitrary or capricious substitution, whereby He thus suffers, "the Just for the unjust, that He might bring us to God."[1] For He already represents our human nature, just as Adam represented it: He acts for us as a parent might act for a young family: He suffers for us as a parent would suffer for his child. We claim our share in this His representative Nature by that act of adhesion which we call faith; and He answers and ratifies our claim by His gifts of grace through the Christian Sacraments. Thus when He suffers, we too suffer by implication; when He dies, we share His Death; when He makes satisfaction to the eternal moral laws for the misdeeds of that nature which He has assumed, we who wear it, and have been the real culprits, make satisfaction too. "God made Him to be sin for us, Who knew no sin, that we might be made the righteousness of God in Him."[2] And thus we are "justified freely by His grace, through the redemption that is in Christ Jesus, Whom God hath set forth to be a propitiation, through faith in His blood."[3]

This is that unveiling of the inmost Heart of the All-merciful—the mystery of the Atonement for sin. It is as opening this mystery to the eyes of Christians—as inviting them all and each to come and share it—that Jesus Christ stretches forth His Hands upon the Cross. "Come unto Me," He says, by this silent but expressive action, "all ye that labour and are heavy laden with your sins, and I will give you rest."[4] It is the appeal of love: love the most tender, the most practical, the most disinterested. The most tender: for surely greater love hath

[1] 1 St. Pet. iii. 18.
[2] 2 Cor. v. 21.
[3] Rom. iii. 24, 25.
[4] St. Matt. xi. 28.

no man than this, that a man lay down his life for his friends[1]—especially considering that "when we were yet sinners, Christ died for us."[2] The most practical: since it was "love not in word, but in deed and in truth;"[3] not merely profession, or merely feeling, but after the fashion of true love, the gift of self; and the gift of the best that self can give, the gift of life. The most disinterested; for we could offer nothing to provoke, nothing to reward it; we could and can give nothing that He has not first given us. It is to our sense of this love, so strong, so practical, so disinterested, that He appeals: can He appeal in vain?

Surely, when we review our lives seriously, that which must chiefly strike most men is God's persevering, overshadowing, ever-pleading mercy. Why has He given us life at all? Why has He, by His free grace, made us, when we could do nothing for ourselves, members of Christ, children of God, heirs of the kingdom of heaven?[4] Why should we have been taught to repeat the Creed of His Church, to read His Word, to think about Him as an Example and a Saviour, while we were young? Or, if it has been otherwise with us, and we have only known Him at all in later life, and are only beginning to know Him now, why has He singled us out for this distinguishing mercy; roused us suddenly and sharply from some dream of worldliness or sin; struck down some near relation, wife or child; cut off utterly some source of gain or amusement; bid us see the lightning of His judgments scorch some sinner at our side who was no worse than we; bid us gaze on some servant of His own, already bright with the lustre of His glory, who has had no greater advantages than we, or has had fewer or less; or has guided us, like Augustine, to some one verse in His

[1] St. John xv. 13.   [2] Rom. v. 8.
[3] 1 St. John iii. 18.   [4] The *Church Catechism*.

Word; or has spoken to us by the voice of a friend, who little knew the full meaning of his utterance, some word which has pierced to the depths of our souls, and made life already a different thing to us? What is all this but the perpetual stretching forth of the Hands of the Crucified during all the past years of life, as we look back on it—the incessant appeal of the Uncreated Mercy? And how has it found, how has it left, us? It is still true of us, as of the Jews of old, that all the long day of life Christ has stretched out His Hands to Christians who bear His Name, but who, like their Jewish predecessors, are a disobedient and gainsaying people.

III.

In conclusion, there are two lessons which we may endeavour to make our own.

1. One is particular. Jesus Christ stretching out His Hands in patient compassion on the Cross is a model for all Christians who are in any position of authority. Not only for monarchs, or statesmen, or great officials, but for that large number of us who, in various ways, have others dependent on us, or under our government and influence. Some of us are parents, and have the most sacred duty of bringing up our children; others are schoolmasters, and have voluntarily undertaken to share that duty; others are heads of "houses of business," and have many clerks and young people under their control; others are masters or mistresses of families, and have domestic servants about them. Like the centurion in the Gospel, a great number of Christians are between the two extremes of society, between those who do nothing but command, and those who do nothing but obey; they are men under authority, having others under them, and they say to this one, Go, and he goeth, and to another, Come, and he cometh,

and to their servant, Do this, and he doeth it.[1] It may be but a little brief authority in which we are dressed, but it is authority; and as such, like that of the Queen upon her earthly throne, it is ennobled as a radiation from that Divine Authority which reigns on the Throne of Heaven. It may be little enough in itself, as measured by our social scales of greatness, but be it little or great, it is charged with responsibility; it has a bearing—more or less direct and intimate—upon the eternal destinies of human beings with whom God, in His providence, has thrown us thus into contact. And here, I say, the model for Christian parents, masters, employers, governors, is rather Christ upon His Cross, in anxious pain, stretching out the arms of entreaty and compassion, than Christ upon His Throne finally dispensing the awards of judgment. Mere right, mere "law," mere insistance upon *meum* and *tuum*, may be all very well for a man of the world, now as in the days of Paganism. The children of the Crucified have caught sight, or ought to have caught sight, of a higher ideal. The love which will not take account of dulness or stupidity, not even of stubbornness and perverseness; the love which anticipates the disobedience and the gainsaying, yet stretches out its hands persistently in tender and incessant invitation; the love which is not baulked and chilled by one failure or by two, but which goes on as if it had not failed at all, stretching out its hands in acts of kindness and consideration; the love which gets no interest for its outlay of pain, and grief, and care, which yet shrouds its disappointment as it whispers after the Apostle, "The more abundantly I love you the less I am loved:"[2] this is what Christians in any position of authority should aim at in dealing with those who depend on them. If all their efforts seem failures; if their exertions and their self-denials seem to bring in

[1] St. Matt. viii. 8, 9.   [2] 2 Cor. xii. 15.

VIII]   *the Crucified Jesus.*   135

nothing but a fresh measure of misunderstanding and scorn; what is this but association with the Divine Sufferer on the hill of Calvary, stretching out His Hands through the long hours of His Passion to a disobedient and gainsaying people? Between His case and theirs there is indeed one point of difference, the importance of which is incalculable. Full as His Heart was of tenderness towards His murderers, He needed no mercy for Himself; the thought never could have occurred to His Human Soul that He too would be judged by the measure which He dealt out to others. With us—with the highest and the best—how utterly otherwise is it! How certain is it that "with what measure we mete it shall be measured unto us again"![1] For a Christian to be forbearing and considerate is hardly disinterested, for, if he be other than this, he cannot hope for the merciful forbearance of God.

2. The other lesson is general. Jesus Christ stretching out His Hands upon the Cross is surely a warning to us at all times, but especially at a season like this. Here we are, on Palm Sunday, at the very gate of the most solemn Week in the whole year! How many Christians who spent this Week with us last year before the Cross of Christ, have since then passed into the eternal world! How many of ourselves, it may be, will never live to see another Holy Week; will look back from their place in eternity,—be it what it may,— upon this very week as an opportunity which will then have gone for ever. Who knows how it will be with each one of us? Brethren, Christ crucified does indeed stretch His Hands in entreaty and compassion, ready and able to save to the uttermost all that come unto God by Him,[2] all the long day of life. While there is life, there is hope, there is opportunity, there is heaven and happiness within reach of faith, of seriousness of purpose, of

[1] St. Matt. vii. 2.   [2] Heb. vii. 25.

simpleness of heart. But the longest day has its evening; and after the evening comes the darkness of the night. Christ crucified, it has been said, has no Redemptive relations with the dead: He has either redeemed them, or they are beyond the reach of Redemption. As the soul passes the gate of eternity, the Pierced Hands of Christ, Which during the long day of life have been outstretched upon the Cross, seem to detach themselves, and to fold together as if for judgment.

"There is no repentance in the grave,
Nor pardon offer'd to the dead."

Carry this thought, I pray you, into the solemnities of the coming Week. Begin now, on Palm Sunday, and accompany your Saviour through each stage of His bitter Passion, with the thought of eternity clearly before your souls. If the exhortations to which you listen from human teachers rouse conscience during these sacred hours into activity; if the scenes on which you dwell,—the scenes of woe and of victory, the Words, the Wounds, the darkened sky, the awful silence,—speak to your souls as if there had come over them some breath from another and a distant world; if, as on Tuesday next,[1] human art gives guidance or impetus to hallowed feeling, and, for a while, you lose sight of the material and transient present, in the keener sight of that world which is beyond sense, and which does not pass away,—O pray that these higher glimpses, emotions, convictions, may not die away like the vast array of unfruitful feelings which make up so large a part of life; pray that they may become resolutions, starting-points for a new, a changed, a higher level of existence, the reverse of past years of disobedience and contradiction. What will it avail to have thought much, felt much, hoped for much, in Passion-tide, if at Easter

[1] The reference is to the special service held in St. Paul's Cathedral on the Tuesday Evening of Holy Week, when Bach's "Passion-Music" is rendered.

all, or nearly all, is forfeited,—if we disobey the Will and gainsay the Truth of our Crucified Master, just as before? Why should He, the dying Son of God, almost year by year, have to repeat the complaint of centuries over Christendom, over Christian souls, over your soul and mine, "All the day long have I stretched out My hands unto a disobedient and gainsaying people"? It need not be so, since He is more than willing to help us; it must not be so, unless all is to be irretrievably lost.

SERMON IX.

THE SOLITUDES OF THE PASSION.

Ps. xxii. 11.

O go not from Me, for trouble is hard at hand, and there is none to help Me.

THIS is one of the cries of the Ideal or Superhuman Sufferer, of Whose agonies, both of mind and body, we have so complete a picture in Psalm xxii. Many attempts have been made to explain this Psalm by some of the circumstances of the life of David, or the life of Hezekiah, or of other persons in Jewish history who have combined eminent piety with great misfortunes. But these attempts, one and all, have been unsuccessful. The Psalm describes a kind and degree of suffering of which we have no records in the Old Testament, and to which, most assuredly, nothing in the known life of David at all corresponds. Yet there is no doubt whatever —as the best scholars agree—that the Psalm is from David's own hand; and the question is how David could have ever brought himself to write as though he were himself feeling and thinking as he here describes. The answer is that the picture of a Great Sufferer presented itself to David's soul; took possession of it—such entire possession that (as in the highest natural poetry may sometimes happen) the writer forgot himself, and lost himself in the subject which possessed him. The words were David's words, but the thoughts, the experiences, the hopes, the fears, the anguish, the exultation, were those of another and a higher than David. David was but a copyist; David was writing down, for the good of the times to come, what, in his illuminated spirit, he saw with his eyes and heard with his ears. His picture of an Ideal Sufferer was laid up among the sacred writings of Israel; but many centuries had to pass before men could know what it meant, and to Whom it referred.

When Jesus, our Divine Lord, hung dying upon the Cross, He interpreted this Psalm of Himself by using its first verse as the fourth of those Seven last Words which He uttered in those solemn hours: "Eli, Eli, lama sabachthani?" "My God, My God, why hast Thou forsaken Me?" as uttered by the Redeemer in the darkest hour of His Sufferings, give the key to all that follows. Henceforth we Christians read the Psalm as if repeated throughout by Jesus in His Passion or by Jesus on the Cross. As His dying Eye surveys the multitude of human beings, in whom an unreasoning hate of truth and goodness had for the time quelled all other thoughts and emotions, in whom the wild beast that is latent in human nature had asserted his sway with frightful power, Jesus might say, "Many oxen are come about Me: fat bulls of Bashan close Me in on every side. They gape upon Me with their mouths, as it were a ramping and a roaring lion. Many dogs are come about Me; and the council of the wicked layeth siege against Me."[1] As He glances down at His mangled Body, His pierced Hands and Feet; as He feels the parching thirst, the inward collapse, the exhaustion of approaching death; He murmurs, "I am poured out like water, and all My bones are out of joint: My heart also in the midst of My body is even like melting wax. My strength is dried up like a potsherd, and My tongue cleaveth to My gums: and Thou shalt bring Me into

[1] Ps. xxii. 12, 13, 16.

the dust of death. . . . They pierced My hands and My feet; I may tell all My bones."[1] As He listens to the taunts which fall upon His ear; as He watches the doings of the men who crowd around the foot of the Cross on which He hangs; He complains, "They that see Me laugh Me to scorn; they shoot out their lips, and shake their heads, saying, He trusted in God, that He would deliver Him: let Him deliver Him, if He will have Him. . . . They stand staring and looking upon Me; they part My garments among them, and cast lots upon My vesture."[2] As He strains the Eye of His Human Soul to gaze into futurity, to pierce the veil which parts the agony and desolation of the moment from the triumph and the peace beyond; He cries, "The Lord hath not despised, nor abhorred, the low estate of the poor; He hath not hid His face from Him, but when He called unto Him, He heard Him. My praise is of Thee in the great congregation; . . . all the ends of the world shall remember themselves, and be turned unto the Lord. . . . My seed shall serve Him: they shall be counted unto the Lord for a generation."[3] The Psalm is throughout written, as if to order, to describe, as from within, the Sufferings of our Divine Lord upon the Cross; nowhere else in the Old Testament does the Holy Spirit more vividly, in a single composition, "testify beforehand the sufferings of Christ, and the glory that should follow."[4]

In this Psalm there is one feature of our Lord's Sufferings upon which particular stress is laid; I mean His desolation or solitude. It is the keynote of the Psalm; the very first words of which complain, "My God, My God, why hast Thou forsaken Me?" And it finds expression again and again; nowhere, perhaps, more pathetically than in the cry, "O go not from Me, for trouble is hard

---

[1] Ps. xxii. 14, 15, 17.   [2] Ib. 7, 8, 17, 18.
[3] Ps. xxii. 24, 25, 27, 31.   [4] 1 St. Peter i. 11.

at hand, and there is none to help Me." Some centuries after David a Figure passed before the soul of the greatest of the prophets, that shadowed out the same aspect of a superhuman suffering, but from another point of view. It was the form of One coming as from Edom, coming with garments dyed in the vintage of Bozrah—emblems of a struggle which meant wounds and blood—glorious in His apparel, His moral apparel of righteousness and mercy, and travelling in the greatness of His strength.[1] And when the seer gazed intently at this Figure, and asked who He was, the reply came, "I that speak in righteousness, mighty to save."[1] And when a further question was ventured, "Why art Thou red in Thine apparel, and Thy garments like him that treadeth in the winefat?"[2] it was answered—as though this was of the essence of the conflict—"I have trodden the winepress alone, and of the people there was none beside Me."[3] Yes, in His Sufferings Jesus was alone; alone in spirit, though encompassed by a multitude. In His Passion He experienced a threefold solitude: the solitude of greatness, the solitude of sorrow, and the solitude of death.

I.

The loneliness of the great is one of the ironies of human life. The great are lonely because they are great; had they peers and companions they would cease to be what they are in relation to those around them. This holds good of greatness in all its forms, whether greatness of station, or greatness of genius, or greatness of character.

(a) Take the word "great" in its most popular but least warrantable sense. What is the case of the "great" in station? The solitude of the throne is proverbial. Not that the monarch is without companions; from the

[1] Isa. lxiii. 1. [2] Ib. 2. [3] Ib. 3.

nature of the case the monarch can command companions as can no other person in the realm. No court in the world is wanting in deferential ministers of the Royal will, whose business it is to furnish companionship to Royalty, whose hourly effort is to carry out the wishes of the Sovereign, and to thwart or screen from his sight all that may traverse his passing inclinations. But companionship such as this is perfectly compatible with solitude. That free, buoyant intercourse of mind with mind, of heart with heart, that entire reciprocity of sympathies which knows no limits save those which are imposed by truth and charity, is banned by the exacting etiquette of a court; is hardly, if at all, possible for the occupants of a throne. The "divinity which doth hedge a king" has its drawbacks, and is costly. A monarch is always more or less of a solitary; alone in his joys, alone in his sorrows; reverence and envy conspire to deprive him of his rightful share in the hearts of men around him. And this solitude of the throne—let us not forget it—is one reason for the claim of its occupants upon the prayers and charity of the Church; this tribute of the best sympathy is one means of redressing the privations and of lessening the dangers of a great position, occupied for the public benefit.

(β) Then, again, there is the greatness of genius. Even when genius unbends, and is fruitful and popular, even when it ministers to the enjoyment and instruction of millions, it is by instinct solitary; it lives apart. The mountain peaks which are the crowning beauty of a vast and fertile plain purchase their prerogative elevation at a great cost; they are cold, bleak, inaccessible. Genius lives in distant realms of thought; genius lives amidst flashes and aspirations which do not exist for others; in the presence of these, it is alone. We may be sure that a man like Shakespeare was familiar with much which he never thought of communicating to the quiet, sensible, commonplace people among whom, for the most part, he passed his days. In his highest and deepest thought he was, from the nature of the case, a solitary.

(γ) Then there is greatness of character. This is the most legitimate use of the word; and this true greatness might seem at first sight to be very far from solitary,—to be, on the contrary, unselfish, communicative, beneficent. Undoubtedly such greatness draws to itself human hearts, and wins human interest.

Yet how often are there features in a really noble character which, when they become plain to the mass of mankind, repel rather than attract. The unswerving adherence to known truth; the resolute sacrifice of immediate advantage to the claims of principle; the flashes of severity which radiate from the purest and highest love,—these are not popular qualities.

History is full of examples of men whose benevolence and kindliness and activity have at first won general applause and admiration, but who have been deserted, hated, denounced, perhaps even put to death, when the real character of their greatness was discovered. Such a man was Savonarola. His story has been made familiar to Englishmen—we may well and gratefully remember in this place—by the pen of Dean Milman. Savonarola, amid imperfections which are inseparable from our human weakness, was one of the greatest religious teachers that the world has seen. He aimed, as all sincerely Christian minds must aim, at carrying Christian principles into the public and social life of man. He held that politics might be no less Christian than personal conduct. The people which had welcomed his teaching with passionate enthusiasm assisted at his cruel and ignominious death. Savonarola was too great even for Florence. And there have been few ages in the world's history where this lesson has not repeated itself;

and where integrity of character and elevation of aim have not experienced the alternate vicissitudes of popular favour and popular dislike, or even violence. Certainly our own age and country are not exceptions to the rule.

Now our Lord in His Passion was great in these various ways. He was indeed, as it seemed, "a worm, and no man; a very scorn of men, and the outcast of the people;"[1] and yet, as He said before Pilate, He was a King;[2] and He felt, as no other can have felt, the isolation of His Royalty. Then His mental Eye took in vaster horizons than were even suspected to exist by any around Him; He had meat to eat that they knew not of,[3] in this as in so many other ways; He lived in a sphere of thought which was for them impossible. And above all, in character He was not merely courageous, true, disinterested, loving—and this in a degree which distanced the highest excellence around Him — He was that which no other in human form has been before or since: He was Sinless. Thus, as He went forth to die, He was in a solitude created by the very prerogatives of His Being; His elevation above His fellows itself cut Him off from that sympathy which equals can most effectively give; and hence one motive of the prayer of His Human Soul to the Father, "O go not from Me, for trouble is hard at hand, and there is none to help Me."

II.

There is the solitude of greatness; but there is also the solitude of sorrow. Certainly sorrow is a link of human fellowship; sooner or later, all men suffer; man is born to trouble as the sparks fly upwards.[4] No condition of life, no variety of temperament, can purchase

[1] Ps. xxii. 6.   [2] St. John xviii. 27.
[3] St. John iv. 32.   [4] Job v. 7.

IX] *The Solitudes of the Passion.* 145

exemption from this universal law of suffering. To some it comes as the chastening which is necessary to perfection; to others as the penalty which is due to sin; but sooner or later, in whatever shape, it comes to all. Yet, though suffering is universal, no two men suffer exactly alike. There is the same individuality in the pain which each man suffers that there is in his thought and character and countenance; no two men, since the world began, among the millions of sufferers, have repeated exactly the same experience. This is why human sympathy, even at its best, is never quite perfect: no one merely human being can put himself exactly, by that act of moral imagination which we term sympathy, in all the circumstances of another. Each sufferer, whether of bodily or mental pain, pursues a separate path, encounters peculiar difficulties, shares a common burden, but is alone in his sorrow.

"Each in his hidden sphere of joy or woe
Our hermit spirits dwell."[1]

Especially was Jesus our Lord solitary in His awful Sorrow. We may well believe that the delicate sensibilities of His Bodily Frame rendered Him liable to physical tortures such as rougher natures can never know. But we know that the mode of His Death was exceptionally painful. And yet His bodily Sufferings were less terrible (it might seem) than the Sufferings of His mind. The Agony in the Garden was of a character which distances altogether human woe. Our Lord advisedly laid Himself open to the dreadful visitation; He embraced it by a deliberate act; He "began to be sorrowful, and very heavy."[2] He took upon Him the burden and misery of human sin,—the sin of all the centuries that had preceded and that would follow Him—that He might take it to the Cross and

[1] *The Christian Year.* Hymn for the Twenty-fourth Sunday after Trinity.
[2] St. Matt. xxvi. 37.

K

expiate it in Death. As the Apostle says, "He bore our sins in His own Body on the tree."[1] But the touch of this burden, which to us is so familiar, to Him was Agony; and it drew from Him the Bloody Sweat, which fell from His forehead on the turf of Gethsemane, hours before they crowned Him with the thorns or nailed Him to the Cross.

Ah, brethren, we endeavour to enter into the solitary sorrows of the Soul of Jesus, but they are quite beyond us. We may, at some time in our lives, have found ourselves in a family circle, when a heavy blow has just fallen on it, and have noted the efforts of the younger children to understand the gloom or misery of their elders. The elders know what has happened. They know that all upon which the family depends for daily bread is irretrievably lost. Or they know that some loved one—a father, a mother, an eldest child—has just been taken away, it may be by a swift and terrible catastrophe, and they have no heart to speak. Or they know, worst of all, that some misery worse than death, some crushing burden of shame and sorrow, has fallen on the family through the misconduct of one of its members. And so they sit, silent in their grief; and the young children gaze wistfully up into their faces, as if trying to make out what is so strange and so beyond them, as if wishing to sympathise with what is to them an incomprehensible woe. They are doing their best; they are concerned at beholding the sorrowing faces; they note the subdued tones, the quiet movements, the hushed sighs, the darkened room: but alas! they are trying to understand what they cannot understand; they are but touching the fringe of a sorrow that is above them. And so it is, brethren, with all of us, in presence of the Sorrows of Jesus Christ, expiating the sins of a guilty world. Before Him we are, indeed, but children; happy if

[1] 1 St. Peter ii. 24.

we share their simple and free sympathies, but certainly, like them, unable to do more than watch, with tender and reverent awe, a mighty burden of misery which we cannot hope to comprehend. All that we can do is to lay to heart the words which sound everywhere in believing souls around Gethsemane and Calvary: "Is it nothing to you, all ye that pass by? behold and see, if there be any sorrow like unto My sorrow?"[1]

III.

Lastly, there is the solitude of death. Death, whenever it comes to any, must be an act in which no other can share. Even if I die at the same moment with another, I cannot sympathise with him in the act of dying; I have no solid reason to presume that each of us would even be conscious of what is happening to the other. Death strips from a man all that connects him with that which is without him; it is an act in which his consciousness is, from the nature of the case, thrown back upon itself, and absorbed in that which is occurring to itself. A dying man may be distracted up to the moment, but not in the moment, of death. Warm-hearted friends may press around him; well-remembered objects may be placed before his failing eyes; at one deathbed, the prayers of childhood, at another, so it has been, soft strains of familiar music, may fall upon the ear. But when the soul, by a wrench which no experience can anticipate, breaks away from the bodily organism with which, since its creation, it has been so intimately linked, it enters upon a lonely path, which may, indeed, be brightened by the voices and the smiles of angels, but into which no human sympathy can follow.

Few things, my brethren, are so tragic as the sharp

[1] Lam. i. 12.

contrast between the crowd that may surround a dying man, and the necessary solitude of the soul in death. When the cholera, many years ago, struck its victims in a crowded drawing-room, the world was hushed with a passing awe; but the same contrast may be found under more accustomed circumstances. What can be more pathetic, for instance, than the deathbed of the French statesman who played so great a part under the Republic and the First Empire, and who lived down into the boyhood of those among us who are yet in middle life? Talleyrand passed the last forty-eight hours of his life sitting on the side of his bed—he could not bear to lie down—and leaning forward on two servants, who were relieved every two hours. In that posture he received, on the morning of the day on which he died, King Louis Philippe and his Queen; and he never for a moment, we are told, forgot what was due to the etiquette of the Court: he received his visitors with the distinction and the attentions to which they were accustomed. Outside his room, in the antechamber, all that was distinguished in the society of Paris was assembled; Talleyrand's death was viewed as a political and social event of the first importance. Politicians, old and young, even grey-haired statesmen, crowded the hearth and talked with animation; while young men and young women exchanged bright compliments that formed a painful contrast with the deep groans of the dying man in the adjoining room. Talleyrand, who was first a bishop and then an apostate from Christianity, made some sort of reconciliation with Heaven: God only knows its real value. But no sooner had the long agony terminated in death than (to use the words of the narrative) it might have been supposed that a flight of rooks was leaving the mansion; such was the eagerness with which each rushed away to be the first to tell the news in the particular circle of which he or she was the oracle: and the corpse of Talleyrand, lying in those deserted rooms, was a visible emblem of the solitude of the soul in the act of death.

Nor can we refer to such a subject to-day without reminding ourselves that only three days since death has claimed as its own a man whom the Church of England will always honour with affectionate reverence.[1] It is for those who had the happiness of knowing him intimately to say, as no doubt they will say, what Bishop Selwyn was in his private life and conversation; what were the thoughts, the enthusiasms, that gave impulse and shape to such a splendid life. We, who have reverenced him from afar, can merely note that his was a figure of Apostolic proportions; that he was one of that comparatively small band of men who reproduce, in our age of clouded faith and softness of manners, the virtues and the force by which long centuries ago the Christian Church was planted on the ruins of heathendom. Surely many of us have accompanied him with the reverent sympathy of our prayers, in his last hours of pain and weakness: nor can we doubt that for him the solitude of death has been brightened by all that our gracious Master has in store for those who, by their words and their lives, turn many to embrace His righteousness and His truth.[2]

In the Death of our Lord Himself it might be supposed that this sense of solitude would be escaped. Living in hourly communion with the Father, and surrounded by hosts of angel guardians, how, we may ask, could He taste of the solitude of death? Was not His Human Nature so united to His Divinity that even in death the Union was not forfeited? And how is this reconcilable with the supposition that He experienced the loneliness of dying, as we men experience it?

[1] George Augustus Selwyn, Bishop of Lichfield (and previously Bishop of New Zealand), died April 11th, 1878.   [2] Dan. xii. 3.

The answer is that our Lord, by a deliberate act, became "obedient unto death."[1] Whatever might have been the law of His Being—as Sinless Man, united to a Higher Nature—He did not, if I may dare so to say, claim its privileges. He laid Himself open without reserve or stint to all the ills to which our flesh is heir, without at all excepting its last and lowest humiliation. He selected as a mode of dying that which conspicuously involved most pain and shame; and He would not most assuredly defeat His purpose by sparing Himself that accompaniment of death, which causes so much apprehension to us sinful men—its solitariness. He might have prayed to His Father for twelve legions of angels;[2] but He would be alone. He might have enjoyed unceasingly the joy of those who always behold the Face of the Father in heaven;[3] but He willed to share the agony of the souls who cry in their last moments—some, we may be sure, every day that passes—"My God, my God, why hast Thou forsaken me?"[4] He submitted Himself to all those elements of our nature which sterner characters affect to scorn; to its sense of dependence, to its craving for sympathy, to its consciousness of weakness. "O go not from me, for trouble is hard at hand, and there is none to help me," is the natural language of the feeblest sufferer in the poorest lodging in London; but it was also the language of our Divine Saviour, contemplating, with true human apprehension, the loneliness of approaching death.

Yes! when as on this day He rode in triumph towards the Holy City, surrounded by a great multitude who cried "Hosanna," and spread the branches of the palms and the garments which they wore along the path of His advance,[5] even at this moment of seeming triumph He was really alone. He knew what was before Him; the

[1] Phil. ii. 8.   [2] St. Matt. xxvi. 53.   [3] Ib. xviii. 10.
[4] St. Matt. xxvii. 46.   [5] Ib. xxi. 1-9.

surging multitude around was for Him as if it was not. We may see men in Cheapside, in the middle of the day, when it is difficult to force a passage along the footway from this Cathedral to the Bank, in whose faces some unconcealed care or some absorbing passion proclaims their virtual solitude amid the crowd. "Never less alone than when most alone" is the motto of the soul as it gazes upwards towards the heavens; "never more alone than when least alone" is the motto of the soul when, under a great stress of pain or doubt, it looks down towards the earth. The crowds which sang "Hosanna" as Christ entered Jerusalem, and the crowds which cried "Crucify Him," as He passed along the Way of Sorrows, touched but the surface of His awful Solitude, as He rode on, as He walked on, to die.

This solitude of our Lord in His Passion is surely full of comfort for us. It shows us first that at the moment of death, and before it, the best Christians may experience a desolation of spirit which is no real gauge of their true condition before God. Many of the best men in the Christian Church have done so; and it has been supposed by those who do not sufficiently reflect upon the teaching of the Passion that this desolation of the soul must needs imply its rejection by God. No conclusion can be less warranted. The confident assumptions of a deathbed which follows upon a life of disloyalty to known duty or truth may indeed be only physical illusions: but the anguish of a saintly soul, which fears, on the threshold of eternity, that God has left it to itself, is but a token of conformity to the Divine Saviour.

And, secondly, we see in the solitude of Jesus Christ crucified a warrant of His sympathy with the dying. "In that He Himself has suffered, being tempted, He is able to succour them that are tempted."[1] Nothing that we

[1] Heb. ii. 18.

may experience, in His good will, no anguish of soul, no weariness or torture of body, has been unexplored by Him Who overcame all the sharpness of death before He opened the kingdom of heaven to the great company of the faithful. May He take pity upon us, His weak and erring children, and suffer us not, at our last hour, for any pains of death, to fall from Him.[1] May He "look upon us with the eyes of His mercy, give us comfort, and sure confidence in Him, defend us from the danger of the enemy,"[2] and so bring us to our eternal home, for His own infinite merits.

[1] Prayer in the Order for the Burial of the Dead.
[2] Prayer in the Order for the Visitation of the Sick.

SERMON X.

THE SILENCE OF JESUS.

ST. JOHN xix. 9.

Pilate saith unto Jesus, Whence art Thou? But Jesus gave him no answer.

TO-DAY we enter on the nearer consideration of the Passion of our Lord and Saviour Jesus Christ; and among its various and awful incidents none is more calculated to rivet our earnest attention than the silence which He observed at certain times during His trial. This silence was not by any means unbroken; but it was so deliberate—we may dare to say, so peremptory—that it has clearly a meaning that is all its own. We cannot but recall the contrast which is presented by St. Paul before the Sanhedrim,[1] before Felix,[2] before Agrippa.[3] To St. Paul, a trial in which his liberty or his life is at stake is above all things a great missionary opportunity, which he improves at once, and to the utmost of his power; and we remember how, as he reasons of "righteousness, temperance, and judgment to come," the tables are strangely turned, and Felix, the representative of earthly justice, trembles before his prisoner.[4] To us, in our short-sightedness, it may have seemed that something else than silence might be looked for from the Divine Master; from His tender charity for the souls of men; from the deep emotion

[1] Acts xxiii. 1-9.   [2] *Ib.* xxiv. 1-25.
[3] Acts xxvi. 1-29.   [4] *Ib.* xxiv. 25.

which, as we know from what passed in Gethsemane, moved the depths of His Human Soul. But no! He is silent. His judge asks Him, Whence art Thou? And instead of regarding the question as affording Him an opening for proclaiming the momentous truth, Jesus gave him no answer.

I.

If we try to place ourselves, by an effort of sympathetic imagination, in the position of one of our fellow-creatures placed on trial for his life, and before judges at whose hands he had little to look for in the way of consideration or mercy, we can understand that the silence of a perfectly innocent man might be natural, for more reasons than one. Our English law does not allow a prisoner to be cross-questioned; but the practice of other countries is different, and the records of the French Revolutionary tribunals during the Terror of 1793-94 supply instances of what I mean. Instances, indeed, might be multiplied to almost any extent: since, both in its habit of inflicting undeserved suffering, and in its way of meeting what has to be endured, human nature remains the same from age to age.

First of all, an innocent prisoner on his trial might be unable to say anything out of sheer bewilderment. For the first time in his life he finds himself in a position unlike any he had ever distinctly pictured to himself before. He knows that he is in danger, although his conscience tells him that he is innocent of the alleged crime. He is surrounded by officials who are practised hands at manipulating evidence, whereas he himself is only a novice. He sees danger everywhere—sees it in quarters where it does not at all exist; he loses the control of his judgment, of his common-sense, of his faculties generally; his head reels, he only perceives at intervals what is going on. He cannot remember what he would; he cannot keep his feelings from intruding themselves boisterously into matters where clear, cold thought is above all things wanted; and so his efforts to think become irregular and turbid; he cannot think consecutively, or with any approach to clearness and force; he tries to think, but all becomes blurred and confused, and he feels instinctively that should he endeavour to speak, his speech would only express and exhibit this inward confusion. So he is silent—not on principle, or anything like it—but in virtue of the instinct of bewilderment.

Akin to the silence of bewilderment is the silence of terror: and this silence, under the circumstances we are considering, is far from uncommon. Fear is a passion which has immediate and decisive effects upon the bodily frame. Even in the lower animals the sense of imminent danger will not seldom arrest all power of movement. The sacred writer tells us that, in man's case, fear is "a betrayal of the succours which reason offereth."[1] Under an overmastering sense of terror, speech becomes impossible: the thought and feeling which prompt man to speak are directed upon a single object with concentrated intensity; in this dumb horror nothing is possible, save inarticulate expression, if indeed that is possible. Nothing is more common—in natures of a certain nervous organisation and temperament—than this silence of fear.

But when an innocent man keeps his head clear, and is so constituted that a new and alarming situation has no terrors for him, he may yet be silent, from a motive of mistaken prudence. He knows that skilful adversaries will take every possible advantage of his words: some chance expression may escape him which is capable of being twisted into aspects which had never occurred to the speaker; he may say too little, or he may say too

[1] Wisd. xvii. 12.

much; he may so excuse as to accuse himself, or he may imply guilt, by saying something without saying enough. There is a safety he feels in silence; silence gives no advantage to the prosecutor which he did not possess before; silence, after all, is silence, and there is no more to be said of it. Pilate seems to have thought that this was our Lord's motive, and he tried in his blundering way to show its practical imprudence, and to reason Jesus out of it. "Speakest Thou not unto me? knowest Thou not that I have power to crucify Thee, and have power to release Thee?"[1] It was indeed an astonishing miscalculation; but natural perhaps in a Pagan magistrate, and under the circumstances.

Once more, there is the silence of disdain. The prisoner is before judges who represent brute force, and nothing more; neither right, nor truth, nor virtue. He is conscious of his innocence; he knows that his innocence is, in their eyes, his crime. Between his ideas of truth, of honour, of excellence in all its higher forms, and the world of ideas in which they live and work, there is no common term. He could speak if he chose; he knows not what fear is; he is in complete possession of his faculties; his thought is clear, and he is prepared for the worst; he is convinced that nothing can be gained by silence. He could, if he so willed, pour forth into a torrent of burning words the indignation of an upright character, confronted with official cruelty and with regulated wrong. But to whom, or rather to what, would the expostulation be addressed? Where would be the moral intelligence to do him justice? where the living moral sense that he could hope to rouse? Why should he expend the strength of his righteous passion upon those whom vice and time between them have rendered too stupid or too wicked to read its meaning?

[1] St. John xix. 10.

No; he will restrain himself: his is the lofty silence of a judicial disdain.

II.

None of these motives for silence, it is plain, will account for that of our Lord before Pilate.

His was not the silence of bewilderment or of fear. From the moment of His arrest in the garden until the last of the seven words upon the Cross, our Lord, it is plain, has His thoughts and His words entirely at command. If He speaks, it is with the tranquil decision which marks His language at the marriage feast of Cana,[1] or at the raising of Lazarus.[2] Every word, if we may dare thus to speak, tells; and the force of what He says lights up the high and solemn meaning of His silence. As to fear, what room for it was there in One to Whom Caiaphas and Pilate were but passing ministers of evil; and Who, as His eye rested steadily on the invisible world, would assign to what was greatest or worst in this its true meed of insignificance? How much lies in that saying, on the way to Calvary, "Know ye not that I can pray to My Father, and He shall presently send Me more than twelve legions of angels?"[3]

Nor was the silence of our Lord dictated by a false prudence. He knew that all things that were written concerning the Son of Man must be accomplished.[4] He foresaw His Death; He foresaw the stages through which He would pass on His way to the Cross and the Sepulchre; if, for a moment, the flesh was weak in Gethsemane, the spirit was always willing:[5] there was no room for prudence of this kind before Caiaphas or Pilate. Nay, what our Lord did say, would have appeared to a looker-on highly imprudent. When Caiaphas asked Him if He were the

---

[1] St. John ii. 1-8. [2] Ib. xi. 38-44. [3] St. Matt. xxvi. 53.
[4] St. Luke xviii. 31. [5] St. Matt. xxvi. 41.

Christ, the Son of God, He answered in words which at once issued in His condemnation by the Sanhedrim: "I say unto you, Hereafter shall ye see the Son of Man sitting on the right hand of power, and coming in the clouds of heaven."[1] When Pilate told Him that he had power to adjudge Him to liberty or to death, He answered, "Thou couldest have no power at all against Me, except it were given thee from above."[2] Silence would have been more prudent than such speech as this, if the object had been to save His life, and we must look elsewhere for the explanation.

Need it be added that, in Jesus Christ, silence could not possibly have expressed disdain? In Him such a feeling towards any human soul was impossible. Between the highest and the best, on the one hand, and Himself on the other, the distance was indeed immeasurable. But He looked out upon all with a boundless pity; had He not come to seek and to save that which was lost?[3] In His Heart, so warmly human in its sympathy, so Divine in its comprehensive embrace, there was no less a place for Caiaphas and Pilate, if they only would take it, than for the Magdalene, or for Peter, or for St. John. No. It is profanation to suspect disdain in Jesus Christ. Scorn, whether it speaks or is silent, is the certificate of shallowness: and Jesus is the Eternal Wisdom. Scorn, whether it speaks or is silent, is a note of the supremacy—if only for the moment—of the pride of self: and Jesus, He is the Infinite Charity.

III.

These were not the reasons for the silence of Jesus: but that it had a reason is plain from its deliberate character. Think over the incidents of the Passion. To the vain and mocking Herod He would say nothing

---

[1] St. Matt. xxvi. 64.   [2] St. John xix. 11.   [3] St. Matt. xviii. 11.

whatever.[1] Of the false witness produced before the Sanhedrim, and before Pilate, He will take no notice—not the slightest.[2] But when Caiaphas asks Him, whether He is the Divine Messiah—Caiaphas, who as High Priest, should have at once recognised and pointed out to the people the true Messiah when He came—Jesus speaks. He repeats that ancient oracle of Daniel, which the Jewish doctors referred to Messiah as the Judge of the world: and Caiaphas knew well, only too well, what He meant.[3] When Annas questions Him about His disciples and His doctrine, He points frankly to the public character of His work:[4] and to Pilate himself He explains both the unworldly character of His kingdom and the prime object of His appearance among men as a witness to the truth. Only when Pilate had jestingly asked, "What is truth?" only when Pilate had prostituted his magisterial sense of justice to prejudices which he did not affect to respect, and had scourged Jesus, and brought Him forth crowned with thorns, and in a robe of purple;—only then to the question, half-anxious, half-insolent, "Whence art Thou?" Jesus returned no answer. He was silent.

What is silence?

Silence in a man, in full possession of his faculties, and in his waking hours, is much more than the absence or failure of speech; it has a positive meaning. It is the deliberate suspension of speech; it is the substitution of that which in human life is the exception for that which is the rule. Surely, brethren, in us men silence is less a foil to speech than speech to silence.

What is speech?

It is the display, in a form which strikes upon one of the senses, of the whole complex activity of the soul: of its thoughts, its feelings, its resolves, its apprehensions.

---

[1] St. Luke xxiii. 8, 9.   [2] St. Matt. xxvi. 59-63; xxvii. 12-14.
[3] St. Matt. xxvi. 63, 64.   [4] St. John xviii. 19-21.

Speech is the dress which the inner life of the soul takes when it would pass into another soul: and if we were not so familiar with it, we might well be astonished at this wonderful and almost uninterrupted process whereby thought and feeling are being all the world over perpetually embodied in sound, and thus projected from mind to mind, from soul to soul, so as to establish and maintain a correspondence, if not a community, of inward life. As we listen to the most ordinary conversation, we may observe all the powers and faculties of a soul pass forth before us arrayed in the dress of language. Thought and reason appear in the choice and copulation of adjectives and substantives, in the delicate manipulation of particles and adverbs, and in all the varied machinery of the sentence; and will emerges in its imperative moods; and desire in optative moods; and purely animal impulse, it may be, in interjections. Unconsciously, but most truly, does the soul reveal itself to our senses in language; and this self-revelation is an instinct rather than a deliberate effort in the immense majority of human beings. And thus we see the significance of silence. Silence is the arrest of this almost incessant activity; and its import consists in this: that the whole productive force which results in language is felt to be still there and at work, although for the moment advisedly restrained from self-expression. There is nothing in the silence of that which never spoke —the silence of a statue, or the silence of an animal; but we, most of us, know, that not the least of the solemnities of gazing on the face of the dead is the thought that those lips will never again, here in this world, give expression to the inward life of a soul. And a sudden, resolute, emphatic silence on the part of a living man has in it something of this solemnity; it means at least as much as—probably much more than—any possible continuance of speech. And, plainly, this meaning is more and more emphatic as we ascend in the scale of minds: it means most in those men whose qualities of head and heart give them a preeminent right to speak. What then must it mean, when we pass beyond the frontiers of humanity, and find ourselves with One in Whom the Eternal Word or Reason spoke through human lips—One in Whom, as His Apostle says, dwelt all the treasures of wisdom and knowledge?[1] How shall we dare, as some have dared, to think that we can at all fully explain His silence, still less that we can assign it to a single motive? We can at best understand it very imperfectly; but we may endeavour, without irreverence, to give some account of it, in the light of His own Teaching and His Eternal Person.

1. Our Lord's silence meant first of all a rebuke. Pilate had asked a question, which it was not for him or for such as he to ask and to expect an answer.

Most of us know what it is to have made this kind of mistake, at least once in our lives, if not more than once. We are in company of a friend whose kindness encourages us, so that we feel at our ease; we say just what comes into our head. Conversation flows on, from this topic to that, easily, listlessly, pleasingly—and at last we ask a question, when, lo! there is silence. We have, out of curiosity, or in sheer thoughtlessness and gaiety of heart, uttered words which could not be answered, at least then, and to us. We have touched the nerve of some very tender feeling; we have probed to the quick some old and nearly-forgotten wound; we have put forth the hand, which, after a long interval of years, has first essayed to lift the veil that had long shrouded some secret or some sorrow, it was hoped, until the end.

There are others, it may be, who might have asked that question without causing such sharp pain as we; others nearer, dearer, more loved and trusted, with more tact and

[1] Col. ii. 3.

gentleness, more recognised right to enter the precincts of deep and tender feeling: but we, alas! must feel that words have passed our lips which have created a new relation between us and the heart to which they were addressed, words which could only be met by silence.

It would, we feel, be a relief to be reproached in words that we could hear. No words, however severe and cutting, could mean all that is meant by that terrible silence; since that silence means that thought has entered upon a region of wondering pain that is beyond language, and about which, therefore, nothing can be said. This is what happens in daily and private life, and it may enable us to enter into one aspect of our Lord's silence before Pilate. In itself, Pilate's question was not necessarily a wrong one; but it was not a question for Pilate, and under the circumstances, to ask. Had the scene been the upper chamber, and St. John the questioner, and the question the same in substance, yet thrown into such a form as love and awe would dictate, it would assuredly have been answered: love always means illumination. Jesus reveals His secrets to the importunity of love. But when Pilate, in the confident temper of a highly-placed officer who was not accustomed to be crossed in his purposes, ventures, in his crass Pagan ignorance, on ground thus sacred, thus supremely awful—stands there face to face with the Infinite and the Eternal, robed and crowned with the sorrows of a world of sin, and utters his frivolous, petulant, "Whence art Thou?" just as if he was talking to a neighbour who lived in the next street—what was possible save the rebuke of silence?

2. For, secondly, our Lord's silence was not merely a rebuke; it was very instructive. It was the sort of silence which, under certain circumstances, tells us much more than we could learn from speech. Speech will sometimes fail to say what should be said, simply because it cannot

be said. We are so familiar with the use and the capacities of God's great gift of speech that we perhaps find it hard to think that speech cannot say anything. Yet the world of thought and the world of fact are alike greater than speech can compass. And as the generations pass, and the languages of men continually enlarge their resources for recording fact and thought and feeling, they fail to keep pace with man's progressive discovery that beyond the utmost reach of language there are regions at whose existence human language can only hint. All that is near to us, all that is a matter of direct experience, whether to the senses or the mind, and much beyond, which belongs to the realm of abstract reason, or of pure imagination, can be compassed and described by human speech. But there are thoughts which just visit the mind now and then, and which language cannot detain and shape; thoughts at which it can only vaguely hint, if indeed it can do as much as that; truths and facts of whose existence we are only so far cognisant that we know them to be beyond the compass of language. When St. Paul was caught up into Paradise he reached a sphere in which he heard unspeakable words, which it is not lawful for a man to utter.[1] When the Corinthian Christians spoke during their religious assemblies in mystic tongues, they were in reality touching upon the fringe of a district of spiritual truth which could not submit to the trammels and limits of the accustomed speech of man. When we try to pass these limits, language becomes confused and vague, not because there is no real object to be described, but because we have no resources at command for the work of description. Pilate asked our Lord, "Whence art Thou?" The Evangelist had replied by anticipation, "In the beginning was the Word, and the Word was with God, and the Word was God. All things were made by

[1] 2 Cor. xii. 4.

Him; and without Him was not anything made that was made. And the Word was made flesh, and dwelt among us, and we beheld His glory."[1] And the Christian Church has echoed this reply, "I believe in one Lord Jesus Christ, the Only-Begotten Son of God, begotten of His Father before all worlds, God of God, Light of Light, Very God of Very God, Begotten, not made, being of One Substance with the Father, by Whom all things were made, Who for us men, and for our salvation came down from heaven."[2] But does not even this momentous language hint at the transcendent reality rather than describe it? Does it not employ metaphors drawn from human relations, and words that have had a great place in human philosophies, to put us on the track of a truth which is really beyond the tongue of man fully to set forth? And if this be so with Christian creeds, after all these centuries of thought and worship, how was Pilate's "Whence art Thou?" to be answered in terms which would convey any such a hint of the tremendous reality as might be possibly suggested, at least upon reflection, by the silence of our Lord?

3. Once more, our Lord's silence was the silence of charity. Knowledge is not a blessing where it only adds to the responsibilities of guilt, or where it is certain to be misused. We should all of us agree that there are just now people up and down Europe who are none the better for knowing something of the properties of dynamite; and a wise and kind father would not begin the education of his little boy by showing him how to fire off a loaded pistol. It is no disloyalty to the cause of education, or to the ultimate value of knowledge to all human minds, to say that certain kinds of knowledge—even the most valuable—are not blessings to men in particular states of mind. Before food can do good, we must be sure that it can be digested: the soil must be prepared before the seed can

[1] St. John i. 1, 3, 14. [2] The Nicene Creed.

grow. Why is it that the most precious of all books, the Bible, only furnishes to many thousands of persons in this country materials for ribald profanity? Because it is put into their hands without any accompanying care to see that it can be appreciated; "sown broadcast," as people say, on all soils alike, and therefore furnishing, to minds that are at once clever and godless, admirable occasions for the indulgence of purely irreligious humour.

This was not our Lord's method. He warned His disciples against giving that which was holy to the dogs, and against casting pearls before swine.[1] He taught upon a principle of consideration for the mental condition of His hearers, sometimes plainly, and sometimes in parables. He taught men, so says His Evangelist, as they were able to bear it.[2]

Brethren, and especially you who have in any way to instruct others, depend on it that to withhold from men the burden of knowledge which they will certainly abuse, is the true work of charity. Pilate, though he was ruler of the land, was, for all religious purposes, a child, if, indeed, we may say so much as that about him. And just as you would keep a beautiful and delicate work of art out of the way of a child, who does not understand its value, and would certainly pick it to pieces, so would our Lord not commit a truth which is not fully comprehended even by the intelligence of Angels to the half-indolent, half-insolent curiosity of Pilate. "Whence art Thou?" What did Pilate expect to be the reply to that question? "Whence art Thou?" What would Pilate have made of the true reply to that question? Surely it was the same Charity which taught what moral beauty means in the Sermon on the Mount, and which opened the spiritual world to the Apostles in the upper chamber, which, when Pilate asked, "Whence art Thou?" was silent.

[1] St. Matt. vii. 6. [2] St. John xvi. 12.

The Silence of Jesus.

Surely, as we contemplate our Lord silent before Pilate, we cannot but feel His incomparable Majesty. He is crowned and robed in derision; crowned with thorns, and robed in purple; but these outward symbols of humiliation and shame do but set forth the more the moral splendours that shine within. Yes, assuredly, Lord Jesus, not only in the moment of Thy bright Transfiguration before the eyes of Thy Apostles, not only in the hour of Thy Resurrection triumph, not now only, when Thou sittest at the Right Hand of the Father, while all that is mightiest and wisest in the realms above bows down before Thee in utter admiration, but also when in Thy Passion Thou standest—deserted, speechless, dumb—before Thy human judge, Thou art the King of Glory, O Christ, Thou art the Everlasting Son of the Father.[1]

[1] *Te Deum Laudamus.*

SERMON XI.

THE ASS AND THE FOAL.

St. Matt. xxi. 3.

And if any man say ought unto you, ye shall say, The Lord hath need of them.

YOU will remember that these words form part of the instructions which our Lord addressed to the two disciples whom He desired to take the necessary measures for His solemn entry into Jerusalem on Palm Sunday. They were to go into the village over-against them, no doubt into Bethphage; and there they would "find an ass tied, and a colt with her;" these they were to loose and to bring them to our Lord. If any remonstrance was made, they were to make a reply which, as they were instructed, would put an end to further resistance or discussion. "If any man say ought unto you, ye shall say, The Lord hath need of them; and straightway he shall send them."

It may, perhaps, at first occur to some of us, that this incident is too incidental—too subservient and preparatory to the Great Entry into Jerusalem itself—rightfully to occupy a main place in our thoughts on a day like this. But it will appear, I trust, as we proceed, that this apprehension is not well grounded. We are, in fact, no good judges of the relative importance of words and acts in a Life so altogether above and beyond us as is that of our Lord Jesus Christ.

In such a Life, our common notions of what is of first importance, and what only secondary, do not apply, at least with anything like certainty; it is safest to assume that, on this sacred ground, nothing is incidental, nothing subsidiary, nothing unimportant. It is at least possible that the charge to the disciples, which preceded the public entry, has as much to teach us as the entry itself; at any rate, we may observe that of the more obvious lessons which it suggests, there are three which appear very markedly to claim attention.

I.

Our Lord's words, then, illustrate, first of all, the deliberateness with which He moved forward to His Agony and Death. When He sent the two disciples for the ass and the foal, which were tied up in the street of Bethphage, He was, as He knew, taking the first step in a series which would end within a week on Mount Calvary. Everything accordingly is measured, deliberate, calm. He first brings into play His power of immediate prophecy, —of prophecy that is directed upon an object in the near future, which could not have been anticipated by the exercise of a man's natural judgment—just as He did a few days after, when He told the disciples to follow a man bearing a pitcher of water, who would show them the way to the room prepared for the Last Supper. He already sees the ass and the foal in the street of Bethphage, and He sends for them. That He should contemplate riding at all is remarkable; there is no earlier or later notice in the Gospels of His moving from place to place, except by walking—to walk was the symbol of His poverty and of His independence! Now, however, He will ride on an ass; and there is a reason for His doing so. He sends for the ass and the foal, because the prophet Zechariah had introduced these animals into his description of the coming of the King of Zion to His own city,[1] and in a prophecy which the Jewish interpreters, from the first and without hesitation, applied to the Messiah. In ancient days, the sons of the judges rode on white asses;[2] the ass was used by Ziba,[3] Shimei,[4] Mephibosheth,[5] Ahitophel,[6] by David's household,[7] by the old prophet of Bethel.[8] David himself and the sons of David rode on mules,[9] in order to mark their royal station without altogether deserting the old tradition; Absalom in his rebellion introduced chariots and horses;[10] Solomon brought thousands of horses from Egypt.[11] The appearance of the horse, familiar to the Assyrians, to the Egyptians, even to the Canaanites, as a feature to the state and apparatus of the Jewish kings, marked the rise of a monarchy which aped the fashions, and would fain have rivalled the power, of the great Pagan monarchies of the East. The horse is in the Prophets a symbol of worldly power; "I will cut off the chariot from Ephraim, and the horse from Jerusalem,"[12] is a prediction of the fall of the worldly monarchy. The ass fell into discredit as the new heathen ideal of royal splendour was increasingly accepted, so that in the last days of the Jewish monarchy the burial of an ass was a proverb for a disgraced end.[13] There was no recorded instance of a king of Judah or Israel riding on an ass. That the King Messiah should come to Zion riding on an ass, meant, for the Jewish people, that He was to have a kingdom not of this world; that He was to be a prophet-king, whose outward bearing should recall those ancient days in which the Lord Himself had been Israel's King[14]—the days which preceded the establishment of the monarchy.

[1] Zech. ix. 9.   [2] Judg. x. 4; xii. 14.   [3] 2 Sam. xvi. 1.
[4] 1 Kings ii. 40.   [5] 2 Sam. xix. 26.   [6] Ib. xvii. 23.
[7] 2 Sam. xvi. 2.   [8] 1 Kings xiii. 13, 23, 27.   [9] 2 Sam. xiii. 29; xviii. 9.
[10] 2 Sam. xv. 1.   [11] 1 Kings x. 26-28.   [12] Zech. ix. 10.
[13] Jer. xxii. 19.   [14] 1 Sam. xii. 12.

Hence the great amount of attention which was fixed on this passage of Zechariah by the Jews: hence our Lord's care for its literal fulfilment.

Men have often asked why the two animals were wanted, and they have observed that St. Mark and St. Luke speak only of the colt. The answer is, not that the foal, not yet broken in, might behave more quietly when its mother was beside it, but that the prophetic passage of Zechariah, so dear to the memory and imagination of the Jewish people, might be rendered before their eyes into a realised picture. Zechariah's redundant language does plainly speak of two animals, not of one ;[1] and therefore our Lord sent for two. The two animals were symbolical; the disciplined ass under the yoke, and the wild unbroken colt, each had its meaning. The ass itself, an unclean, ignoble, debased drudge, as the Jews deemed it, was a picture of unredeemed man, enslaved to his errors and his sins ; but then, within the human family, the Jews had been under the yoke of the law, and were so far broken in; the undisciplined heathen were like the wild unbroken colt.[2] It was thus essential to the full meaning of our Lord's action that He should ride, first on the one animal, and then the other: while the whole circumstance of the entry into Zion, on the part of Zion's king, as conceived of by Zechariah, was preparatory to Zion's deliverance through suffering. When then our Lord sent for the ass and the colt, He solemnly entered on the group of associations which prophecy had traced around His Passion: it was the beginning of the end; it was the first step in the procession to the Cross. "All this was done, that it might be fulfilled which was spoken by the prophet, saying, Tell ye the daughter of

---

[1] Zech. ix. 9.
[2] Cf. *Commentary on the Minor Prophets*, by E. B. Pusey, D.D. Zech. ix. 9. pp. 556-59.

Zion, Behold, thy King cometh unto thee, meek, and sitting upon an ass, and upon a colt the foal of an ass."[1] With most men, as we know, it is otherwise. "They think that their houses shall continue for ever, and that their dwelling-places shall endure from one generation to another, and call the lands after their own names."[2] During the years of health and strength, human nature still whispers to itself, "Tush, I shall never be cast down, there shall no harm happen unto me."[3] And when this is no longer possible, how often do we put off the thought of death! We try to disguise from ourselves its gradual approach; we do anything in our power to postpone it: we diet ourselves, we change the air, we give up, if we can, our more exacting employments; we struggle against the inevitable; we hope against hope. There have indeed been, in many, if not in all, generations, noble exceptions to the rule; men who, knowing what they were doing, have gone out to meet death, armed with a strong sense of duty, or inspired by an heroic resolve. Such was the old Roman, whose name was dear to his countrymen for many a succeeding century, who when he was sent back as a captive from Carthage to recommend a discreditable peace, and with the knowledge that failure would entail on him a death of torture, deliberately advised them to reject the proposed terms.[4] Such have been soldiers, who have volunteered for a forlorn hope; doctors, who have, perhaps within our own knowledge, undertaken duties which they knew must cost them their lives; Sisters of Mercy, who have nursed cholera patients, and laid them out for burial, when their nearest relatives have deserted them. In these and like cases the moral glory of our Lord's deliberate and voluntary

---

[1] St. Matt. xxi. 4, 5.   [2] Ps. xlix. 11.   [3] *Ib.* x. 6.
[4] The Embassy of Regulus is beautifully described in Cicero *De Officiis*, iii. 27.

suffering rests in its measure on our human weakness; the great difference is that, with Him, there is no trace of the pressure either of unforeseen outward circumstances, or of sudden heroic impulse from within. He knows that He is going to die, and He gives His orders just as quietly as though He were sitting at the marriage-feast of Cana. He might at any moment withdraw Himself from the tempest of insult and agony that will presently be poured on Him; but His heart is established and will not shrink until He see His desire upon those spiritual enemies[1]—sin and death—whom it is His mission to subdue. The twelve legions of angels are waiting; He has but to summon them;[2] but though He already sees and feels all that is awaiting Him, He sends into Bethphage for the ass and the foal.

It is this deliberateness in His advance to die, this voluntariness in His sufferings, which, next to the fact of His true Divinity, gives to the Death of our Lord Jesus Christ its character of a sacrifice for the sins of the whole world.[3] If it was to be the offering, not merely of an Immaculate Body, but of a perfectly resigned and holy Will, the Victim must say, at each stage of it, "A body hast Thou prepared me; then said I, Lo! I come to do Thy Will, O God."[4] And this is what our Lord does throughout; it is the motive of His last utterance on the Cross: "Into Thy hands, O Lord, I commend My spirit;"[5] it is the motive of the very first measure He takes, when entering on the preliminaries of His Sufferings, and sending into Bethphage, in obedience to Zechariah's prophecy, for the ass and the colt.

II.

Our Lord's words illustrate, secondly, the exacting nature of His claims. "If any man say ought unto you,

---

[1] Ps. cxii. 8.   [2] St. Matt. xxvi. 53.   [3] 1 St. John ii. 2.
[4] Heb. x. 5, 7.   [5] St. Luke xxiii. 46.

ye shall say, The Lord hath need of them." No doubt the owner of the animals had work for them to do; in any case, they were his. Yet here is a demand, at first sight, not unlike the requisitions, as they are called, of an invading army, when "might becomes right;" when the ordinary rights of property are swept aside at the bidding of a hostile and superior force; and men have to furnish provisions, lodgings, horses and carriages, furniture and equipages, under pain of suffering the extremities of war, if they refuse. Here, too, was a requisition in its way: "Ye shall find an ass tied, and a colt with her: loose them, and bring them unto Me. And if any man say ought unto you, ye shall say, The Lord hath need of them; and straightway he will send them."

What is the justification of this demand?

A modern German Socialist writer, Weitling, traces here the right of those who are in want to help themselves out of the possessions of their well-to-do neighbours, and he laments the false refinement of our days, when the disciples would have been at once arrested and charged with theft before the nearest magistrate. This writer's idea is that our Lord was really what would now be called a communist, and that He claimed the ass and the foal as really belonging to the community of which he was a member. This account of the matter would ill accord with our Lord's solemn proclamation, that He came not to destroy the moral law, but to fulfil it.[1] He certainly did not abrogate "Thou shalt not steal."[2] Yet the eighth commandment is unmeaning, unless property, in the sense of private property, is of moral right; you cannot steal that which belongs to nobody in particular, and on which every one has an equal claim. The community of goods described in the early part of the Acts of the Apostles[3] was a very different thing from communism; it was a fruit of the

[1] St. Matt. v. 17. [2] Exod. xx. 15. [3] Acts iv. 32-35.

spontaneous action of Christian charity; it rested upon the voluntary surrender of their private rights by the first Christians. In one of his sermons, three and a half centuries later, St. Augustine describes a very similar state of things in his own household at Hippo.[1] Every one who entered it voluntarily subscribed a declaration by which he disposed of his property in favour of a common fund, which supported them all; and any one who, after this, claimed to be the owner of any sort of property, was expelled from the community. But this, like the life of the first Christians, was a very different thing from the communism which denounces property as immoral, and which would confiscate it to public purposes, whether its present owners would or no. Property, it might be shown, if this were the time and place to do so, is not an arbitrary or vicious product of civilisation; it is an outcome of forces which are always at work in human nature and life; it is a formation or deposit which human industry is always accumulating; it is an original result of the terms on which men—at once industrious and free—live together as members of a society. It has its duties, no doubt, as it has its rights; its duties are not really matters of choice, any more than its rights are matters of sentiment; but if property is in any sense imperilled, if communism is ever destined to get the upper hand in modern Europe, it will be because the holders of property have thought only of its rights, and have forgotten its duties. Nevertheless, while its rights may for high moral purposes be surrendered voluntarily, they are rights which may be retained and insisted on; and they cannot be violated without doing violence to the nature of things, without breaking the eighth commandment of the Decalogue.

 This then brings us back to the question of the principle on which our Lord claimed the ass and the colt in the

[1] St. Aug. *Serm.* ccclv. vol. v. p. 1381 (ed. Ben.).

street of Bethphage. It is a question which can only be answered in one way—namely, that Christ was all along the true Owner of the ass and the colt, and that the apparent owner was but His bailiff. "The Lord hath need of them." How would the owner of the animals have understood this reply? We cannot doubt, from the general tenor of the narrative, that the owner was in some sense a disciple; that Christ foresaw not merely the presence of the ass and the colt in the street of Bethphage, but the state of mind of the person to whom they belonged, and that by "the Lord" the owner of the ass would have understood "the Lord Messiah." Not merely Messiah "the Master," but Messiah "the Lord"; not here merely "the Son of Man," His favourite description of Himself, but the Lord, the word being employed, no doubt, in the original language which was used of the Lord Jehovah. "The Lord hath need of them." He claims what He has lent for a while; He resumes what has always been His own; we hear the voice of the Being to Whom man owes all that he is and has, "Whose we are, and Whom we serve."[1]

Certainly, my brethren, this claim of our Lord's implies His Divinity, but it is a very modest claim when compared with others which He made on those who heard Him. To ask for a man's cattle is little compared with asking for his affections, his thoughts, his endeavours, for the surrender of his will, for the sacrifice of his liberty, for the abandonment, if need be, of all earthly happiness, and of life itself. Yet nothing less than this was meant by the warning that a man may have to hate father and mother, and wife and children, for His sake and the gospel's;[2] nothing less than this by the stern sentence, "No man having put his hand to the plough, and looking back, is fit

[1] Acts xxvii. 23.
[2] St. Luke xiv. 26; St. Mark viii. 34, 35.

for the kingdom of God;"[1] nothing less than this by the peremptory command, "What is that to thee? Follow thou Me."[2] Christians, at any rate, if they are still Christians, can only feel and express surprise at our Lord's requiring the ass and the colt, if they have forgotten what He asks of themselves as a condition of any serious discipleship, and how this demand throws any claim upon their property entirely into the shade.

At this season, indeed, we think of our Lord's claims upon us less in the light of His Divine Person than of His Redeeming Work. He has a right to make them, not merely as our Lord, but as our greatest Benefactor; not merely as having created us by His Power, but as having redeemed us by His Blood. Assuredly, in these solemn days on which we are entering, He does not claim our service chiefly as the Infinite and the Eternal, He claims it as the Incarnate and the Crucified. Has He then no right to some return for those thirty-three years of humiliation and toil; for that long Agony of Soul and Body in which they ended; for sufferings so various, so violent, so subtle, so protracted, above all, so voluntary; for a tragic Death, each incident in which seems to plead to the Christian heart,

"This have I borne for thee,
What doest thou for Me?"

It is not exaggeration, it is simple Christian feeling, with its eye on the Cross of the Divine Redeemer, which sings—

"Were the whole realm of nature mine,
That were an offering far too small;
Love so amazing, so divine,
Demands my soul, my life, my all."

And if conscience whispers to you or me that He has need of something which we have not yet given Him,—of our substance, of our time, of the work of our hands or of our brains, is it possible that we can hesitate as to the answer?

[1] St. Luke ix. 62. [2] St. John xxi. 22.

III.

And, thirdly, our Lord's words show how He can make use of all, even the lowest and the last; nay, how, in His condescension, He makes Himself dependent on them for the fulfilment of His purposes. It was of the ass and the colt that He Himself said, "The Lord hath need of them." What was the need? Was it that He was too tired at this particular time to ascend the Mount of Olives on foot, or that He desired, in going to meet the multitudes who were eagerly waiting for Him, to be raised above the accompanying crowd of disciples around? These were very subordinate elements of the need, if elements of it at all; He wanted the ass and the colt, as we have seen, that He might enact before the eyes of the people the literal fulfilment of Zechariah's prophecy. This ass and colt, insignificant in themselves, had become necessary to our Lord at one of the great turning-points of His Life; they were needed for a service, unique and incomparable, which has given them a place in sacred history to the end of time. They were to be conspicuous in that great Sacrificial Procession (for such it was) in which He, the Flower and Prince of our race, moved forward to yield Himself to the wild wills of men, who to-day can shout "Hosanna!" as to-morrow they will cry "Crucify!"

The needs of God! It were surely too bold an expression, if He had not authorised us to use it: we might well shrink from implying that anything is necessary to Him, Who is alone complete in Himself, and is the Source of all that is. Yet there they stand—the words, "The Lord hath need of them." He needed the ass and foal in the street of Bethphage. We ask, almost with impatience, Could He not have done without them? In one sense, —Yes; in another,—No. He might beforehand have so ruled matters as to make their service unnecessary. He might—so we may reverentially suppose—have originally inspired His prophet to colour the picture of the future somewhat differently; to throw into another form those predictions, whose behests, in an after age, He would Himself obey. But when the prophetic word had gone forth, it could not return to Him empty.[1] Prophecy, being in Zechariah's mouth what it was, the true Messiah could not but obey it. Prophecy being what it was, He did need the ass and foal in order to fulfil it; it was too late, if we may so speak, to raise the question whether the lesson which they taught might have been otherwise rendered into symbol. The ass and the colt might count for little among the villagers of Bethphage; but they had a necessary place marked out for them in the Passion of Christ—a place and a work on that first Palm Sunday, which higher, nobler, more intellectual beings could not have supplied or undertaken.

The needs of God! My brethren, if anything is necessary to carrying out His purposes, it is because He has made it so. He gives laws to the world of nature; and lo! there arises some particular physical necessity, as we call it, that is, to speak plainly, God's necessity that some condition should be obeyed in order to meet the exigencies of a particular law. Health, for instance, has its appointed conditions; they cannot be set aside, without miracle; God has made health depend on food, air, and exercise, and we may dare to say that ordinarily He needs these conditions,—in order to secure it to His creatures. In like manner God has made human society dependent for its wellbeing and coherence upon the maintenance of certain principles and rules, and then a state of things presents itself in which some man, or transaction, or course of events is necessary, if these are to be maintained

[1] Isa. lv. 11.

and society is not to go to pieces. Once more, He has made the strength and continuance of the Christian life depend on an inspired Bible, on an organised Church, on the preaching of the Faith, on duly administered Sacraments. Whether any part of this provision might have been otherwise, consistently with the great purposes of Redemption, it is too late now to inquire. God's declared Will is that they should be necessary, and thus we find Him, as it seems, constantly in need of poor, feeble human instruments in order to give effect to His own high purposes of grace and mercy. "The Lord hath need of them." Whether it might have been otherwise is not for us to ask; our business is to take note of what is,—of the needs of God, which He Himself points out to us.

The needs of God. Yes! And what is much to be remarked is that He often needs those whom we, as we think, if we were in His place, could have dispensed with. We measure Him by our own standard of experience; we know that we habitually depend on intellect, on ability, on wealth, on power, and that we do not want the unintelligent, the feeble, the poor, the uninfluential. We are, whether consciously or not, anthropomorphic in our conceptions of the needs of God : if we had been on the Throne in Heaven eighteen hundred years ago, we should in our stupid way have hoped to convert the world by gaining the good graces of rulers of men like Tiberius and Nero, of literary men like Seneca or Tacitus, and should have taken small account of the fishermen of Galilee. But with Him it is otherwise. The difference between the highest intellect and the narrowest and feeblest is as nothing, because it is a measurable distance when compared with the distance between what we call the highest intellect and the Eternal Mind. The difference between the strongest and the weakest of beings is as nothing when compared with the distance that parts the strongest from the Almighty Strength of the Creator. And He constantly reminds us of this by exhibiting Himself as needing not the great forces which awe thought, or which direct events, or which reconstruct or uphold society, but the humble, feeble, half-perceived, or unseen agencies which are taken no account of by that ordinary human estimate of men and things which passes for wisdom.

Yes! "The Lord hath need of them." Let none hereafter say: "What can God want of me, a mere unit among the millions of the human family? He is not without resources; He raises up great men to carry out His purposes; but I am too insignificant, too remote from the scene and the capacity of effective action to contribute anything to a cause, to a Church, to a world, that is what it is because He has willed it."

No, my brother, the Lord hath need of thee too; though thou wilt not believe it. He might, it may be, originally have dispensed with thee; He might have left thee out of the group of influences which were to work His will in thy day and generation. Thou canst not penetrate the secrets of His predestination; but, as things are, He needs thee; if it were otherwise, thou wouldest not exist. He needs thee for some service, great or lowly, trivial or magnificent, which none else can do; which will not be done, at least as He had designed it, if it be not done by thee. God's abstract power of dispensing with each of His creatures, or with all of them put together, is one thing; His actual plan of governing the world, as expressed in the series of forces and events amid which we live, is another. In fact, He does not release Himself, except upon critical occasions, from the empire of His own rules or laws; and if this or that agent, to whom He has assigned some special work or service, drops out of his place, the omission is not supplied by miracle; the work is left

XI] *The Ass and the Foal.* 181

undone, the immediate, though not the ultimate, purpose of the Creator is frustrated.

If this is an awful, it is surely still more a very consolatory, thought. Numbers of persons are oppressed by the conviction that they are of little use to anything or anybody; that God has no work for them to do: that they belong to the waste of the moral world, not to its legitimate and productive substance. Let them think, when these gloomy thoughts take possession of them, of the ass and the colt on Palm Sunday. For all of us, the weakest and the humblest, there is a place and time of special service, to be rendered sooner or later to the Eternal King, Who condescends not merely to expect, but to need it. For that hour we have been created; towards it we have been tending, consciously or unconsciously, during the years of life; and at last it comes; perhaps it passes; perhaps it never repeats itself. Happy we if we are only ready to give and to be given to Christ when He deigns to ask for us; to contribute our little all to His triumphant advance across the centuries, on His errand of beneficence and judgment, among the sons of men.

May He enable us all during this Passiontide to understand the freedom of His atoning Suffering for us; to yield what we can in answer to His demands upon our love; to be sure that we, too, have some work to do in His kingdom, which can be done by none other, and which, if done faithfully, He will own.

SERMON XII.

POPULAR RELIGIOUS ENTHUSIASM.

St. John xii. 12, 13.

Much people that were come to the feast, when they heard that Jesus was coming to Jerusalem, took branches of palm trees, and went forth to meet Him, and cried, Hosanna: Blessed is the King of Israel That cometh in the Name of the Lord.

OUR Lord's entrance into Jerusalem on Palm Sunday was one of the most important events in His whole earthly life. It was the great public act by which He entered upon the duties and sufferings of the week in which He died for the salvation of the world: and by it He gave notice, if I may so say, to the faithful, and to mankind at large, of what He was about to do and to suffer. Palm Sunday is the solemn introduction—if the metaphor is allowable, it is the overture—to the week which follows; and it anticipates, but with due reserve, the solemn tragedy which it introduces. And so this is one of the few events in our Lord's Life which is described by all the four Evangelists. Approaching the Passion from very different points of view, each Evangelist is alive to the unique character of the entry into Jerusalem, as a proceeding which is marked, on the part of our Lord, with even more deliberation than are His actions, always so deliberate, on other occasions. Each Evangelist mentions the animal on which our Lord rode, in fulfilment of prophecy; each repeats, with but slight variations from the rest, the Hymn of praise which was sung by the people who accompanied Him; each is careful to note the great number of persons, some of them disciples, some of them independent lookers-on, who were present, and who were led to take a part, more or less pronounced, in this great demonstration of enthusiastic religious feeling.

I.

The occasion was, indeed, of capital significance in the Life of our Lord; and its bearing upon His Work and Sufferings, and claims upon the faith and homage of mankind have been, from the first ages of Christianity, constantly and earnestly recognised. To-day, however, we may, perhaps with advantage, consider it as affording a great display of feelings of reverence and love, on the part of an assembled multitude, which our Lord condescended to sanction and to accept. The governing motive of what took place on Palm Sunday was religious rather than, for instance, social or political. No doubt there was a political element at work in the popular feeling which welcomed Jesus of Nazareth as the expected Messiah. For some generations the Jews had read their national hopes and ambitions into the ancient prophets; and, as a consequence, the idea of the coming Messiah, which the Jews of that day entertained, was largely political. The Messiah was expected to be a great Captain and Ruler of men, by whose genius and victories Israel would be freed from the yoke of his western conquerors, and would become the ruling race in some new and world-wide empire. We cannot assert that no such feeling as this was entertained by any who took part in the demonstration on Palm Sunday; nor can it be denied that there may have been a social feeling at work as well as a political one. Those who did not listen attentively to what our Lord said, and did not look below the surface of His bearing and actions, would have seen in Jesus Christ a social reformer of the highest class, as well as a great philanthropist, endowed with extraordinary faculties for giving effect to His benevolence, so that His earthly presence was a moveable hospital, within whose precincts every form of human suffering might find relief. Such a personage would in all ages and under any circumstances command general interest and devotion.

But when our Lord entered Jerusalem, religious motives had more to do with the welcome that greeted Him than any others. Our Lord addressed Himself to the religious feeling of the people, as distinct from their political hopes or their social gratitude, when He entered Jerusalem riding on an ass. The warrior-politician of Jewish Messianic fancy would surely have been mounted on some richly caparisoned charger, surrounded with chariots and horsemen; the horse, then, as always, in human estimation, the nobler animal, was already in the book of Proverbs,[1] in Hosea,[2] and in Jeremiah,[3] associated with the enterprises and triumphs of war—the horse, in the popular imagination, was ever "prepared against the day of battle." When our Lord, with such forethought and deliberation, chose the ass, He was at once setting aside the foolish political dreams of his countrymen, and was claiming to fulfil Zechariah's prediction of the Messiah's entry into Jerusalem as the King of peace, "Behold, thy King cometh unto thee, meek, and sitting upon an ass, and upon a colt the foal of an ass."[4]

And the action of a large part of the gathered multitude was no less expressive of religious as distinct from political or social feeling. This appears from the circumstance described by St. John in the text—"Much people

[1] Prov. xxi. 31. [2] Hos. xiv. 3.
[3] Jer. xvii. 25. [4] Zech. ix. 9.

that were come to the feast, when they heard that Jesus was coming to Jerusalem, took branches of palm trees, and went forth to meet Him." St. Matthew and St. Mark say that a great multitude cut down branches from the trees and strewed them in the way;[1] and this is sometimes carelessly supposed to be what is referred to in other terms by St. John. In truth—and it is important to mark this—the acts were different, the agents were different, and the objects of the acts were different. The trees by the road-side, whose branches were cut down, would not have been palms (the leaves of which would have been out of reach), and were almost certainly olives. The people who cut them down were coming from Bethany, and the action does not necessarily mean more than the bounding joy and reverence for Jesus which was also expressed by spreading garments along the road of His progress. But the palms, which St. John alone mentions, were not cut down on this occasion, but were brought out of Jerusalem by a multitude which went out to meet the procession advancing from Bethany. These palms had been cut in all probability some days before, and were now festooned with myrtle and otherwise, as was the custom, in readiness for the approaching Passover. They were not strewed along the ground, they were carried in the air before our Lord, and their use on this occasion would have been a proclamation, more or less conscious, that "He is the very Paschal Lamb Which taketh away the sin of the world."[2] Indeed, it would seem that the band which advanced from Jerusalem kindled a new enthusiasm in the pilgrims from Bethany, and then they joined together in singing the hymn of praise, "Hosanna, save now, O Lord: Blessed is He That cometh in the Name of the Lord."[3] This was a third

[1] St. Matt. xxi. 8; St. Mark xi. 8. [3] Ps. cxviii. 25, 26.
[2] *Proper Preface* for Easter Day in the Order for the Holy Communion.

circumstance which marked the religious character of the enthusiasm. The words are from the Psalm cxviii.; they had long been used at the Feast of Tabernacles, and at the Paschal festival; they were connected in the minds of pious Jews with the coming of the expected Messiah; and so, as the mingled company advanced down the slope of the Mount of Olives, and towards the gates of the sacred city, they surrounded Jesus Christ with actions, and they hymned Him in language, denoting at the very least deeply moved religious feelings of thankfulness and love. "Hosanna: Blessed is He That cometh in the Name of the Lord. Hosanna in the highest."

It may be asked how this religious feeling could have been kindled in so large and mixed a multitude of persons. It is plain, first of all, that a main impulse proceeded from the company which came out from Jerusalem, and which was composed of "people that had come to the feast," that is to say, of Jews of the provinces or of the Dispersion, who were generally more devout, more attentive to the guidance of prophecy, and to God's teaching through events, than the Jews who lived in the sacred city. It was the conduct of these Jews which drew from the leading Pharisees the despairing remark, "Perceive ye how ye prevail nothing? behold, the world is gone after him;"[1] and they would have been likely to influence the general multitude more powerfully than could the disciples coming from Bethany. Their homage to Jesus Christ would have been considered by the nation at large at once more disinterested and surprising; and to them probably—among human agencies—must be attributed a large share in the events of the day.

Of course, in so mixed a multitude on such an occasion, there would have been very various degrees of conviction and insight, while nevertheless they all united in recog-

[1] St. John xii. 19.

nising in Jesus Christ something higher than was to be found among the sons of men. On other occasions we find this recognition in the most dissimilar quarters. It was an Apostle who cried, "Depart from me, for I am a sinful man, O Lord;"[1] a demoniac which exclaimed, "We know Thee Who Thou art, the Holy One of God;"[2] a Pagan soldier who observed, "Truly this was the Son of God;"[3] a multitude which agreed, "Never man spake like this Man."[4] From very different levels of religious existence it is possible to recognise some elemental truths; just as the sun in the heavens is visible in the deepest valleys not less than on the summits of the Alps. There was that in Jesus Christ which compelled much religious recognition. That union of tenderness and strength, of lowliness and majesty, of sternness and love, of weakness and power, must have struck many a man who never asked himself what it really meant, yet as unlike anything he had ever seen on earth. Such a man could not have explained himself; but he was not the less under the empire of the impression produced by our Lord's Character: and thus, when an opportunity of giving outward vent to his pent-up feelings presented itself, he would have joined in it, though the words he used went beyond his present insight. Many a man who little knew its full import sang on that day no doubt with a full heart, "Hosanna : Blessed is He That cometh in the Name of the Lord." The enthusiasm which is created by a multitude of men in each one of the units who compose it, is a result of the nature which God has given us. He has made us social beings. He has endowed us with many qualities and dispositions which not merely fit us for companionship with each other, but which require it, in order to our complete satisfaction and wellbeing.

[1] St. Luke v. 8.   [2] St. Mark i. 24.
[3] St. Matt. xxvii. 54.   [4] St. John vii. 46.

When human beings come together in great numbers, this social side of our nature is brought powerfully into play, it may be without our knowing it; instead of thinking of ourselves as individuals, we then think of ourselves as integral parts of a great multitude. There is a contagion of sympathy in great masses of associated men—a contagion of regulated passion—almost a contagion of thought. Mind beats in unison with mind, heart with heart, will with will, under the strain and compulsion of a common object presented to the view of a gathered multitude; it is felt that personal traits, eccentricities, preferences, prejudices are here out of place; what distinguishes a man from his fellows at other times is for the moment lost sight of in the overpowering sense of that which unites him to them; and thus, like reeds before the wind, private feelings, and sometimes even strong resolutions, go down for the moment, and bend in submission before the imperious ascendancy of this common enthusiasm; and a multitude moves as if it were a single body animated by a single soul, with a simple directness and intensity of purpose, towards its goal.

This sense of association is the soul of all powerful corporate action among men. It is the soul of an army: each soldier sees in his comrade not merely another fighting unit, but a man to whom he is bound by the sympathies inspired by common enterprise and danger. It is the spirit which gives influence to a public assembly; since such a body is less dependent for its usefulness on the capacity of the orators who may address it than on the pervading sense among its members of united thoughts, and hearts, and resolves for the promotion of a common object. Is it conceivable that when the highest of all subjects that can forcibly interest human beings is in question, it should have nothing to say to so fertile and powerful an influence? No; wherever human beings have engaged in that noblest of human occupations, the worship of a Higher Power, they have laid the sense of association under tribute; each worshipper feels that he is not alone, face to face with the Awful Object of worship; he knows himself to be engaged in a work to which all around him are devoting themselves; if his thoughts and affections are first of all directed upon God, they are also entwined by sympathy with the affections and the thoughts of his fellow-men around him; and in this felt communion of each with all and of all with each lies the strength of public worship, and to it was granted of old that uncancelled irrevocable charter, "Where two or three are gathered together in My Name, there am I in the midst of them."[1]

It was this enthusiasm arising from the sense of association among the members of a great assemblage of human beings, which our Lord took into His service so conspicuously on Palm Sunday. He had had multitudes before Him not unfrequently before, to instruct, to feed, to bless them; but He had withdrawn Himself from their advances, as when they desired to make Him a King;[2] He saw further than those around Him; He had His own times for reserve and for self-abandonment. To-day He yields Himself to the enthusiasm of the people; He the Lord of hearts and wills, Who knew what was in man,[3] and could control it, bids the surging and uncertain currents of feeling in a mixed multitude of men, on this memorable day, minister to His glory. It is a power called into existence for all time; St. Paul will tell the Corinthians that at the sight of the ordered worship of the Church, a heathen should fall down and confess that God was in it of a truth;[4] St. Augustine will leave on record how, as yet unconvicted, he was touched by the hymns which were sung by the assembled faithful in the Church of Milan.[5] On all

[1] St. Matt. xviii. 20.   [2] St. John vi. 15.   [3] *Ib.* ii. 25.
[4] 1 Cor. xiv. 1-25.   [5] *Confessions*, Book ix. § [VI.] 14.

the mountains of the world, as of old on the slope of Olivet, weak and sinful men shall join henceforth with the choirs of Angels in the worship of Christ's Sacred Manhood—in the ascription to the Lamb that was slain of that praise and honour which is everlastingly His due.[1]

II.

It cannot be denied that the sympathy which is inspired by the sense of fellowship with a multitude of our fellow-creatures may tell in more directions than one. It may be turned downwards as well as upwards: it may become an instrument of violence and wrong. Associated masses of men have at times even achieved gigantic evil. At the bidding of some malignant genius, multitudes of men have again and again in the world's history taken leave of reason and conscience, and have abandoned themselves to those brutal ferocities which, in the absence of conscience and reason, occupy the throne of the human soul.

In many an Eastern city, so well-informed travellers assure us, a chance expression or an unintended gesture, or a wild suspicion, or a word of order dropped by some influential dervish, will fall like a spark upon a mass of inflammable matter; where but now all was peaceful and reassuring, an angry crowd has assembled, whose faces gather blackness, and who threaten or execute some deed of blood. Nor is the terrific power of conscious association for violent crime unknown to our Western civilisation; it may be questioned whether any darker examples of it are to be found than those which the first French Revolution again and again supplies. Human nature being what it is, the precept not to follow a multitude to do evil[2] is never unneeded.

If, then, Palm Sunday places us face to face with a great religious enthusiasm, we cannot help thinking of what will

[1] Rev. v. 11, 12.   [2] Exod. xxiii. 2.

XII]   *Popular Religious Enthusiasm.*   191

follow. The foil to Palm Sunday is Good Friday. What will these people who are strewing the road with their garments and bearing palms before the advancing Saviour, and singing Hosannas to His praise—what will they be doing then ? Will none of them be spitting in His Adorable Face, or buffeting Him, or smiting Him with the palms of their hands ? Will none of them join in the brutal demand that the robber Barabbas shall be preferred before Him ? Will none help to force the Pagan governor to a crime from which he shrinks, by swelling the cry, "Away with Him! Crucify Him! crucify Him" ?[1] Do we not already see in the tears which Jesus sheds, as He passes the crest of the hill, and the city comes into full view, that His Eye is full upon the future; that He knows what is before Him ; that while the agony and the shame in prospect cannot touch the calm depths of His Holy Soul, He does not take what is passing at more than its real worth ; He does not forget the sad and certain fact that the applause of all but thoroughly good men is the exact measure of their possible or probable hostility ? And yet here it is possible to draw a mistaken inference from the whole scene. Does it not prove, men go on to ask, the worthlessness of all corporate religious enthusiasm ? What was the outcome, after all, of these palms, of that path carpeted with robes and branches, of that procession of palm-bearers, of those ringing songs of praise ? What did it lead to practically ? Did it not precede almost immediately the great crime of the Crucifixion ? and may not the condition of popular feeling that led up to the Crucifixion have been a reaction from unnatural religious excitement which preceded it ? Is not religion always a strictly personal relation between man and his Maker, between God and each single soul ? And does not a tempest of feeling, like that on Palm Sunday, tend to obscure this simple and vital truth, and to invest

[1] St. John xix. 15.

what is merely human and almost physical with the semblance of spiritual energy and life?

It is clear, brethren, that at least no Christian can be of this opinion. For, on Palm Sunday, it appears that a like objection was felt by some Pharisees who asked our Lord to rebuke His disciples who were chanting Hosanna. And He said unto them, "I tell you, if these should hold their peace, the stones would immediately cry out."[1]

No, brethren! the religious enthusiasm of a multitude is not therefore worthless because its worth may be exaggerated, or because it may not be lasting, or because it may be succeeded by an enthusiasm which is not religious. It is not a profound view of human nature which explains successive moods of human feeling as a series of reactions,—as though the heart of man must perforce oscillate like a pendulum in a clock with perpetual exactness, first to this extreme of feeling and then to that. Religious enthusiasm, however we arrive at it, has ever a certain value of its own: there is not too much of it in our busy modern world, where the whole thought and energy of the majority of men is unreservedly devoted to the passing but engrossing things of sense and time. Surely it is something, now and then, to rub off if it be only a little of the dust which clogs the wings of the human spirit; surely it is something to escape, for an hour or two if it must be no more, from the cold prison-house of matter in which so much of modern thought, so many modern souls are strictly imprisoned, into the free warm atmosphere of the world of spirits, into the rays of the Love of God. Grant that religious enthusiasm is often misguided, shallow, unchastened, unpractical; effervescent, but unproductive; rising from the heat of the spirit, and then presently dying away; yet surely it is better than the total absence of any thought about, or feeling after, higher things:

[1] St. Luke xix. 39, 40.

better than the unbroken reign of death, which continued forgetfulness of God, on the part of a being made to love and praise Him everlastingly, must surely mean. An hour's bright sunshine on a December day is not the summer : but it reminds us that the sun is there, and it is better than a cloud-bound sky with the temperature below freezing.

And if religious enthusiasm be kindled by the sense of association with a multitude of men who are engaged, each according to his light and strength, in praising the Perfect Being, who are we that we should object? Each man nowadays has his one narrow prescription for the spiritual improvement of his fellows ; God, Who has made us, and Who knows what we are, is more generous and more considerate.

He is not bound to times and places, to petty proprieties and rules, in His vast action upon the spirit of man, when He would draw it towards Himself. Sometimes He approaches it through the operations of reason, sometimes through the yearning of the heart after a Higher Beauty; sometimes He speaks to it in the mysteries of nature, sometimes in the solemnities of history, sometimes even through art, such as music or painting, and not unfrequently, as, in fact, on Palm Sunday, through the felt sympathies of a multitude of human beings. He has, indeed, other and more powerful agencies behind,—His own Holy and Sanctifying Spirit, the Divine and Inspired Scriptures, an organised and teaching Church, Sacraments that are channels of grace and power,—but the wind of His compassion bloweth where it listeth, and its heavenly action is beyond the scope both of our criticism and our approval.

But undoubtedly it is better to regard any such warmer feelings which God may in His mercy give us from time to time, not as ends in themselves, not as great spiritual attainments or accomplishments, but as means to an end beyond. The religious feeling which at times takes possession of multitudes of men, which raises them above their ordinary level, and makes them fancy themselves capable of acts or sacrifices which, in their cooler moments, would seem to be impossible, is like a flood-tide—to be made the most of while it lasts, but not to be counted on as lasting. Like the tide, it will assuredly recede, and, therefore, what is to be done by its aid, must be done at once. What is wanted is not merely hymns and psalms but the obedience which marks true discipleship, and the practical resolutions which give to obedience reality and shape. It is especially desirable to bear this in mind at this sacred season, when all hearts in which Christian faith is a living power are stirred to the depths by the remembrance or the contemplation of the Sufferings of the Redeemer of the world. How shall any Christian follow the solemn service which will be held in this Cathedral on Tuesday evening,[1] and not kindle at the thought of what the Eternal Son has achieved for sinners ? How shall we listen on Good Friday to the Words of Christ hanging on His Cross, and not desire to live as men who have been bought with a price,[2] even infinite in its value ? If God, in His mercy, does grant to us such thoughts and desires as these, will they not be enhanced by the knowledge that they are shared, in various degrees, by thousands at our side,—shared by millions whom we do not see with our bodily eyes, but who, throughout Christendom, are with us engaged in thankful remembrance of the Great Sacrifice? Surely the risk is, not lest we should be too richly endowed with such feelings as these ; but lest, having them, we should let them run to waste instead of turning them to account ; lest we should sing Hosanna to-day, with

[1] The service in St. Paul's Cathedral on Tuesday in Holy Week, when Bach's "Passion-Music" is rendered.   [2] 1 Cor. vi. 20.

more or less sincerity, only to cry "Crucify," by relapse into some old sin a short while hence. What is needed is resolution taken in the strength of God the Holy Spirit and after earnest prayer. Resolution to do, or to give up doing, that one thing which conscience, having its eye upon the Cross, may prescribe. If God gives us warmer feelings, let us humbly and sincerely thank Him; but let us also pray with the Psalmist, "Try me, O God, and seek the ground of my heart: prove me, and examine my thoughts: look well if there be any way of wickedness in me, and lead me in the way everlasting."[1]

[1] Ps. cxxxix. 23, 24.

SERMON XIII.

RELIGIOUS EMOTION.

St. Matt. xxi. 9.

And the multitudes that went before, and that followed, cried, saying, Hosanna to the Son of David: Blessed is He That cometh in the Name of the Lord: Hosanna in the Highest.

IN our Lord's public entrance into Jerusalem on Palm Sunday, five days before His Crucifixion, two things, among others, are especially remarkable. The first, the emotion of the multitude that welcomed Him. The second, the practical worthlessness of much of this emotion, as shown by all what followed.

I.

That which calls forth emotion in a multitude of men is first of all the consciousness of having a common object. And it is natural to ask ourselves, Why should a multitude of persons have left their homes, and have gone out to meet our Lord on His Entry into Jerusalem? If they had believed all that we Christians know to be the truth about His Work and Person, it would have been easy to account for their enthusiasm. But for them He was merely a new Prophet, with a certain reputation attaching to Him among the peasantry of a northern province. London is not generally forward to echo the judgments of Wales or Northumberland; and why the approach of the Prophet of Nazareth to the Jewish capital should have provoked a public demonstration, and have been the occasion of a great public holiday, is at first sight unintelligible.

The answer is that the appearance of a new prophet was an occurrence beyond all others grateful to the Jewish people, at least in the later times of their history. The nations of the ancient world, like those of modern times, had each of them a specific enthusiasm which was roused by the occurrence of particular events, or the appearance of a particular sort of personage. Accordingly, what the foundation of a new colony was to Carthage, or the conquest of a new province to Rome, or the completion of a masterpiece by a poet or sculptor to Athens—that and more was the appearance of a prophet, or even of a man who claimed to be so, on the soil of Palestine. For Israel was the people of Revelation, just as Carthage was the home of commercial enterprise, and Rome the seat of Empire, and Greece the nurse of art and of letters. Israel knew itself to be the people of Revelation; that was its distinctive glory among the nations of the world; and of this Revelation, which had been made not once for all at the beginning of its history, but gradually during a long sequence of centuries, in which first this and then that addition was contributed to it, the prophets were mainly, and in later times exclusively, the organs. When a prophet appeared the nation expected to learn something that it did not know before about the Will of God: about His Nature, His Attributes, His Ways; about its own destinies and prospects; about the fortunes of other nations around it. And especially when the days of its own national glory had passed, and Palestine had come to be only a province of the great Empire of Rome, the Jews fell back with more and more attachment on all that recalled their great religious past, and a new prophet received a welcome which would certainly not have been given him in the days of David or Jehoshaphat. Often indeed it happened that this public enthusiasm was grossly abused, and that the people followed some worthless adventurer until he led them to the brink of political catastrophe. But their devotion to the Baptist was a fair test of the popular temper:[1] once let it be proclaimed that "a great prophet hath risen up among us, and the Lord hath visited His people,"[2] and the heart of Israel, the depository of God's ancient Revelations, and the expectant heir of His Revelations to come, was at once touched. To look on the prophet's face, to listen to his words, men would leave their occupations and their homes; and so universal was this feeling that it was strong enough to set aside the poor opinion which then, as now, the inhabitants of a capital commonly entertained for the judgment of provincials. This was the object which brought the multitude together—the attraction which the reported appearance of a new prophet always exercised over the countrymen of Isaiah and Jeremiah—the vague hope of hearing some new utterance of the Mind of God.

The multitude thus came together in quest of a common object, and then a second source of emotion came into play, viz., the sense, which was thus roused in each individual man, that he was one of a multitude. To be a unit in a multitude, gathered together for a common purpose, stirs the heart and soul of man,—in some cases consciously and powerfully, in all cases to some extent. There are faculties and inclinations in each of us—social instincts we now call them—which are roused into active conscious self-assertion when we find ourselves surrounded by a number of our fellow-creatures. While we are alone, or living only with a few, the social instincts are more or less dormant in average men; but when a man is brought

[1] St. Matt. iii. 1-6. [2] St. Luke vii. 16.

into intimate contact with many others, assembled together for a common purpose, that which is merely personal in him falls into the background, and all that associates him with others comes to the front. We all know as an abstract truth that we are each of us members of the great human family spread throughout all climes and countries of the world; but this conviction is a very shadowy one until it is in a manner thrown into a visible and concrete form by our becoming part of a great assembly of human beings: mind thinking side by side with mind; heart throbbing side by side with heart; will resolving, struggling, nerving itself side by side with will; as though individual life had merged itself for the time being in a common life, or at least that each man in the multitude were leading two lives at one and the same time, a personal life and a corporate or social one, while of these the latter was for the moment by far the more powerful and constraining.

The emotion which is produced by a sense of belonging to a great multitude is a force which no reasonable man will underrate. In all free countries this is shown by the jealousy with which men guard the right of public meeting. Often enough the thought which is produced at a public meeting is much less entitled to real attention, much less thorough, finished, and true, than that which a solitary student works out alone in his library. But in the meeting there is the element of emotion, which more than atones for what may be defective or turbid in the thought, since it is a real source of strength. It is not only that two men are stronger than one, but each man is stronger through this fellowship with the rest; his sense of brotherhood, thus brought home to him by the presence of his fellow-men, quickens and enlarges his stock of power, whether of head or heart: he is more of a man for being thus in close contact with his brother men. This is the secret of what they call the spirit of the corps in the army; this is, in part, though not, by any means, altogether, the secret of the value of public worship. Every such assembly as that which is gathered here to-day, invests, or may invest, each person who composes it with a force which he would not have if he were alone: a great congregation of men, believing in One Lord, and hoping through His Mercy for a blessed life after death, and loving Him because He is what He is, and other men for His sake, is not merely an aggregate of praying souls, but a great productive source of spiritual sympathy. As we meet within these walls the pettier aspects of life surely fall away, and we lose ourselves in the vision of "one Body and One Spirit, even as we are called in one hope of our calling, One Lord, one faith, one baptism, One God and Father of all, Who is above all, and through all, and in all;"[1] we see before our eyes an earthly representation of that great multitude which no man could number, of all kindreds, and nations, and people, and tongues, standing before the Throne of God and of the Lamb, with palms in their hands, and singing the new song of the Life Eternal.[2] In a great congregation the fire of a sacred brotherhood passes from soul to soul: it is easy to understand how much would be lost by forsaking "the assembling of yourselves together, as the manner of some is."[3] No doubt, too, on that first Palm Sunday, the Jewish multitude, because it was a multitude, was conscious of an emotion all its own, an emotion distinct from that which was created by the purpose that had drawn it together, and from that which followed on the common act of homage to Jesus which it provoked.

To these sources of emotion—the quest of a common object, and the sense of forming part of a multitude— a third must be added: a common action. This com-

[1] Eph. iv. 4-6.   [2] Rev. vii. 9, 10.   [3] Heb. x. 25.

mon action is the product of previously existing emotion, and it reacts in greatly increasing it. And the first common action of a multitude moved by deep feeling is exclamation. It matters little who supplies the watchword: it is uttered, it is taken up, and becomes common property. When the Christians of Milan were in doubt whom to elect for their bishop, and Ambrose, a layman governor of the city, was present, simply to keep order, a little child cried out, "Ambrose is Bishop." So exalted was his character, so obvious was the fitness of the appointment, that the cry was at once echoed on all sides: "Ambrose is Bishop!" In ignorance of the real speaker, it was even said to be the suggestion of an Angel: and in spite of his sincere resistance, he was within a week ordained and consecrated Archbishop of Milan. A multitude, having vaguely before it a common purpose, and animated by that emotion which the sense of numbers of itself produces, soon finds a voice. The suggestion may, too easily, come from below. Who was it that first cried " Crucify Him!" on the day of Calvary? Who was it who suggested, at a critical moment, that the mob of Paris should march on the Tuileries? It is sometimes easy to lead, as always to follow, a multitude to do evil. For evil or for good, a multitude finds a voice; and then this voice, raised in rude but substantial harmony under the presence of a common body of feeling, reacts powerfully upon every member of that multitude. We all of us know the difference between a hymn sung by a single performer, or by a select choir, and a hymn sung in unison by four thousand people. In the latter case it is a sensible embodiment of the feeling of fellowship in a common object; and public worship is a spiritual blessing in the proportion in which it can succeed in appropriating this great power of common spiritual effort embodied in voice. The ancient Christians set great store on this. St. Ambrose compares the responses of the people, as they sang the psalms in public worship, to the breaking of the waves at regular intervals upon the sea-shore:[1] and St. Augustine has told us how much the hymns sung by St. Ambrose and the people of the Church at Milan touched his heart and drew him up to God, when he was yet some way from his conversion.[2]

So no doubt it was at our Lord's entry into Jerusalem. Perhaps one of the disciples, thronging round our Lord, gave the signal: from them it spread to the crowd around. "The multitudes that went before and that followed cried, saying, Hosanna to the Son of David: Blessed is He That cometh in the Name of the Lord: Hosanna in the Highest." It was at once a prayer and an act of praise: it was vague enough to be used by those who knew least about the new Prophet, while yet it satisfied those who knew most about Him: it expressed the twofold feeling in the minds of the multitude, who were at once delighted with a new Ambassador from above, and withal hopeful that He might brighten their national future. But as it rose upon the breeze, from the lips of the multitude who thronged around the advancing Redeemer, it must have quickened the emotion that produced it, and raised it to its highest point of intensity and fervour. Each man who joined in it felt, as we may feel, how much lies in that word of the Psalmist's, "My praise is of Thee in the great congregation."[3]

The temper of us Englishmen leads us to regard emotion with a certain distrust; and in the last century there was a school of writers who especially attacked its connection with religion. The one great object of their apprehension might have seemed to be religious enthusiasm. Religion, they said, ought to be based entirely

---

[1] St. Ambrose, *Hexaem.* iii. 9.
Confessions of St. Augustine, Book ix. §[VI.] 14. [3] Ps. xxii. 25.

upon reason: and reason is the traditional foe of enthusiasm and all its ways. An English prelate wrote a work, in which he claimed for the Church of England a superiority over Methodism on the one hand, and Roman Catholicism on the other, on the ground that while these religious systems encouraged enthusiasm, the Church of England was free from it.[1] Few good or prudent Churchmen in the present day would think that a very effective apology for the English or any other Christian Church; but it represented the temper of a cold and somewhat heartless age—a temper, from the prevalence of which the Church unhappily did not altogether escape. Strange indeed we must deem it that any Christian with the New Testament in his hands could bring himself to denounce religious fervour or emotion, or could regard it as anything but a great and precious gift of God. How can we read the Gospel accounts of the raising of Lazarus,[2] or the description in the Acts of the Apostles of St. Paul's farewell to the presbyters at Ephesus on the shore at Miletus,[3] without being conscious that the tenderest feelings of our natures are stirred, much more powerfully than our reasoning faculty? And if religion undertakes to improve man as a whole, how could she ignore the life of feeling and address herself exclusively to the life of thought? Certainly, emotion is not necessarily religious; but the best and highest use of emotion is in the service of religion, to which, indeed, it contributes some very important elements. What is it that constitutes the felt difference between hard morality and really religious conduct? The presence of emotion. What is it that makes the mental attitude of us Christians towards the truths of faith so different from that of a man of science or of letters towards the conclusions of philosophy?

---

[1] Dissertation on Enthusiasm, by Dr. Green, Bishop of Lincoln.
[2] St. John xi. 1-44.   [3] Acts xx. 17-38.

Emotion. What is it within the soul that speaks to God in true heart-felt prayer? Emotion. What is the undefinable charm which everywhere marks the active operation of religion on the human heart? Emotion. What is it that now and then visits us, we know not how or why, and for the time makes us better, nobler, truer, than our wonted selves? Viewed from without, it is emotion. Surely, brethren, we, most of us, do not live so near to Heaven that we need nothing to lift us up out of the earthly nets in which our poor spirits get so often, as it seems, hopelessly imbedded and fixed; surely we are too often bound and chained down to the life of sense and the life of habit, which is based on and intertwined with sense: and a lever that can give our hearts and minds a few hours' liberty to regain something of that air of Heaven which God created them to breathe must be a blessing. Reason, after all, is only a faculty of the soul: a royal faculty, if you will, but by no means able to do duty for the whole complex life of man in the matter of religion: and when men have attempted to base religion wholly upon reason, religion soon has shrivelled up into the proportions and likeness of a thin philosophy that has vainly endeavoured to secure the approbation of a few coteries of learned critics, at the cost of forfeiting all claim whatever to touch the heart of the mass of mankind. That which swayed the Jewish multitude as they sang Hosanna before Jesus Christ on Palm Sunday was a deep emotion; and, so far as it went, it was assuredly a great blessing—at least a great possible source of blessing —for all who took part in it.

II.

The religious value of emotion is beyond question; but the circumstances of our Lord's entry into Jerusalem appear to show that emotion by itself may not be worth much; that it requires other things as well if it is to be healthy in itself, and if it is to last. For we know that five days after there was emotion enough of a very different kind on the other side of Jerusalem; nor is it possible to doubt that it was shared in by some of those who had taken part in the Hosannas of Palm Sunday. What is it that emotion needs if it is to be retained in the service of true Religion?

1. First, then, religious emotion must centre in a definite conviction. Emotion is called out by some fact, whether it be an event or a person; but if the emotion is to last this person or event must be constantly present to the mind as real and definite. If the emotion is called out by a momentary impression, which presently becomes vague and indistinct, and then dies away, the emotion will share the fate of the impression, and will accompany it in the process of dissolution. Unless we Christians have a clear and definite idea about the Divine Person and Redeeming Work of our Lord Jesus Christ, about the power of His Precious Blood to wash away our sins, the presence of His Spirit to renew our hearts and lives, the virtue of His Sacraments to unite us to His Sacred Manhood in time and for eternity,—a few pulsations of objectless emotion will not help us long. Here is the value of the Christian Creeds: they fix in clear outline before the soul of the believer the great objects of his faith, which rouse in him movements of love and awe: they resist the tendencies of unassisted emotion to lose itself on what is vague and indistinct: they place before him God, in His Essential Threefold Nature, and in His Redeeming and Sanctifying work, and in this way they sustain the living emotion of the soul directed towards God, as revealed by Himself. The Creeds are not a series of detached propositions: they are a collection of statements which correspond to a living whole. To an un-

believer a creed only suggests the reflection : How many propositions—dogmas—for a man to believe ! To a believer, before whose soul's eye the Divine Object described in the Creeds is livingly present, a Creed suggests the reflection : How impossible to omit any one of those elements of a description which the Reality demands !

Now it is at least probable that a great many of the people who accompanied our Lord on His entry into Jerusalem had very vague ideas of what—I do not say He is, or claimed to be, but—even of what His countrymen imagined Him to be. They joined the crowd because others around them did so : they were carried away by the impulse of the moment : others cried Hosanna, and they did : others cut down branches, and they threw themselves into the spirit of the moment, and followed the example. But the day declined, and they re-entered the Holy City and returned to their homes; and little remained with them in the way of a definite impression. The emotion of Palm Sunday had passed, for this among other reasons, because it had had no very definite object; and they were ready for another emotion—of a very different character—"when the chief priests would persuade the multitude that they should ask for the release of Barabbas and destroy Jesus." [1]

2. Next, religious emotion must not be divorced from morality and conscience. It is not necessarily connected with them. In the old Pagan world some of the most emotional forms of worship—such as those which came to Rome from Syria and Egypt—were also most closely allied with culpable forms of self-indulgence. And in Christendom the transition is easy—only too easy—from ardent religious emotion to very serious transgressions of the Divine law. The fact is that the raw material of the two opposite impulses is sometimes the same : the passion

[1] St. Matt. xxvii. 20.

which when sanctified by grace pours itself out in adoration of the Eternal Beauty may easily, in its natural and selfish form, become an instrument of man's deepest degradation. Our composite nature, half-angel, half-brute, lives on the frontier of two worlds, and the impulse which may raise it to the Heaven of heavens is but a transformed and spiritualised form of the impulse that may bury it in all that is lowest and foulest on earth.

Thus from time to time the world is startled by some great misconduct on the part of persons who have shown more or less devotion to religion; and men speak as if what had happened was as wonderful as it is startling. The explanation probably is that the religion in question was all emotion, having no relation to conscience and conduct. Philip II. of Spain, and Louis XIV. of France, had their times of sincere religious emotion—though we know what they were at other times too. And many people in this country who talk of their being justified by faith, ought, if they spoke quite accurately, to speak of their being justified by transient emotion. When St. Paul teaches us that faith is the condition of our justification,[1] he means by faith not a mere movement of the intelligence, not a mere throbbing of the heart, not even an act of trust, but an adhesion of the whole inward being of man, of mind and heart, of will and of affection, to Jesus the Perfect Moral Being, Who obeyed the Divine Will even to death for love of us men. This is a very different thing from feeling "warmed up," as people speak, after attending a very exciting service, and then going home to our old habits and states of mind; a different thing from bearing branches of palm-trees before the Redeemer, and going back to Jerusalem to obey the leading Jews when they are preparing to crucify the Lord of Glory.[2]

[1] Rom. v. 1.   [2] 1 Cor. ii. 8.

There is much need for thinking of this just now, when we are entering the most solemn week in the Christian year. No man in whom the Christian sense is yet at all alive can pass through Holy Week with entire indifference; can be heedless and heartless, while Christendom is on its knees, throughout the world, before the Cross of Christ. If anything can touch a man, it is surely God's "inestimable love in the redemption of the world by our Lord Jesus Christ," which has placed within our reach "the means of grace," and which endows us with "the hope of glory:"[1] it is the long and tragic history of the Passion, with its incalculable depths of shame and pain, willingly undergone for the love of us sinners, each and all. We may be but as among those who stood at the outer edge of the crowd on Palm Sunday, yet we must have some share in the emotion which the Object before us, the thousands around us, the sacred language of the Church, so powerfully and variously suggest. It is impossible not to believe that of the thousands who here in the heart of London, during this past week, have left their engrossing occupations to listen for a few minutes to the eloquent and sincere voice that day after day has set forth with unaccustomed power the mystery and virtue of the Cross of Christ, within the walls of the Cathedral,—some have not felt an enthusiasm to which they had before been strangers, and have desired to live hereafter more purely for the glory of their Crucified Lord. How important it is that their feelings should attach themselves to definite convictions, and should take shape in some real practical effort,—in the determination to form a new habit, to renounce a bad practice, to put on in some true way the new man who after God is created in righteousness and true holiness.[2] This emotion has not, believe it, dear brethren,

---

[1] The *General Thanksgiving*; Book of Common Prayer.
[2] Eph. iv. 24.

been vouchsafed you for nothing; do not let it die away; do not part with it, only to meet it again, as one of your forgotten responsibilities in the hour of judgment.

Again, on Tuesday evening next, the particular commemoration of our Saviour's Sufferings, which has now become annual in St. Paul's, will take place;[1] and a great German genius of a past age, set forth by English skill and genius of the present day, will doubtless, as in former years, draw numbers within these walls. On these occasions music does her noblest work as the handmaid of religion; and many a man, whom sermons fail to reach, finds his spirit awed and soothed by the language of harmonies which carry him far beyond the world of sense and time. Alas! how great will be our failure to have done anything real for God's glory, if those who come here are thinking only or chiefly of the music, and little of Him whose Sacred Sufferings it is designed to recall. How poor and worthless will have been the expenditure of emotion, if it should lavish itself altogether on the artistic performance, and never cross the threshold of the outer chambers of the spiritual world! Æsthetic pleasure with a beautiful service differs altogether from the joy and satisfaction of the soul, when really in His presence to Whom all services should lead: this sort of Hosanna may always be easily and swiftly followed by "Crucify Him! crucify Him!" May our Crucified Lord enable all who are present on Tuesday evening at the "Passion-music" to do true and heartfelt honour to His sacred Sufferings: to turn any warm or tender feelings that He may graciously vouchsafe to them to some practical account; and to prepare themselves all the more carefully and reverently for the solemn hours of agony and silence on Good Friday, and for the transcendent joys of a good conscience at the Communion of Easter morning.

[1] *i.e.* The Service at which Bach's "Passion-Music" is rendered.

SERMON XIV.

THE TRAITOR-APOSTLE.

ST. MATT. xxvi. 24.

It had been good for that man if he had not been born.

PALM SUNDAY, as it brings before us our Lord's solemn entry into Jerusalem before His last Passover, suggests a great many subjects for reflection, but none more entitled to our attention than the great variety of characters who may be joining, apparently with an absolute unity of purpose, in the services or the devotions which are appropriate to a great religious occasion. The narratives of the entry into Jerusalem distinguish between the parts taken by the Disciples on the one hand, and by the general population on the other; but all co-operated to promote a common purpose—namely, the glory of the Son of David at His solemn approach to the Holy City. The conduct of the multitude has often been pointed to as an illustration of the fickleness of popular opinion; the men who to-day cried "Hosanna to the Son of David" would be shouting five days hence, "Crucify Him! crucify Him!" But the Disciples, who could claim a larger knowledge and a nearer intimacy, who thronged around their Master as His immediate attendants or bodyguard, were they altogether secure from any such infirmity or vacillation of judgment or purpose? Was there no risk lest any of them should exchange the mood of loyalty and devotion for a different attitude towards their Master when the hour of trial should come? We know, my friends, how that question must be answered. The time was not far distant when Christ's first Apostle denied Him;[1] when, at any rate for the moment, all His disciples forsook Him and fled;[2] when of the chosen twelve one only in the hour of danger stood near His Master's Cross of shame.[3] The fear of man and the fear of pain and death will account for this weakness of our Lord's first followers; but these motives would not account for a more startling failure of loyalty which was to be witnessed in the circle that immediately surrounded Him. Side by side with John, who was to stand beneath His Cross; side by side with Peter, who, after denying Him, would repent with bitter tears; side by side with Andrew and James the Greater and the Less, and Thomas and Bartholomew, and Matthew and Philip, and Simon and Jude, there was another, who with them had walked up the long steep road from Jericho, had witnessed the miracle whereby Lazarus was raised from the dead at Bethany, and who now, no doubt, waved his palm branch, and chanted his Hosanna like the rest. Still a member of the Apostolic College, still in closest intimacy with the Divine Redeemer, but already within three days of the Betrayal,—there walked and sang in that solemn procession advancing towards Jerusalem, Judas Iscariot.

"It had been good for that man if he had not been born." It has been observed that our Lord Himself says the sternest as well as the most tender things that are recorded in the Gospel. He would not bequeath to a disciple the responsibility or the odium of proclaiming truths against which human nature, conscious of its real condition, will always rebel. He did not leave it to an Apostle to announce the unrepentant sinner's doom. And He

[1] St. John xviii. 25-27. [2] St. Matt. xxvi. 56. [3] St. John xix. 26.

described the moral characteristics of men and classes and populations who came before Him during His ministry. Chorazin and Bethsaida, though on the sacred soil of Palestine, were, He said, in a worse case than the Pagan cities of Tyre and Sidon.[1] Capernaum, though exalted unto heaven, would be cast down to hell.[2] The Scribes and Pharisees, though sitting in the seat of Moses, were "fools," "hypocrites," "whited sepulchres."[3] Herod on his throne was yet a "fox."[4] But nothing that our Lord ever said of any class of men, or any one human being, approached in its severity this saying about Judas.

They were sitting, He and the Disciples, at the Paschal meal, as the twilight was deepening towards the night. They ate almost in silence; scarce a word was spoken that was not necessary to the ceremony. Suddenly He broke in on the stillness with a saying which carried dismay to the hearts of all present: "One of you shall betray Me."[5] Each, even the most sincere, must have feared lest he should be capable of committing the unparalleled sin. Each was to feel for a moment his liability to a crime of which another might be guilty. Each by his question, "Lord, is it I?"[6] implied withal his consciousness of innocence. Then our Lord proceeded to declare solemnly His approaching self-sacrifice, and the agency by which it would be brought about. He answered and said, "He that dippeth his hand with Me in the dish, the same shall betray Me. The Son of Man goeth as it is written of Him; but woe unto that man by whom the Son of Man is betrayed! it had been good for that man if he had not been born. Then Judas, which betrayed Him, answered and said, Master, is it I? He saith unto him, Thou hast said."[7]

Concerning no other human being is so stern an utter-

---

[1] St. Matt. xi. 21.   [2] Ib. 23.   [3] Ib. xxiii. 13-30.
[4] St. Luke xiii. 32.   [5] St. Matt. xxvi. 21.
[6] St. Matt. xxvi. 22.   [7] Ib. 23-25.

ance on Divine authority placed on record. It cannot be explained—against the whole drift of the passage—as though our Lord meant that it would have been good for Himself if Judas had not been born : nor yet as a proverbial saying which should not be taken too literally, since this is to mistake the profound seriousness of purpose with which our Lord used the gift of human speech. Nor does it merely predict that Judas, like such servants of God as Jeremiah or Job,[1] would in a moment of transient despondency curse the day of his birth, since Jesus Himself confirms and utters this judgment of the despairing Judas; it is the Most Merciful Himself Who says, "It were good for that man if he had not been born." As we think over the piercing words, we see how they close for ever the door of hope: since, if in some remotely distant age there were in store for Judas a restoration of his being to light and peace, beyond that restoration there would still be an eternity, and the balance of good would preponderate immeasurably on the side of having been born. It must be good for every human being to thank God for his creation,—for the opportunity of knowing and loving the Author of his existence,—unless such love and knowledge has been made, by his own act, for ever impossible.

I.

Now, first of all, observe that there are sayings about Judas which might seem to imply that his part in life was forced on him by an inexorable destiny. St. John says that Jesus knew from the beginning who should betray Him.[2] Our Lord asked the assembled Apostles: "Have not I chosen you twelve, and one of you is a devil ?"[3] In His great Intercession, He thus addresses the Father:

[1] Jer. xx. 14; Job iii. 3. [2] St. John vi. 64. [3] Ib. 70.

"Those that Thou gavest Me I have kept; and none of them is lost, save the son of perdition."[1] And at the election of Matthias, St. Peter points to the destiny of Judas as marked out in prophecy: "His bishoprick let another take:"[2] and he speaks of Judas as going to his "own place."[3] This and other language of the kind has been understood to represent Judas as unable to avoid his part as the Betrayer: and the sympathy and compassion which is thus created for him is likely to blind us to a true view of his unhappy career.

The truth is that at different times the Bible looks at human lives from two very different and, indeed, opposite points of view. Sometimes it regards men merely as factors in the Divine plan for governing the world—for bringing about results determined on by the Divine Wisdom; and when this is the case, it speaks of them as though they had no personal choice or control of their destiny, and were only counters or instruments in the Hand of the Mighty Ruler of the Universe. At other times Holy Scripture regards men as free agents, endowed with a choice between truth and error, between right and wrong, between a higher and a lower line of conduct: and then it enables us to trace the connection between the use they make of their opportunities and their final destiny. Both ways of looking at life are of course strictly accurate. On the one hand, it belongs to the sovereignty of the Almighty and Eternal Being, that we, His creatures, should be but tools in His Hands: on the other, it befits His Justice that no moral being, on probation, should suffer eternal loss save through his own act and choice. The language of Scripture about Pharaoh illustrates the two points of view. At one time we are told that the Lord hardened Pharaoh's heart,[4] that he would

---

[1] St. John xvii. 12.   [2] Acts i. 20.
[3] Acts i. 25.   [4] Exod. ix. 12; x. 20.

not let the Children of Israel go; at another, that Pharaoh hardened his own heart.[1] The same fact is looked at, first from the point of view of what was needed in order to bring about the deliverance of Israel; and next from the point of view of Pharaoh's personal responsibility. St. Paul stands at one point of view in the ninth chapter of his Epistle to the Romans, and at another in the twelfth. It is no doubt difficult, if not impossible, with our present limited range of knowledge, to reconcile the Divine Sovereignty in the moral world with the moral freedom of each individual man. Some of the great mistakes in Christian theology are due to an impatience of this difficulty. Calvin would sacrifice man's freedom to the Sovereignty of God; Arminius would sacrifice God's Sovereignty to the assertion of man's freedom. We cannot hope here to discover the formula which combines the two parallel lines of truth, which meet somewhere in the Infinite beyond our point of vision: but we must hold fast to each separately, in spite of the apparent contradiction. If our Lord, looking down upon our life with His Divine Intelligence, speaks of Judas, once and again, as an instrument whereby the Redemption of the world was to be worked out, the Gospel history also supplies us with materials which go to show that Judas had his freedom of choice, his opportunities, his warnings, and that he became the Betrayer because he chose to do so.

II.

Secondly, Judas's career illustrates the power of a single passion to enwrap, enchain, possess, degrade, a man's whole character.

The most Christian poet of our day contrasts the bliss

[1] Exod. viii. 15, 32.

of the Mother of the Redeemer with the sad lot of the mother of Judas—

> " Sure as to Blessed Mary come
> The Saints' and Martyrs' host,
>
> To own, with many a thankful strain,
> The channel of undying bliss,
> The bosom where the Lord hath lain,
> The hand that held by His ;
> Sure as her form for evermore
> The glory and the joy shall wear,
> That robed her, bending to adore
> The Babe her chaste womb bare ;—
>
> So surely throes unblest have been,
> And cradles where no kindly star
> Look'd down,—no Angel's eye serene
> To gleam through years afar."

Then he tells how

> " Christ's Mother mild
> Upon that bosom pitying thought,
> Where Judas lay, a harmless child,
> By gold as yet unbought."[1]

Judas, we must suppose, had his good points, or he would never have become, by his own act, a disciple of our Lord Jesus Christ. He was not in the position of those of us who are born of Christian parents, and are by Baptism made members of Christ in their infancy, without being consulted. He chose to follow our Lord, when to follow Him implied no gain or credit, and at least some risk of unpopularity or danger. This would seem to show that he must have had some eye for, or capacity of, understanding excellence; that he must have had some pleasure in associating with the good; that he cannot, at any rate at one time in his life, have been wanting in moral courage, self-denial, and a spirit of enterprise for public religious objects.

Judas had one vice or passion—the love of money, carried to a point which filled his thoughts and controlled the

[1] *Lyra Innocentium*, ii. 13.

action of his will. When this propensity first showed itself we do not know: the germ of it may have been already lodged in his soul when he left his home to follow our Lord Jesus Christ. Certainly he had at first no opportunities for indulging it. Those great operations of modern finance, by which thousands, or even millions of money are transferred from hand to hand, or from one great firm to another, never, it need not be said, flitted before the imagination of this Galilæan peasant; nay, when he first became an Apostle, the rules under which the Twelve set to work forbade their providing gold or silver or brass in their purses, or scrip for their journey.[1] At a somewhat later period, when our Lord was joined by Joanna the wife of Chuza, Herod's steward, Susanna, and others, who ministered to Him of their substance,[2] a common fund would seem to have been formed, and, either because he was thought to have natural aptitudes for the work, or because he desired it, Judas became the treasurer; he had the bag.[3] That bag contained, probably, at most a few of the small copper coins that were struck by the Roman procurators or by the Herods. But the magnitude of any passion in the human soul is altogether independent of the limits of its opportunity for indulgence. Tyranny is as possible in a cottage as on an Eastern throne; though it may have to content itself with more restricted gratification. Envy, pride, sensuality, maliciousness, though they may be gratified on a vast area, and with terrific results to millions, or within the narrowest limits of a very humble lot, are, as passions, in the one case what they are in the other—powers that overshadow and gradually absorb all else in the soul, and give it throughout the impress and colour of their own malignity. Just as there are bodily diseases, which, at first unobtrusive and unnoticed, and capable of being extirpated if taken

[1] St. Matt. x. 9, 10. [2] St. Luke viii. 3. [3] St. John xii. 6.

in time, will spread and grow until first one and then another limb or organ is weakened or infected by them, so that at last the whole body is but a habitation for the disease which is hurrying it to the grave; so in the moral world one unresisted propensity to known wrong may in time acquire a tyrannical ascendency that will make almost any crime possible in order to gratify it.

It is a neglect of this truth—a truth which may be verified by a very little observation of human nature—that has led some modern writers to attempt a revision of the account of the character of Judas which is set before us in Holy Scripture. They think that that account does not explain so tremendous a fall: that the real reasons for it must have been graver, or more numerous, or more complex; that it was profound insincerity from the first; or envy of the moral superiority of Jesus; or resentment secretly cherished for some warning, or rebuke, or fancied neglect; or even a seeming attachment to the Jewish priesthood, to the Scribes and Pharisees, to the orders of men who were prominent in the old religious life of the country. If it was so, it must be a matter of conjecture: Holy Scripture does not say so. If it was so, we may be sure that the ruling passion gradually enlisted these other motives; drew them up into and assimilated them with itself, like the raw levies of subject states, which a conqueror incorporates with his own disciplined forces. Judas was at bottom, and before all, a man who cared for money more than he cared for conscience, or for virtue, or for God; and it was this fatal propensity which, with or without other contributing causes, but at any rate in the first instance, determined his ruin.

We see this motive in full energy when Mary anointed our Lord's Feet at Bethany. Judas could see in her action no ray of the love which made it so beautiful. He had only one thought,—the money's worth of the box of ointment.

It might have been sold, he said, for three hundred silver pence and given to the poor.[1] Covetousness will often give itself the airs of a far-sighted philanthropy, which protests against the waste of money on what it describes as mere sentiment. Our Lord did not note the fact that Judas was dishonest, and would have had the price of the ointment in his keeping had it been sold. He only observed that Judas would have other opportunities for befriending the poor, and that Mary had used her one opportunity of doing honour to His Burial by anticipation. But Judas understood the rebuke; and no doubt it quickened the determination he had already formed. If he could not have the three hundred silver denarii, he at least might have thirty shekels, about one-fifth of it; and his revenge for the scene at Bethany into the bargain.

III.

Thirdly, the history of Judas shows us that great religious privileges do not of themselves secure any man against utter spiritual ruin. It would, of course, be ingratitude to God to deny that such privileges may and should further our highest interests. But religious privileges only do their intended work when they are responded to on our part by the dispositions which can appropriate and make the most of them; by sincerity of purpose, by a humble, that is to say a true, estimate of self, by sorrow for past sin, by watchfulness, by an especial care not to let any one acquire that preponderant and supreme place in the soul which may render all helps to holiness useless, and may forfeit all prospect of eternal peace.

What religious opportunities could be greater than those which were enjoyed by Judas Iscariot? He was one of those twelve men who were most closely associated

[1] St. John xii. 5.

with the Redeemer of the world during His Ministry. He was admitted to an intimacy which was denied to those of our Lord's first-cousins, "brethren," as they are called,[1] who were not already Apostles; nay, which, when His Ministry had once begun, was denied to His Blessed Mother. Judas shared a Companionship compared with which the purest and noblest intimacies that this earth has known were worthless and degrading. He heard the very Words, he witnessed the very Works, which are recorded in the Gospels. He heard and witnessed many more which have not been recorded. He received upon his understanding and his memory, if not within his heart, the impress of that one incomparable Life revealing itself insensibly, incessantly, by a thousand rays of Charity and Wisdom playing all around it.

How often may we have heard men say, "If I had not to live among the degenerate and inconsistent Christians whom I see around me, if I had lived eighteen hundred years ago with Jesus of Nazareth in His own Galilee, I should be a better man than I am." But is it more certain that this would be so than that the brethren of Dives, who heard not Moses and the prophets, would have been persuaded by one rising from the dead?[2] If anything could have roused a man to a sense of moral danger we might think that the teaching of Jesus Christ, to which Judas listened, would have done so. Judas must have heard our Lord's warnings about the guilt of unfaithfulness in the "unrighteous mammon."[3] Judas would have listened to the Parable of the Sower, and the explanation how the cares of this world, and the deceitfulness of riches, choke the Word of Truth in the soil of the soul.[4] Judas may well have thought that the saying, "Ye cannot serve God and mammon;"[5] or the proverb, "It is easier for a camel to go

[1] St. Matt. xii. 47; xiii. 55.   [2] St. Luke xvi. 31.
[3] St. Luke xvi. 11.   [4] St. Matt. xiii. 1-22.   [5] Ib. vi. 24.

through the eye of a needle than for a rich man to enter into the kingdom of heaven,"[1] were meant for him. Judas was even one of those who asked the question with regard to this proverb, "Who then can be saved?"[2] But the very greatest religious advantages do not compel the understanding to be sincere, or the conscience to be sensitive, or the affections to be warm and quick, or the will to be straightforward and vigorous. Judas lived in the closest intimacy with Jesus; but this intimate relation with Jesus did not save Judas from a crime compared with which that of the Jewish rabble, and the Roman soldiers, and Pontius Pilate, and the Chief Priests and Pharisees, was venial :—it did not save him from becoming the betrayer.

Surely this is a most serious consideration for those who are already, by God's great goodness and mercy, privileged to know much of religious truth, and to have much to do with the duties and privileges that more especially belong to Religion. Especially, as I would remind myself, does it concern us of the clergy, who are necessarily associated more closely than other men with the works, the advantages, and the truths that belong to Religion; who have to use the language of Religion; and who may too easily assume that this of itself implies an immunity from moral and spiritual disaster, that is by no means assured to us. Who does not know, or may not easily discover, that this necessary familiarity with holy things has dangers which are peculiarly its own; that it may easily foster a mechanical and formal temper which robs language of its sincerity, and prayer of its power and efficacy, and a man's inner life of the strong and pure motives that alone ennoble it; that, unless there be great watchfulness over what is going on within, as well as care to do and say sincerely what has to be said and done in

[1] St. Matt. xix. 24. [2] Ib. 25.

the way of outward duty, almost any measure of spiritual ruin is only too possible? And what is true of clergymen is true of all who have knowledge of and contact with the things of Religion. To be close to Jesus Christ may be to be as St. John; but it may be to be as Judas. Let us, one and all, not be high-minded, but fear.[1]

If any one, whose business it may have been to study the infidel literature of our day, should set himself to inquire whence have come the most intelligently bitter and deadly thrusts at the power and work of our Divine Master, he will not, I think, find that they proceed from the layman, who has perhaps known nothing of religion in his early years, and has been kept throughout life by a thick integument of prejudice from making any real acquaintance with it in his later life. No! rather will they be found to come from men who have been trained, or even cradled, amid sacred associations: from the teacher in a Christian school; from the seminarist who was looking forward to Ordination; from the Divinity student who was destined to occupy, or who already occupied, a professor's chair; from the companions and associates of those who have had most to do with kindling among their contemporaries the sacred flame of religious conviction.

In order to betray religion effectively, a man must have been, in some sense, intrusted with it: he must have explored and shared its sacred secrets; he must not only have studied it from afar; he must have taken it to his heart. Everybody does not know enough to be a Judas —enough to pierce religion in the part which, to the common apprehension, shall seem to be most vulnerable, or where the sensitiveness of Christian faith will be most deeply pained. Every one does not know enough to be sure where Jesus will be found after dark,—under the

[1] Rom. xi. 20.

olive-trees in the Garden; enough to lead a rude company of followers, all of them indignant, but most of them uninformed, down across the steep valley of Jehoshaphat, and up again to the gate of Gethsemane, and then to go straight to the Object of their search, without hesitation or error, and utter the "Hail, Master"[1] which is to show them their intended Victim.

Observe, too, in the betrayal of our Lord, the survival of religious habit when the convictions and feelings which make Religion real have passed away. Judas betrayed the Son of Man with a kiss.[2] The kiss was a customary expression of mingled affection and reverence on the part of the disciples when meeting their Master.

To suppose that Judas deliberately selected an action which was as remote as possible from his true feelings is an unnecessary supposition. It is more true to human nature to suppose that he endeavoured to appease whatever there may have been in the way of lingering protest in his conscience, by an act of formal reverence, that was dictated to him by long habit, and that served to veil from himself the full enormity of his crime at the moment of his committing it. In like manner, brigands in the south of Europe have been known to accompany deeds of theft, and even murder, with profuse ejaculations, whether of piety or superstition: and cases have been known further north of picking pockets when the thief and his victim were kneeling or sitting side by side in a Church or meeting-house. In these instances Religion may be employed, not simply as a blind to an immoral act, but as a salve to a protesting conscience; the passing thrill of emotion seems to do something towards reducing the magnitude of the crime which accompanies it.

The kiss of Judas! It has become a proverb for all those procedures whereby, under the semblance of outward

[1] St. Matt. xxvi. 49.   [2] St. Luke xxii. 48.

deference for Religion, or of devotion to its interests, its substance and reality are sacrificed or betrayed. The general conscience of mankind is still too alive to the importance of basing human life on sanctions that are drawn from a higher world, to welcome, or even to permit, attacks upon all Religion, on the ground of avowed hostility to it. Accordingly, its opponents generally assume some garb of discipleship: they commonly profess an interest in it to which its ordinary professors or defenders are strangers: if they attack its doctrine, they are only anxious to remove what they conceive to be excrescences, and to restore in its purity some creed which they attribute to the earliest times: if they assail its discipline, it is in the interests of some theory of personal liberty which they would have us believe is essentially bound up with real piety; if they would confiscate its material revenues to some secular purposes, they assure us that what they really have at heart is the restoration of the Church to a condition which shall satisfy their ideal of apostolical poverty.

A religious reason is generally produced for the abandonment of any interest, truth, or duty of religion. Eternal Punishment is set aside out of anxiety to assert God's Mercy: the Pardon of penitent sinners from devotion to His strict Justice: Sacraments are depreciated under cover of our profession of lofty spirituality: practical energy is decried for the honour of some doctrine, certainly not St. Paul's, of Justification by Faith. Something of the nature of a kiss is required by public opinion in Christendom in order to disguise the process of delivering Jesus to His would-be murderers: so that even the most extreme forms of infidelity find it necessary to preface an assault upon fundamental truth, of vital import to the very heart and life of religion, by an expression of concern for a very transcendental essence of religion which is to survive, and indeed to profit by, the rejection of the particular truth which is being assailed.

But this affectation of interest in religion on the part of its opponents belongs only to particular phases of public opinion. The professed friends of Jesus are always in danger of betraying Him. The Scribes and Pharisees, the Roman soldiers, Pilate and Herod, could apprehend, insult, torture, condemn, crucify our Lord; but they could not betray Him. For this it was necessary to be more or less in His confidence. We Christians can do Him a more deadly injury than can any who know Him not, and have no part in Him.

Let us put each before himself the misery that it will be if He, Who made us for Himself, and Who redeemed us and sanctified us, that we might be His in time and in Eternity, should pronounce any of us, for such a reason as this, to be one who had better not have been born. Let us reflect that it is not impossible for us to incur the sentence which was uttered over the fallen Apostle by the Most Merciful. We may be nearer acting the traitor's part than, in our security, we think: the outward signs of the gravest effects in the spiritual world are, like the kiss of Judas, often insignificant enough: a word, a smile, a slight act performed or omitted, even a shrug of the shoulders, may leave on another spirit an impression that will last throughout Eternity. And if we would escape this misery let us do one thing,—aim at, long for, pray for, a single aim in the service of God. St. Bernard used often to ask himself the question which our Lord put to Judas, "Friend, wherefore art thou come?" Why hast thou been created and placed in this world at all? why hast thou been made a member of Christ in Baptism? why hast thou been led by Providence to this or that state of life? Art thou here to do thy own will; to live without obeying any above thee; or wouldst thou indeed serve God, and by labour and suffering prepare for His Everlasting Presence? " Friend, wherefore art thou come?"[1] If we would sincerely press that question home, how different might be the aim and the perfectness of our work throughout each day; secular occupation, intercourse with others, prayers public and private, Communions,—all would receive a new elevation from the dread lest, through vanity, or insincerity, or worse, we should after all have our part with the traitor.

And if we will often ask ourselves this question, it will make and keep us watchful over what is going on within our souls. Where this watchfulness is lacking, vices may spring up, and grow unobservedly, until they have eaten out love, moral force, spiritual beauty; leaving only the external semblance of what once was life, and biding their time for the occasion which, by one fatal crime, shall discover to the world and to the conscience itself the dread reality of an utterly perverse and apostate will. Nobody ever became very bad indeed all at once; and to grapple with tendencies to evil before they have had time to acquire the strength which can enlist the passions in their service, and make a home and empire within the soul, is indeed the part of Christian prudence. Let these words of our Redeemer, which fell to no purpose on the ear of Judas, sink deep into our souls; lest for us too His Precious Blood should have been shed in vain. "Try me, O God, and seek the ground of my heart: prove me, and examine my thoughts. Look well if there be any way of wickedness in me; and lead me in the way everlasting."[2]

[1] St. Matt. xxvi. 50. [2] Ps. cxxxix. 23, 24.

SERMON XV.

THE ECONOMY OF RELIGIOUS ART.

St. Matt. xxvi. 8, 9, 10.

But when His disciples saw it, they had indignation, saying, To what purpose is this waste? For this ointment might have been sold for much, and given to the poor. When Jesus understood it, He said unto them, Why trouble ye the woman? for she hath wrought a good work upon Me.

IT was on the Saturday before our Lord's Death that He was anointed at Bethany. He came to Bethany on the Friday evening, that He might spend a quiet Sabbath-day there, before making His entry into Jerusalem on what we now call Palm Sunday—that is, to-day,—and meeting all that was to follow. He rested at the house of Simon, a leper, it is probable, whom He had Himself healed, and possibly, although this is far from certain, related to the family of Lazarus; but whether as their father, or as the husband of Martha, it is impossible to determine. When He came, the love and devotion of those villagers who were His disciples led them to welcome Him with a public entertainment; it is plain from the literal force of the text that He was present in the house of Simon, as a Guest among other guests. There He reclined between the two trophies of His power: on this side was Lazarus, silent, reserved, self-involved, as became one who had passed the portals of the grave, and had seen sights at which the living can only guess; and on that side was Simon, who, by His special grace and mercy, had escaped from the terrible scourge of leprosy. There He reclined; and Martha, no doubt, as in her own home, would have waited on all the guests, but especially on Him : but where was Mary ? She was absent when the Feast began; but on a sudden she appears: St. John names her;[1] St. Matthew and St. Mark call her simply "a woman,"[2] that they may concentrate the attention of their readers, not upon who she is, but upon what she does. She enters with a box or vessel, worked in calcareous spar or alabaster, and containing the ointment known to the ancient world as *nard*, the most celebrated, probably, of ancient scented ointments, and as such alluded to, where we should expect the allusion, in the Song of Solomon.[3] She "brake the box," says St. Mark;[4] that is, she broke the narrow neck of the vessel, or in some way removed the seal which prevented the perfume from evaporating; and then she poured the contents of the jar or box first upon the Head, and then, St. John tells us, on the Feet,[5] of Jesus. To anoint the head and clothes on festive occasions, however little in keeping with modern manners, was the custom of the ancient world,—Roman, Greek, Egyptian. In the tombs of Egypt there may be seen to this day paintings which represent slaves anointing guests as they arrive at the house of their entertainers; and alabaster jars have been found in these mansions of the dead, retaining traces of the ointment which once had filled them.

So Naomi desires her daughter-in-law Ruth to anoint herself, by way of getting ready for Boaz;[6] and Solomon bids a man, in his joy of heart, let his garments be always white, and let his head lack no ointment;[7] and when he says further that a good name is better than precious ointment,[8] he says a great deal for a good name, because

---

[1] St. John xii. 3.   [2] St. Matt. xxvi. 7; St. Mark xiv. 3.
[3] Song of Sol. i. 3, 12.   [4] St. Mark xiv. 3.   [5] St. John xii. 3.
[6] Ruth iii. 3.   [7] Eccl. ix. 8.   [8] *Ib.* vii. 1.

the use of such ointment was a first requisite of Jewish respectability. There was nothing extraordinary, then, in the mark of respect shown to our Lord by pouring ointment on His Head; but St. John says that Mary anointed the Feet as well as the Head of Jesus. This meant something more intense, more passionate, than an act of conventional welcome; and now that the box was opened, and the scent, as St. John notes, filled the whole house,[1] it was impossible not to be sensible of its delicacy and richness. If the act had been a common act; if the ointment had been common ointment, the incident might have passed without notice; but as it was, there were ill-natured eyes looking on across the table, and unfriendly criticism was at work, and pretty sure to make itself heard.

I.

My brethren, it is to the observations which were made on this act of Mary, and to the way in which our Lord treated the critics, that I wish to direct your attention this afternoon.

1. First of all, what was the criticism? The act of Mary, it was said, was a wasteful act. "To what purpose is this waste?"—or, as it might be rendered, this destruction?—"for this ointment might have been sold for much, and given to the poor." Or, as St. Mark and St. John report the words: "The ointment might have been sold for three hundred Roman silver pence or more"—the denarius was the current silver coin throughout the Roman Empire—"and given to the poor."[2] The point of the criticism was that there had been an outlay of valuable material for no practical purpose; that there had been a culpable indulgence of mere feeling, mere sentiment, when what there was to give ought to have been given to the cause of human want and human suffering. There

[1] St. John xii. 3.   [2] St. Mark xiv. 5; St. John xii. 5.

was a very poor population at this date in and about Jerusalem, to which the speaker would have been understood to allude. No doubt the criticism was uttered in a sharp, harsh voice, designed to make Mary thoroughly uncomfortable at what she had just been doing, and by provoking our Lord's attention, to get Him, as eminently a friend of the very poor, to condemn her too.

2. Next, who were the critics? St. Mark, for reasons of his own, does not care to name the speakers: some who were there, is all that we learn from him. St. Matthew gives us a nearer view; he tells us that the speakers were disciples: "When His disciples saw it, they had indignation, saying, To what purpose is this waste?" St. John brings us into the very scene itself. Everything of the kind begins with one person, and is taken up by others. And we should probably be less ready to repeat the ill-natured stories which go floating about the world, and growing larger and more malicious as they float on, if we only knew the weak or wicked source from which in many cases they originally spring. Nothing is more infectious than ill-nature; generally speaking, a very few people supply the world with the raw material on which it works.

Who began to criticise the act of Mary? St. John tells us that it was "Judas Iscariot, Simon's son, which should betray Him."[1] Judas was the first speaker; the other disciples, overawed by a clever sneer and a strong will, assented,—they assented, at any rate, by a low murmur of approval, or by their looks, or by a silence which under the circumstances could not be mistaken. Practically, then, whoever spoke or did not speak, the disciples present were all of them, in different degrees, the critics.

3. Thirdly, what was the real motive of the criticism on the act of Mary? Now, as regards Judas, St. John is very explicit: "This he said, not that he cared for the

[1] St. John xii. 4.

poor, but because he was a thief, and had the bag, and bare what was put therein."[1] Judas was treasurer of the common fund of alms, out of which our Lord and His immediate followers supported themselves; and St. John, who had every means of knowing the truth, from his intimacy with Jesus, says plainly that Judas was dishonest, and used the common fund for his own purposes. It has been suggested that the common purse was empty at this time, from whatever cause. Judas was anyhow annoyed at what he regarded as the withdrawal of three hundred silver coins from a fund on which he was accustomed to draw for private purposes. But, like other dishonest or sinful people, he felt that it was prudent to affect a respectable motive; so, for the time being, he set up for a large-hearted philanthropist, who had a particular concern for the sufferings of the poor, and it was in this capacity that he led the chorus of complaint at what had been done by Mary, in anointing the Feet and the Head of our Lord Jesus Christ with so very costly an ointment.

The motives of the disciples who agreed with Judas would have been different; there is not the slightest reason for suspecting them of insincerity. They were guilty—if that term may be used—of a want of moral courage, or of an error in judgment. Of a want of moral courage, if, as I suggested, Judas overawed them by the sheer force of bitter and noisy vehemence, and they agreed with him, in order to avoid a disturbance, just as easy good-natured people, who have not yet got any very firm hold on principle, will always do under such circumstances. Of an error in judgment, if, not yet knowing the real character of Judas, and thinking that there was something in what he said, after all, which deserved attention, they begged, with respectful deference, that an act of too lavish ex-

[1] St. John xii. 6.

penditure might be disowned by their Master, and the person responsible for it rebuked.

They probably were entirely persuaded that to pour this very costly preparation upon His Head, and even upon his Feet, was to be guilty of an unpardonable extravagance. It might have been turned into bread for the starving poor; and when they said so they thought, no doubt, that they were saying what He, their Master, under ordinary circumstances, might be expected to say Himself. Was He not notoriously the friend, the associate, the champion of the poor? Was He not the enemy and the denouncer of selfish luxury, of subtle self-pleasing, of the sacrifice of duty to sentiment, of the sacrifice of moral obligations to social or religious or conventional form? Whatever led Him to be silent now they at least would speak out, in the firm belief that their view was a sensible one. Criticism of this kind is very plausible; it may seem at first sight irresistible, but it is false.

It was set aside very summarily indeed by Jesus, when they appealed to Him to sanction it. He did not balance between Mary and her critics; He did not admit that there was something in what they said, and that Mary's zeal had outrun her discretion. He placed Himself between her and the disciples; His first care is to make her cause utterly His own. He is wounded in the wounded Mary. He is troubled in her perplexity. "Why trouble ye the woman? she hath wrought a good work on Me." He will not make any admission in favour of her judges, while He acknowledges her act in terms which He never applied to any other human action during the days of His flesh. If her act was not wrong, it would at least have appeared to Mary's critics to be insignificant; but Jesus has deigned to confer on it an immortality of glory, unlike any other mentioned in the Gospels—an immortality for which statesmen and warriors and authors have sighed in vain. "Verily I say unto you, Wheresoever this Gospel shall be preached throughout the whole world, there shall also this deed, that this woman hath done, be told for a memorial of her."[1]

II.

Why does our Lord speak of Mary's act in terms like these? He Himself tells us: "She hath wrought a good work on Me." Why, we again ask, was the work good? He tells us that it was good for two reasons.

1. It was good, first of all, as being a work of faith. The guests at the feast of Bethany, most of them, notwithstanding the recent miracle which had summoned Lazarus from his grave to a seat at that very table, were living as most men live: they were living in the present, without a thought of the future; they were living in the visible, without a thought of the unseen. Mary looked higher than the world of sense; deeper into the future than the passing hour. She knew what Jesus had said about His Personal claims to be before Abraham,[2] to be One with the Father;[3] and she took Him at His word. She knew that He had foretold His Death,[4] and Burial,[5] and Resurrection;[6] and she took Him at His word. As He sat at that board, eating and talking like every one else, it was not every soul that could set aside what met the eye of sense and discern the reality; not every one who could see that there was that beneath the form of the Prophet of Nazareth which is worthy of the most passionate homage of the soul; not every one who would reflect that ere many days had passed, that very Form would be exposed upon a Cross to the gaze of a brutal multitude, while Life ebbed slowly away amid overwhelming agony and shame. Mary did see this. "In that she poured the ointment on My

[1] St. Matt. xxvi. 13.   [2] St. John viii. 58.   [3] Ib. x. 30.
[4] St. Mark x. 32-34.   [5] St. Matt. xii. 40.   [6] Ib. xx. 19.

Body, she did it for My Burial." " My Burial ! " How the words must have jarred upon the ears of the company; almost as much as would an allusion to death in a speech at a great City dinner. What an irony there is in the contrast between this solemn allusion and the festive scene around! There they were reclining at the board, rejoicing at the restoration of their friend Lazarus; and lo ! the acknowledged Lord of Life, the Raiser of Lazarus from the grave, is discussing the proprieties of His own Funeral. Well may they have wondered. Mary knew that all was natural and in order. "*My* Burial!" Does Jesus read into the act of Mary a deeper meaning than she had made plain to herself, or is He assisting her to recognise her motives, her real motives, indistinctly realised though fully acted on? Probably the latter is the true account. If in the Judgment Hall and on the Cross the Messiah was to be before the eyes of men as a worm, and no man, a scorn of men, and the outcast of the people,[1] He was, Isaiah had foretold, to be with the rich in His Death.[2] Nothing that earth could yield would be too precious to anoint, after the manner of the ancient world, that Sacred, that Loved Body of Jesus; and if Mary could not be near Him then, she would anticipate the dreadful moment while yet she might; she would see in Him, though He was still among His friends, the dying Crucified, and she would lavish on Him her very best. " In that she hath poured this ointment on My Body, she did it for My Burial."

2. Mary's act was good, our Lord says, for a second reason. It made the most of an opportunity which would not recur. The disciples, following the lead of Judas, pleaded the claims—the sacred claims—of the poor against the act of Mary. Our Lord glanced at the promise in Deuteronomy that the poor should not perish

[1] Ps. xxii. 6. [2] Isa. liii. 9.

out of the land:[1] "Ye have the poor always with you." Certainly He does not deny their claim,—He Who had said to the rich young man, "Sell what thou hast, and give to the poor, and thou shalt have treasure in heaven, and come, follow Me,"[2]—He Who on His Judgment-Throne makes deeds of mercy done to the poor deeds done to Himself—forgetfulness of the poor forgetfulness of Himself.[3] But He does say, "Do not plead a duty which is always pressing, and which can always be discharged, against the claims of an extraordinary demand upon faith and love." "Ye have the poor always with you, but Me ye have not always." Once only would Jesus die; once only could He be prepared by loving hands for Burial; once only would He sit at that feast in Bethany, in that solemn, awful stillness which befitted the near approach of the storm when sin and hate were to do their worst upon Him—that faith and love might claim their rights and prepare for the end. It was Mary's happiness that she knew the preciousness of the moment; that she made the most of it.

3. Our Lord gives no other reasons than these, and they will be sufficient for Christians, as coming from the King of the moral world. But a utilitarian age will still ask a further question: it will ask how an action of this particular form could be thus in itself a good work from a spiritual and religious point of view, could be other than a wasteful expenditure? If Mary had saved her ointment, but had said in her enthusiasm that she believed in the Divinity of Jesus, that she anticipated and was preparing for His approaching Death, would not this have been enough? Might not the same amount of good have been done, and the price of the ointment given to the poor at the same time? Was it not really waste? Waste is, of course, a relative term. Before we know

[1] Deut. xv. 11.   [2] St. Matt. xix. 21.   [3] Ib. xxv. 36-45.

whether a particular action involves waste, we must know what the agent thinks is best worth aiming at. Those who are engaged in great enterprises generally appear wasteful to those who confine themselves to small ones. Those who think only of sensual enjoyment cannot understand the sacrifices which men will make for intellectual objects; they who are happy in a private station cannot enter into the willingness of public men to give time and money for unremunerative objects, as they seem; and in the same way, the worldly cannot understand the proceedings of the earnest believer; and the cold or apathetic in religion have no key to the meaning of loving devotion. Men live in worlds of thought and effort so different, that the life of one is as unintelligible to the mind of another as the proceedings of a bird would be to an observant fish; and this being so, waste is plainly a term which is used by hardly any two people in the same sense. For Mary, Judas's hoard was wasted; just as Judas complained of the waste of Mary's ointment. But was Mary's act really wasteful? When our Lord commended it, was He commending a pointless form, involving a lavish outlay? Look closer, and you will see that Mary illustrates a great law of the moral and spiritual world; namely, that truth and goodness are largely promoted among men by indirect means. We see this in God's Providence, in His making a way for religion by the advance of civilisation. Civilisation, as we all know, is not Religion; it is human life organised and embellished in the best way, and with a view to the wellbeing, here in this world, of the greatest number. But civilisation is frequently a pioneer or a fellow-traveller with Religion; civilisation needs Religion for its own purposes in order to get motives strong enough to hold and make good the ground which it has won from animalised savage life; and Religion, on the other hand, is under obligations to civilisation, to the arts and the knowledge which it brings, and which are all of them helpful to the propagation of the Faith. And thus it happens sometimes, though not always, that the attention of men or of races is won for Religion by the march of civilisation; civilisation is thus, while it seems to exist for its own sake—it is, I say, as it were, in the Hand of Providence, the box of precious ointment which is poured on the Head and the Feet of Jesus. We men are impatient at the process sometimes; we do not see the connection between the two things; we wish Jesus to be honoured and acknowledged without wasting the labour of years, perhaps of centuries, in the slow travail of social reconstructions, or of material and intellectual progress. We do not see why its railroads, and its schools, and its new courts of judicature, and its press, and its inheritance of a new world of ideas, which are European, no doubt, but not religious, should precede the conversion of India to the Faith of Jesus Christ. We think, perhaps, that if we could revise the action of God's providence it would be different; we should not allow this waste of energy upon that which has no traceable connection with the other world. We have not yet learnt the value of indirect witness or indirect services to truth; Mary, with her precious ointment, was really doing the same work as St. Paul preaching on the Areopagus at Athens.[1] But it takes time and thought to see this.

We may see the same law in Education. If you teach a child a truth or a duty directly; if you say, "This is true," "That is right," the child may or may not learn the lesson; it will depend upon his confidence in or love for the teacher, upon his docility of temper, upon his power of being attentive and humble at the same time. But the child is often best taught by an act which only makes him think, which is unintelligible to him, and excites his

[1] Acts xvii. 22-31.

curiosity, perhaps his indignation, till he has found out the true reason for it. He sees something quite out of the way, and, as he thinks, extravagant; the precious ointment is poured upon the Head of Jesus and upon the Feet of Jesus too, and the child wants to know why. He gets his answer, and the consequence is that he learns his lesson much more surely than if it was taught him in a direct way. For his mind is active and not passive in the process; he goes out to find truth instead of having it pressed on him. His reason, as well as his imagination, is reached, and his memory is tenacious of that which had excited his surprise when first he witnessed it.

The same principle will explain the use which the Church of Christ, ay, and the Bible, have made of art. Art is not religion: it may be profoundly anti-religious or irreligious; but it may also be a missionary and an apostle. Take poetry,—the first and highest of the arts. How much of the Bible is poetry! No poetry that ever was written is more beautiful, as poetry, than Isaiah. Yet Isaiah might have said what he did say much more briefly if he had written out what he had to say in prose, like newspaper paragraphs; and there are no doubt some persons who read him now as they would read an Act of Parliament, and who would rather not have had to get at his meaning through his poetry; who are inclined in their inmost hearts to say of his incomparable majesty and pathos: "To what purpose is this waste of words? This language might have been economised, and the surplus saved might have been devoted to some other useful subject!" And if such advice has not been taken by anticipation, why is it? Why, but because He Who made us knows that, side by side with our sense of truth, we have a sense of beauty; and that our sense of beauty may most persuasively minister to our apprehension of truth.

XV] *The Economy of Religious Art.* 239

So, again, with music, and painting, and sculpture. Each of these arts is a natural handmaid of religion. The Psalms were, many of them, intended to be sung to an instrumental accompaniment by their inspired authors; and the fine arts, as we call them, were profusely lavished under Divine direction upon the Tabernacle and the Temple. It may be said here too—Why this waste? Why could not David have read his Psalms instead of singing them? Why could not Solomon have dispensed with the services of Hiram of Tyre, and the skilled workmen?[1] The same thing has been said from age to age about the music and the temples of the Christian Church. "God," men have said, "is a Spirit; and they that worship Him must worship Him in spirit and in truth."[2] Most true: but the question is not as to what is of the essence of real accepted worship; the only Master in the school of prayer Who can teach to any purpose is God the Holy Ghost; but the question is, Whether art may not lead the way to the school in which He teaches—whether it is not like the pot of ointment—a witness to the future and the invisible? Certainly, for those who see Christ in His Church, who believe with St. Paul that it is His Body, the fulness of Him That filleth all in all,[3] it is natural, as it was natural to Mary, to bestow on it our costliest and our best. Nay, it appears to me that noble souls, fired with a love of Christ, are at times anxious, like Mary, to bid defiance to the world by doing Him some public and extraordinary homage; there are times when they can no longer contain the love for Him, the Eternal Beauty, which consumes them, and they rejoice to ignore the criticisms of a Judas, or the criticisms of weak-minded disciples whom Judas misleads. They fall down before Him, and break the box which contains their all, and pour it, in

---

[1] 1 Kings v. 2-18; vii. 13-51.   [2] St. John iv. 24.
[3] Eph. i. 22, 23; Col. i. 24.

their passion, not on His Head merely, but on His Feet as well, out of their love for Him.

The criticism which our Lord rebukes has not died away with the age of the Apostles. The false utilitarianism which keeps the bag, and grudges every penny that does not go into it, constantly asks, "To what purpose is this waste?" How often is the cause of the poor at home pleaded against the cause of Missions!—as if one form of charity did not really help another; as if interest in the spiritual needs of the heathen did not really go hand in hand with interest in the temporal and spiritual needs of the home poor; as if the spirit of charity or the spirit of devotion could be thus divided against itself, and set one object against another in unnatural rivalry.

"To what purpose is this waste?"

It was said to me, not very long ago, that it is morally wrong in us to set about the completion of St. Paul's, while London, and especially the East End of London, presents to our view such a mass of poverty and misery. "When all the poor have good houses to live in, and plenty to eat; when pauperism has been absorbed into the ranks of honest poverty, and poverty is being really dignified and enriched by well-paid labour,—then, if you like, you may complete your Cathedral. But until then," the critic will go on saying, "these mosaics—those marbles, that gilding—might have been sold for much more than three hundred pence and given to the poor." Who can doubt that if the speaker had been at the feast in the house of Simon the Leper at Bethany he would have agreed very energetically with the disciples, and have denounced Mary and her work?

To all such criticisms our Lord's words are an eternal rebuke. He has condemned once and for ever the cold judgments which a narrow utilitarianism, even though it may own His Name, would pass upon the generous emotions of devout hearts. Their pure feeling has its language, which is unintelligible to those who do not share it, but which is read in the skies. If we do not enter into the enthusiasms of others, let us fear, at least, to criticise them: they may be very high above ourselves in the kingdom of grace. If our own service of God is meted out by a rigid rule, if it is incapable of those generous outbursts of love such as was Mary's act at Bethany—this is hardly a cause for self-congratulation. Our own temperament may be a real element in our personal responsibility : it can be no safe measure of the acts of others.

III.

Let me conclude with two particular applications.

On Tuesday next, please God, St. Matthew's account of the Passion of Jesus Christ, as set to music a century and a half ago by the German composer, Sebastian Bach, will be rendered in this Cathedral. There are two ways of looking at such an enterprise as this. One is to regard it simply as a musical entertainment, with a certain appropriateness to the time of year and the place, which is offered to the public by the clergy of St. Paul's. I have seen it so described; but if this description were a true one, you would have a right, my brethren, to ask the question with some warmth, To what purpose is this waste ? Was it then for this—for the mere promotion of a noble art—that these sacred walls were raised by our forefathers, and that this church is maintained among the living millions of this great Metropolis ? Is this an object which would have been owned by the great Apostle whose name we bear—the man who determined to know nothing among his converts save Jesus Christ, and Him Crucified ?[1] I trow not. From a religious point of view,

---

[1] 1 Cor. ii. 2.

art which has no object beyond itself—art which has no ambition higher and nobler than artistic perfection—is waste: it does nothing for man in his deepest relations and capacities; it has no bearing upon the Eternal world. The only way of looking at such an enterprise as ours which is compatible with our duties towards you, my brethren, and towards our Lord and Master, is to treat it, not as a concert, but as a religious service: as an effort, through the ministry of sublime and pathetic music, to bring the successive incidents of our Lord's bitter Passion and Death for us sinners more closely home to our hearts and feelings. If it does that, it will not be waste. If it does that it will earn, not merely the good words of the musical journals, but the acclamations of the Angels in heaven and the approval of our Lord. If it does that, for even a few souls out of the multitude, we shall feel that the box of ointment has not been poured forth in vain.

There are many persons so constituted that for them music means nothing; it is merely a scientific form of noise. There are others who delight in it, but only as art; to whom it suggests nothing beyond itself. Very well, let them stay away: clearly they will not be helped if they come here; a love of music is not necessary to being in a state of grace: they may go to heaven just as well without music as others with it. But let them not judge what they do not understand, after the fashion of narrow disciples, and at the bidding of a Judas, who wishes no good to religion at all. What we want in these days especially is generosity—the generosity which can understand that all characters, all souls, are not framed in one mould; which can bear with a fervour higher and intenser than its own, and proportionately strange in its self-expression; which, in any case, can believe and hope the best when it cannot itself follow.

Lastly, and in any case, with this day begins the most solemn week for serious Christians in the whole course of the year, the week which is consecrated, every day of it, as Good Friday is especially, to the contemplation of our Saviour's Sufferings and Death. It is a time for being, if possible, much alone; for earnest prayer over and above our usual devotions and the regular Services of the Church; for avoiding all the distractions of pleasure and business that can be avoided; for getting deeper into our own souls, closer to our God, in union with His Suffering Son. There will not be wanting voices around us, whispers in our own hearts to ask the purpose of this waste of strength and time: but, brethren in Christ, heed them not. Nothing is wasted on earth that lays up ever so little in heaven; and if we have any true sense of what is due to our Crucified Lord, we shall open our hearts to the influences of the time—to the strength, the tenderness, the clear-sightedness, the fervour, which come from close contact with the Cross. And I am mistaken if, to some at least, there does not come also the desire to join with Mary in bringing some alabaster-box of ointment of spikenard, very precious, ready for the Redeemer's Burial— some one generous act, done for His dear sake, to His Church or to His poor, done to Him in them, done in forgetfulness of the present, and in the thought and view of the Eternal Future—done in the conviction that He will accept and bless what love for Him can offer, and that His Blessing makes all human judgments a matter of entire indifference.

SERMON XVI.

THE LIVING WATER.

ST. JOHN. iv. 13, 14, 15.

Jesus answered and said unto her, Whosoever drinketh of this water shall thirst again: but whosoever drinketh of the water that I shall give him shall never thirst; but the water that I shall give him shall be in him a well of water springing up into everlasting life. The woman saith unto Him, Sir, give me this water, that I thirst not, neither come hither to draw.

THERE is no scene in our Lord's earthly Life in which it is easier to bring Him vividly before our eyes than that which gave occasion to these words. He was walking from Judæa along the great road through Samaria; and in the middle of the late autumn day, weary with His journey, He sat down—the language exactly expresses His attitude—resting on the edge of, and so leaning over, a well, at the mouth of the valley which led up to the ancient city of Shechem. The well is there now at this very hour, recognised as beyond dispute by the most sceptical of travellers as the well of Jacob, the well of the conversation in St. John's Gospel. It is just 9 feet in diameter, and 105 feet in depth, and in the spring-time there is commonly about 15 feet of water in it. This well had a history: it was a relic of the age of the Patriarchs. It had been dug by Jacob, partly to mark his possession of the spot, just as in Southern regions of Palestine Abraham had dug, and Isaac had cleared and repaired similar wells, partly as a sheer necessity for great cattle-owners, as were the ancestors of the race of Israel,

The Living Water. 245

tending their flocks and herds under an Eastern sun. The Samaritans loved and revered this particular well; believing themselves, not very accurately, to be the children of Jacob and Joseph (they were really converted heathens with Gentile blood in their veins), they looked on this well as a connecting link with their presumptive ancestors. As the disciples left their Master sitting on the well's brink, and wended their way up the narrow valley towards the city in which they were to buy provisions for their remaining journey, down the same valley there came a Samaritan woman, veiled, and with a pitcher, to draw water; just as Rebekah, as Rachel, as Zipporah had drawn it elsewhere in the ages before her. She came, and the Stranger asked her to give Him a little water to drink; and she, marking the dialect or accent of His speech, and knowing how, for more than four long centuries, a fierce religious feud had separated the Jews from the Samaritans, expressed her surprise that He should claim at her hands a token of neighbourly, almost— for so the Easterns deemed it—of religious communion. Our Lord does not answer her question: He had come on earth not to argue but to teach: He answers not the inquiry which fell upon His human sense of hearing, but the deep unexpressed yearnings of the soul of the speaker, which He could read, when not a word was uttered, in all its hidden misery. "If thou knewest the gift of God, and Who it is that saith to thee, Give Me to drink; thou wouldest have asked of Him, and He would have given thee living water."[1] She knew of no living water but that which lay just 90 feet beneath them, at the bottom of the ancient well of Jacob. She could not understand how the Stranger who had "nothing to draw with" could promise her the clear spring water out of that well. And if He was thinking of another well, with living water in it,

[1] St. John iv. 10.

purer and more refreshing than this, was He claiming to be greater than the patriarch of the race,—" Our father Jacob, which gave us the well, and drank thereof himself, and his children, and his cattle " ? Again Jesus speaks,— in answer not directly to her spoken question but to the questions of her inmost soul,—" Whosoever drinketh of this water shall thirst again, but whosoever drinketh of the water that I shall give him shall never thirst: but the water that I shall give him shall be in him a well of water springing up into everlasting life." What the Speaker exactly meant the woman of Samaria can only have vaguely apprehended. But she felt at least that He was speaking of some water with properties far more exhilarating and precious than any of which she knew. She knew that she, for many weary years, had toiled down to that well of Jacob, and back to the city, day by day, with a laggard step, and with a heavy heart; and it seemed to her as if she might somehow be relieved from her thankless toil, from her aching sense of misery: "Sir," she cried eagerly, "give me this water, that I thirst not, neither come hither to draw."

I.

It will do us good, my brethren, if God gives us His Blessing, to ask what was this water of which Jesus spoke, and of which the poor woman so earnestly desired to drink. We Christians, of course, look at our Lord's earlier Words in the light of His later Revelations; and we are not reading into them meanings which they will not bear because we ascribe to Him, and to those whom He commissioned to speak for Him, a consistency of language which warrants us in interpreting one utterance by another,—the earlier by the later, the scanty intimation by the explicit assertion.

1. Observe, first of all, the nature of this gift of which

Christ speaks. Our Lord calls it a "well of water,"—and "living water." This expression had already an ascertained sense in the Hebrew Scriptures: it meant pure water ceaselessly rising from a spring, as opposed to still or stagnant water. Such was the water—it is the same expression—which Isaac's servants found when they digged again the old wells which the Philistines had stopped in the valley of Gerar:[1] such was the water over which, according to the Jewish Ritual for the cleansing of the leper, one of the offered birds was to be killed in an earthen vessel.[2] And although the exact expression does not occur, the idea of water running from a spring as a source of life and health is prominent in such visions as those of Ezekiel, who beheld an abundant stream pour forth under the Gate of the Temple at Jerusalem, and then flow eastward;[3] or of Joel, who told "how a fountain should come out of the House of the Lord, and should water the valley of Shittim;"[4] or of Isaiah, seeing deeper into the future, and exclaiming to the coming generations, "With joy shall ye draw water out of the wells of Salvation."[5] There is much else to the same purpose in the Old Testament; and the banished Apostle in vision gathers up its completed meaning when he tells how the Angel showed him "a pure river of the water of life, clear as crystal, proceeding out of the Throne of God and of the Lamb."[6]

If the question be asked what it was precisely that our Lord meant by the "living water" here, we have to consider that He, especially in St. John's Gospel, speaks of Himself as the Life: the Being, that is, Who quickens, upholds, and invigorates movement and growth in the souls of men. As the Life, He is, He says, the Food of men;[7] as the Life,

---

[1] Gen. xxvi. 17-19.   [2] Lev. xiv. 50-52.   [3] Ezek. xlvii. 1.
[4] Joel iii. 18.   [5] Isa. xii. 3.   [6] Rev. xxii. 1.
[7] St. John vi. 32-34, 48-52.

He is also the Resurrection;[1] as the Life, He claims to rescue alike from moral and physical death; "all that are in the graves shall hear His voice;"[2] as the Life, He bids all who would live indeed to come to Him, cling to Him, feed on Him.[3] Doubtless the figure of water is used especially in Holy Scripture as a physical likeness of the cleansing action of the Divine Spirit: but the Spirit of Christ is so termed because it is His work to graft us into Christ's Human Nature; and Christ Himself is termed by St. Paul a "quickening Spirit,"[4] with reference to His thus becoming an inward gift. Nor in the words "living water" does there seem to be any clear, or at least primary, reference either to Baptism, by which Christ's Life is originally imparted, or to faith, by which it is received. It is the gift, not the method of its bestowal, which is here in question: and Christ is His own gift, as He is His own message, His own Gospel: He has nothing higher to announce, nothing better to give us, than His Adorable Self. But as we dwell on it, the figure which our Lord employs suggests vividly to us the characteristics of His gift.

2. A well of living water is, in the first place, always fresh. It does not stagnate like rain-water, it does not become brackish or foul; the new supplies which, minute by minute, burst upwards from the soil, keep it pure and clear. So it is with Christ. History is a great storehouse of buried memories, some of which are galvanised into a momentary life by our antiquarians, but which soon die away again from the grasp of memory, since they belong to a past age, and do not answer to our wants or correspond to our sympathies. But eighteen centuries ago One appeared Who spoke words which have the same incisive and trenchant force, the same exquisite and mysteri-

---

[1] St. John xi. 25. [2] Ib. v. 26-29.
[3] St. John vi. 35, 40; vii. 37. [4] 1 Cor. xv. 45.

ous attraction, as if they were the novelties of yesterday. His several actions and His life as a whole speak to the nineteenth century as they spoke to the first, provoking sharp hostility now as then, but then as now winning their way to sure empire over true hearts. He is, in short, ever fresh and young; and such as He is in history, such is He also within the sanctuary of the heart. In that vast treasure-house of the dead—the human soul,—amid all that is stagnant, all that belongs to the irrevocable past, all that bears on it the marks of advancing change and corruption, amid the thoughts which pall, the memories which depress, the forms of feeling which once quickened within us the highest and most subtle enjoyment, but which have long ceased to move, or which are roused now into a momentary life only to create something like repugnance,—there is, I dare to say it, for Christians one thought which is ever fresh, one memory which is ever welcome and invigorating, one train of feeling which kindles within the soul into a burning tide the keenest and purest passion: it is the thought, the memory, the love of our Lord and Saviour. Just as literary men have said that if they had to choose one book in the world which should furnish them, in the absence of all others, with high interest and enjoyment, and that unfailingly, they would choose the Bible; so within the soul the thought, the memory of the One Perfect Being is the one warrant of a continuous refreshment, because He is more than a thought or a memory—far more; because He is a living Presence. A Well of Water—that is His own figure—He lives within regenerate souls in His perpetual freshness: as He was guaranteed against seeing corruption in the tomb,[1] so much more, now that He has risen, is He proof against its ravages; the centuries pass, but He renews His youth; life waxes and

[1] Ps. xvi. 10; Acts ii. 24-27.

wanes, but He smiles on its sunset not less refreshingly than on its springtide. "Thou art the same, and Thy years shall not fail,"[1] and "With Thee is the Well of Life."[2]

3. A spring of water is also in continual motion; and herein also Christ is true to His own metaphor. He is in History, He is in the Soul of Man, ever different and yet the same. As the sky presents the same outline of clouds on no two days on which we observe it, and yet is the same sky; as the sea, visit it as often as we will, never looks quite as it looked before, yet is ever the same; as the smallest jet of water, whose volume never varies, yet presents us minute by minute with an infinite variety of forms; so is it in the world of spirits with the Presence of Christ. He is movement, and yet identity. He is to us what He was to our forefathers; yet He is ever displaying new aspects of His Power and His Perfections to those who hold communion with Him. He is at one and the same time Stability and Progress: here preserving the unalterable lines of His One Perfect Revelation of Himself, there leading us on to new and enriched perceptions of its range and its significance.

As He is Himself movement, so He is the Source of movement. He has set the soul of man in motion, and kept it moving. He has quickened the very intelligence which would fain drive Him from His throne. For the truths which He has brought to us have moved the soul of man to its depths—moved it so profoundly, that whether men accept these truths or not, they cannot rest as though they had not heard them. As it is said in the Gospel of His last entry into Jerusalem, that when He had entered "all the city was moved,"[3] so is it with His entrance into the soul. Faculties which had been dormant for years are stirred to meet Him, and He keeps them in motion, because He Himself is perpetually ex-

[1] Ps. cii. 27.   [2] Ib. xxxvi. 9.   [3] St. Matt. xxi. 10.

hibiting new aspects of His Power or His Beauty. It is said sometimes of the Christian Creed that it ensures the stagnation of honest thought. Undoubtedly in one sense it does arrest thought; it gives a fixed form to our ideas on subjects of the highest importance; it fixes them thus in the Name and with the Authority of the All-Wise. We Christians are not now discussing the Divine Attributes or the destiny of man as if these were matters upon which the light of certainty had never been thrown; but fixed thought is not the antagonist of active thought, any more than the wall or rim of the well is hostile to the movement of the water which springs up within. Those who have had anything to do with education must know how often a naturally stupid and dull person has been quickened into intelligence, at least on one set of subjects, by learning to take a deep practical interest in religion. The vast ideas which the Christian Creed contains, when once they are living realities to the soul, move it to its very depths—God, Eternity, the past, with the account to be given of it, the future, with its mighty hopes and fears, Christ's love in Redemption—these things cannot become more than words to any and leave the soul unmoved.

4. And thus a well of springing water fertilises. All around the edge the green verdure tells the story of its life-imparting power. And here too Christ is the great fertiliser of the soul of man. He has made human thought capable of productions which could not else have been produced. Dante and Shakespeare are in their different ways distinctly His creations. He has fertilised affection: family life, as we understand it in Europe, is His work: His Authority is reflected in the Christian Father, His Tenderness in the Christian Mother, His lowly Obedience in the Christian Child. Above all, He has fertilised Will; He has made it capable of new measures of self-sacrifice; of heroism and self-sacrifice,

prosaic and unnoticed more often than conspicuous; heroism and self-sacrifice which, but for Him, would never have existed.

Ah! if by any national infatuation in the years to come, we should try to do without Him, we should soon discover even in the matters of this life the magnitude of our mistake. When human thought has nothing upon which it can seriously fix itself beyond the province of sense; when human affection is forbidden to spend itself on any form that is not earthly, palpable, material; when the human will is invigorated by no motives that are drawn from a higher world than this,—human life will soon become barren and unfruitful: we shall gradually but surely exchange the civilisation of Europe for the civilisation of China or Japan. We are so accustomed to the sun that we take its light and warmth as a matter of course; but we do not rack our imaginations by thinking what the world's surface would be without it. Yet be sure that the world would not then be more forlorn and lifeless to the eye of man than to a spiritual eye is the soul of a man or a nation which has lost the Presence of Christ.

II.

Note, secondly, the seat or scene of this gift. The water that I shall give him shall be "in him." This is the claim and the triumph of Jesus Christ; He does His work in the very seat and root of man's being. Others have done great works—have effected vast changes on the surface of human life. They have founded empires, imposing the will of a man or of a race upon millions of reluctant subjects: they have changed "customs and laws and even languages;" they have altered the whole outward character of a civilisation. Others again have penetrated deeper: they have founded empires not of force, but of ideas: they have so wrought upon and fashioned the shape and setting of human thought, as to reign, long after their death, in the thoughts of millions who never heard their name. But Christ has done more even than this. He is more than the Founder of a kingdom: more than the Author of a world-wide philosophy. He penetrates beyond the sphere of force and the sphere of thought to the very centre of the soul. A government may be obeyed, while it is hated : a philosophy may be accepted while no personal allegiance or love is felt for its author. Christ reigns, when He reigns, not merely over men's conduct, not merely over their ideas, but in their hearts: He places Himself at the very centre of their souls; in that inner sanctuary of consciousness whence thought and feeling and resolve take their origin, He raises His throne. He is there not merely as a Monarch, but as a Friend ; not merely as a Force, but as a Source of Life ; it is not an iron hand the pressure of which the Christian feels ; it is a sense of buoyancy, of invigorated power, of kindled affection, of enlarged and enlarging thought, as though his own personal being were superseded and another Higher and Wiser than himself had taken possession, and was making him that which of and by himself he could not be.

Yes, this gift is really within man : and hence Christians know, and they only know, the secret of man's dignity. The old heathen philosophies said much, and often said it well, about the human soul. Men speculated on the nature of the soul, the origin of the soul, the connection that subsists between the body and the soul; the probabilities for and against a life of the soul after the death of the body. But they did not really proclaim the dignity of man as man. Much was said about the dignity of particular individuals, classes, races of men : to be a Roman citizen, to have particular blood in your veins, to govern a city or a province—this was great according to the ideas of the ancient world. But nothing was said about the greatness of conquered races, of women, of slaves—of slaves who outnumbered the freemen of the empire, and who were bought and sold and abused and made much of, simply as a form of personal property with no rights of their own, no accorded permission to plead the instincts of humanity, or the claims of justice. Of their dignity nothing was said: though they too were men, with warm hearts and keen intellects, and a sense of what they might be, and a sense of what they were, not less vivid than their masters'. Jesus Christ did not do His work at once; He would not provoke an uprising of the oppressed populations expressing their too natural vengeance amid scenes of fire and blood; He did not talk, as others since have talked, about the rights of man: but He did more. He placed at the very centre of the soul, alike of slave and master, the true sense of its real dignity; the instinct, the irrepressible instinct, of communion with the All-Holy, resulting in an abundant outburst of man's noblest life within; and He left this to do its work as the centuries passed, slowly but surely, as leaven deposited in the unwieldy mass of human society. It has wrought, that leaven, from then till now. It has been heaving visibly—and with no trivial results in our own day—beyond the Atlantic; it has yet work to do, far and wide and deep, ere the work of proclaiming man's true greatness as man is complete. That proclamation will be made in its integrity only when the preciousness of Christ's inward gift to the human soul is the creed of the human race.

Christ's great gift is within; and as this is the secret of His dignity, so it is the source of His spiritual independence. If Christians were dependent on the things of sense the world might crush out—it might have crushed out long ago—the Christian life. I do not deny that the Christian life is largely supported by what meets the eye and the ear. After all, we are what God has made us—men, not angels. I do not deny that the language of the written Word, and the grace of the Sacraments can alone reach the soul through the organs of sense; so that if all copies of the Bible could be destroyed, and the administration of the Sacraments really prevented as well as forbidden, the ordinary means of grace would be cut off. But when driven to bay, and in the last resort, the soul falls back upon a Presence which is independent of sense. The world could proscribe the Christian worship, and destroy the Christian Scriptures; but its legislation is just as powerless against the Presence of the Divine Redeemer in the sanctuary of the soul as against the clouds and the sunlight. It was this which made bonds, imprisonment, death easy and welcome to our first fathers in the faith: they knew that they had not merely in heaven, but within their breasts, One Who would not leave them; One Who was Light when all else was darkness; One Who, while all outward aids were denied, was of Himself a well of water springing up into everlasting life.

III.

The effect of this gift is its last and not its least characteristic. "Springing up into everlasting life:" to render it more exactly, springing up unto the higher life of man, which belongs to the future age of his existence. This is the real effect of Christ's Gift of His Presence to the soul. It does much besides; it makes human thought and feeling, as we have seen, fresh and active and fertile. But its true object is to be found not in the present but in the future; not in the life of this world but of the next. The life of love, directed towards its one worthy Object, begins here, but it does not end here. It is the life of the blessed beings who inhabit the Eternal World: and Christ's gift expands within His people to prepare them for that world. Without it man would not be happy in heaven. Heaven would be hell to those in whom the true Life of the Eternal World has not yet found a place, and whose whole thought and energy is persistently directed towards the things of time and sense.

To some who hear me, it may be, it will occur to think that what has been urged is, as men speak, mystical language,—intelligible no doubt to minds of a particular cast, but not suited to the practical matter-of-fact views of conduct and duty of simple people. You know nothing then, my brethren, of the inner Well of water springing up into everlasting life? It may be there, nevertheless; like the sunshine and the atmosphere, without which your bodily life would be impossible, yet which you do not note. You know nothing, you say, of this inward gift. Then trust those who do. In the days of ancient Greece there were African travellers who penetrated so far as to find that at noonday their shadows turned towards the south. They returned and reported the fact, and it was treated by the historian of the day with entire incredulity. We know that they had simply crossed the Equator; and that their experience is shared by the passengers who crowd every mail-packet that leaves the Cape of Good Hope. But the reports which Christians bring back from the land of spiritual experience are not less certain, or more apparently incredible, than the story of the Greek travellers. The Well of water springing up to the Eternal Life only seems mystical until its reality has been practically ascertained; until, like the Samaritans, men have heard the Inner Teacher themselves, and "know that this is indeed the Christ the Saviour of the World."[1]

[1] St. John iv. 42.

To others, again, it will occur to think: This is all very well for those who have all their way in this life, who take no thought for the morrow, because the morrow is probably well provided for; who occupy themselves with spiritual experiences, because they have leisure and abundance at command. But what of the very poor, the hard-working, the multitudes to whom life is a struggle for existence, to whom each day is like all other days, a long mechanical plodding through monotonous work; to whom each year is like other years, only that energy is fainter, and the margin between the struggler and the dark waters is narrower—those dark waters which are the only home to which despair can look forward? Ah! you say, this talk of inner refreshment rouses indignation in presence of the appalling proportions of human suffering: it is a maudlin substitute for the plain honest duties of active charity, of better education, of improved sanitary regulations, of relief administered to bodily want and pain. If it were so, you would perhaps be right, brethren, in denouncing it. If it were so, you might well doubt whether Christ had really blessed the world by His Gospel. But as matters stand, look around you, and say whether, generally speaking, and in the long-run, the philanthropists and the educators are not also the Christians: whether the inner Spring of water does not fertilise this life, as well as spring up into the moral beauties which prepare for the next. One duty does not proscribe another: and whether a man be poor or wealthy, he equally needs the inner Source of life; and if he enjoys it beyond everything else, it enables him to bear his lot in this world well, and according to his means to bless his fellow-creatures.

Indeed, this it is—the presence or absence of this inward gift—which constitutes the real difference between man and man. The names or titles we bear, the property we inherit or have acquired, the reputation which follows us,—these things are as little our real selves as the coat we put on in the morning and take off at night. That which really belongs to us is within; it is part of that imperishable essence which is man's inmost self,—which does not weaken with disease or die with death—which lives on, somehow, necessarily and for ever. It is here that we have or have not that of which Christ spoke to the Samaritan; that which will last when all else is passing, that which will comfort and sustain when all else is proved of no avail.

To us, too, it may be, Christ comes as He came to her of Samaria, as a Petitioner: He asks us to aid His poor, or to support His Church, or to assist in the propagation of His Gospel; He would place Himself under an obligation to us—" Give Me to drink." And yet it may be that if we knew the gift of God, and Who it is That saith unto us, " Give Me to drink," we should long ago have asked of Him, and He would have given us, as He has given to others, the living water.

It may be that while we are, as was said of a great Jesuit in a past generation, buttresses of the Church, we lack that which alone makes the Church worth supporting. Outward activity and benevolence is no good substitute for the life of the soul; and whether the soul shall live is a question of prayer, of earnest importunate prayer, addressed to Him Who gave us all that, in nature or in grace, we have ever received, and Who only waits for our petitions to give yet more abundantly. Prayer is a question of earnestness: and earnestness is only natural when men have taken the measure of life and death, of the things which are seen and which are temporal, and of the things which are not seen and which are eternal.[1]

[1] 2 Cor. iv. 18.

SERMON XVII.

THE TRUE LIFE OF MAN.

ST. LUKE xii. 15.

A man's life consisteth not in the abundance of the things which he possesseth.

THIS is an instance of our Lord's manner of taking occasion, when a particular incident comes before Him, to proclaim a truth of world-wide import. The truth is broader and deeper than is needed for the immediate purpose: but then, in the eyes of the Universal Teacher, the particular case is not only to be considered in itself; it furnishes an opportunity for proclaiming something that shall concern and interest the world. Our Lord had come to a pause in His public teaching, when it occurred to a Jew who was listening that a person of such influence and ascendency might possibly help him towards attaining a private and domestic object, which he had greatly at heart. This Jew was a younger son, who could not easily forgive his elder brother for enjoying a double share of their father's estate. The elder brother, it is plain, was also one of our Lord's hearers, and likely to be, in whatever degree, attracted by Him; but, on the other hand, it may be taken for certain that he had no mind to part with any portion of his estate, or the appeal against him would not have been necessary. "Master," cried the younger man, "speak to my brother, that he divide the inheritance with me."[1]

[1] St. Luke xii. 13.

Our Lord might, it is clear, have met this appeal by a direct discussion of its intrinsic merit. But in fact, placing Himself at the point of view of the speaker, who could not yet know at all what He Himself really was, He asks what commission He could be supposed to hold for deciding such questions at all. "Man, who made Me a judge or divider over you?" And then, as if glancing at both the brothers—the elder, who held so tenaciously to his legal fortune, and the younger, who was so eager to share it—He rises into a higher atmosphere, and His words become at once instructive to all men and for all time. "Take heed," He said, "and beware of covetousness," for one reason among others, but especially for one—that covetousness involves a radical mistake as to the true meaning and nature of life : "a man's life consisteth not in the abundance of the things which he possesseth." He does not deny that something is needed to sustain physical life; but He has His eye upon the tendency to accumulate a great deal more, and to throw all the energy of thought and work into this accumulation. Man's life consists not, He says, in this kind of abundance, which is made up of things which he possesseth. If we could forget who the Speaker is, some of us might, at the first thought, be disposed to say that this is a truism. No doubt it is. So true is it, that it was a commonplace among the heathen. We may remember the lines in which even the light-hearted poet of the Augustan age tells how "neither house nor farm, nor store of brass and gold, can banish fever from the ailing body, or care from the mind."[1]

Understand life as you will, and the Sacred words correspond with everyday experience, that life is not any-

---

[1] " Non domus aut fundus, non aeris acervus et auri
    Aegroto domini deduxit corpore febres,
    Non animo curas—— "
                              Hor. 1 *Ep.* ii. 47.

thing external to man. Every invalid knows that his physical life consists not in the costly medicines or professional skill which he can command, but in the renewed vigour of his bodily frame and its vital functions. Every student knows that his mental life consists, not in the books on his shelves—not even in the thoughts of other men industriously copied into his note-books; but in the appropriation of these treasures by his memory and his thinking faculty, in their being interwoven with and made a part of the texture and system of his mind. And every Christian knows, or should know, that his spiritual life consists, not in the possession of a Bible, or in the near neighbourhood of Churches and Sacraments, or of Christian friends, or of other religious opportunities, but in that which is "hid with Christ in God;"[1] in the incorporation with his inmost self of that Truth and Grace of which religious opportunities, the highest and the lowest, are but the channels. So obvious is this, that when it is denied that life—something always and essentially internal and personal—consists in that which is distinct from and independent of us, we are at first tempted, if not to ask, yet to think, "Who ever said that it did?" Yes, the saying is a truism. But there are truisms and truisms. There are truisms which are admitted to be such in the conduct as well as by the speech of men. And there are truisms which are never questioned in conversation, and which are rarely acted on. To insist on truisms of the former class is no doubt an impertinence; to insist on truisms of this latter kind again and again, and even with importunity, is by no means superfluous; and the saying of our Lord is undoubtedly a truism of this description. The distinction which He draws between what a man has and what he is, is as obvious, when stated, as it is commonly overlooked. The saying that life consists not in

[1] Col. iii. 3.

what we have but in what we are, is as true as the practice of making life consist not in what we are but in what we have, is common. Intellectually speaking, the world did not need these words of our Lord. Practically speaking, there is no one of His sayings which it could less dispense with. For just consider the two brothers. They both knew perfectly that what our Lord said was true. They had learnt the truth from their own Hebrew Scriptures, and yet they were acting as if it were an ascertained illusion. The determination to retain the larger share of the property, the determination to have it divided if possible, meant that in the practical judgment of both the brothers life did somehow consist in possessing property. All the energy and resolve with which we pursue that about which we feel most deeply was thrown into this question of retaining or dividing that bit of property. Each would have said, no doubt, that his life did not consist in possessing it. Each certainly acted as if it did.

Truism or truth, there is no mistake as to the importance which our Lord attached to what He then announced. He taught it in act as well as by word of mouth. Unlike ourselves, He could determine the circumstances in which He would enter this world, and with which He would surround Himself in it. And what did He advisedly choose? A poor home, poor people for His Mother and Foster-father, poor men for His companions the foxes had holes, and the birds of the air had nests, but the Son of Man had not where to lay His Head.[1] He would not accept consideration and position even from the poor: He would not be made a King or an umpire. And at last He gave Himself up to be stripped even of His poor garments and to die in agony on the Cross. "Ye know," said His Apostle in after years, "ye know the grace of our Lord Jesus Christ, Who, though He was rich, yet for

[1] St. Matt. viii. 20.

your sakes He became poor, that ye through His poverty might be rich."[1] And the wealth which He thus earns for us is largely moral wealth; it lies above all else in making our life consist in something else than the things which we possess.

Certainly, judging from experience, it would seem that there is a constant tendency in our fallen nature to run counter to the truth which our Lord proclaims; to create, if we may so put it, a new centre of gravity in life, so that we come to act and speak and think more with reference to something that is altogether outside us than to the true centre of our existence. And this tendency is a result of that momentous event in the earliest history of our race, which we term the Fall.

For in his fallen state, and so far as he is stripped of God's supernatural grace, man's solitary self is too thin and feeble a spirit to persist in independence of the outer world of matter; it exerts upon him evidently and always a fatal and all but resistless attraction; it attracts him through that side of his composite nature which belongs to it; it lures or draws or drags him down until his personal self, his spirit, is entangled in and detained by it; until, victim as he is of its ceaseless and subtle importunity, he has fallen, at first little by little, but in the end completely, under its sway,—under the empire of material nature. Of this fact the Pantheism of the ancient world, which was at the root of its idolatries, was an expression; it was an unconscious attempt, by way of after-thought, to make man's degradation respectable by decorating it with theory. And within the frontiers of Christendom, wherever the grace of Regeneration has been forfeited, the old attraction is at once felt; modern civilisation imposes on it some characteristic form; society takes the place of wild nature; and life, still practically

[1] 2 Cor. viii. 9.

made to consist in that which is external to man, is also made to consist in that which society prizes most.

Look at our great cities. For millions of human beings the face of nature scarcely exists; they live in these vast centres of population, where man has traced his own ungraceful inscriptions over the fair handiwork of God; and the matter which they extract from the bowels of the earth or which they collect from its extremities, to wield, to mould, to refine, to analyse, to reproduce in a thousand disguises, seems, as they handle it, to thicken the mental air they breathe; to bury thought, imagination, affection, will, in its dull encompassing folds; to penetrate their immaterial being and impregnate it with qualities which might, if possible, even materialise thought; to make man, undying spirit that he is, forget his true value and his destiny, and think of himself as though some grains or nuggets of the matter around him were more precious than he. What wonder if, where little or no light from above illuminates these populations, so conducive by their varied industries to our material prosperity as a nation, but ministering to it so often at so vast a cost,—what wonder if there should be forgetfulness of that wherein man's true life consists: if, when labour is rewarded by wealth, that life should be sought in something altogether external; in the tangible products of his brains or of his hands; in the abundance of acres or houses or railway shares or other symbols of material wealth of which he may have succeeded in possessing himself!

It was for men of this temper, though living in an agricultural district, that our Lord in His condescending mercy uttered the parable about the man whose fields brought forth plenteously, and who proposed to pull down his barns and build greater, and who whispered to his soul that he should take his ease, eat and drink and be merry for many a year to come, and to whom God said, "Thou fool, this night thy soul shall be required of thee."[1]

An intellectual society is apt to congratulate itself on its freedom from the vulgar care for money which is characteristic of a manufacturing town; though it may perhaps be a question whether it is really justified in doing so. But a man who is careless about money for its own sake may still make his life consist in works of art or of literature. The true posture of his mind is to a certain extent disguised from his conscience, because books and pictures are associated with ideas rather than with the money which they will fetch in the market, so in making idols of them the owner may persuade himself that he is a purely intellectual or æsthetic enthusiast. But after all, they are just as much outside him as a heap of sovereigns, and he must part with them at death. What a pathetic description is that of Cardinal Mazarin, rousing himself from his dying bed at Vincennes to take a last look at the treasures which his long ascendency in the councils of the French Monarchy had enabled him to accumulate. When his nurses and doctors were away he rose from his couch, and with his tall figure, pale and wasted, closely wrapped in his fur-lined dressing-gown, he stole into the gallery; and the Count de Brienne, who reports the scene, hearing the shuffling sound of his slippers as he dragged his limbs feebly and wearily along, hid himself behind the curtains. As, in his extreme weakness, the Cardinal had to halt almost at each step, he feebly murmured, "I must leave all this." He crawled on, however, clinging, so as to support himself, first on one object and then on another, and as at each pause, exhausted by pain and weakness, he looked around the splendid room, he said again, with a deep sigh, "I must leave all this." Then, at last, he caught sight of Brienne: "Give me your

[1] St. Luke xii. 16-20.

hand," he said, " I am very weak and helpless, yet I like to walk, and I have something to do in the library." And then, leaning on the Count's arm, he again pointed to the pictures. "Look at that beautiful Correggio, and this Venus of Titian, and this incomparable Deluge of Antonio Caracci. Ah! my poor friend, I must leave all this. Good-bye, dear pictures, which I have loved so well!"[1]

No doubt the most obvious form of the mistake against which our Lord guards us is somewhat of this kind; and yet there are other things besides gold, and acres, and pictures, and books, much less tangible and palpable, yet purely external to man, in which he may make his life consist. Such is reputation; such is social, political, academical, ecclesiastical honour, as the case may be. Many a man, whose natural instincts are too refined to allow him to care keenly for property, is even passionately desirous of honour. Every society has its own standards and certificates of honour. All the expressions of it which meet the eye and which fall upon the ear—decorations, titles, ordered precedence, the delicate and scarcely-hinted compliment, the tone and posture of calculated and restrained deference—these we find everywhere in human life, and not less than elsewhere in the life of a University. The younger of us know the pleasure which is felt at the cheers which follow an athletic victory, or a conspicuous service rendered to the college boat on the river, or a brilliant speech in the Union, or upon the generous congratulations which are called out by expected or unexpected success in the schools. And others, whom years have taught to discipline and restrain the expression of feeling, are yet fully alive to the subtle fascinations of honour, when, perhaps, some post of authority or responsibility is offered them, or some notice taken of them in a

[1] *Mémoires inédits de Louis-Henri de Loménie, Comte de Brienne* (Paris, 1828), ii. 114-117.

very high quarter, or some little work of theirs is favourably criticised in a German periodical, or some warmth of commendation from a living friend commonly chary of his words, and not given to compliments, is indirectly conveyed to them. We all know how largely we prize these things; it is well for us if we do not make our life consist in them; for such honour, in all its forms, is no part of our real selves; it is just as much external to us as the coat we wear on our back, or the shillings in our pocket,—very close to us for the time, but very easily separable, and very certain to be separated. Well for us indeed if we deserve it, even in part; if conscience does not whisper that in welcoming it we are taking that which is not our own; as, indeed, in one sense conscience must always remind us that there is in the last resort only One Being Who can deserve, as only One Being Who can confer, true honour.

> " When mortals praise thee, hide thine eyes,
> Nor to thy Master's wrong
> Take to thyself His crown and prize ;
> Yet more in heart than tongue."[1]

And anyhow, of all earthly honour, as of wealth, it is true that a man " shall carry nothing away with him when he dieth, neither shall his pomp follow him."[2]

There is a kind of monument more than once still to be met with in our old English Cathedrals, which was meant to teach this truth in what would now be called a realistic way. Above, perhaps, lies the figure of a great Prelate, arrayed in his full pontificals, with cope, and mitre, and pastoral staff, possibly raising his right hand as if still in the act of benediction, and surrounded with all the symbols of his high order, and his spiritual and temporal jurisdiction, while carved angels support the broidered cushion on which he rests his head, and with his feet he treads upon the young lion and the dragon—the moral, or

[1] *Lyra Innocentium*, iv. 3.   [2] Ps. xlix. 17.

social, or political opponents of the Church's rule; and
below this figure, so beautiful in form, so emblazoned
with colour, there lies on a lower ledge another. It is a
well-nigh naked corpse, emaciated almost to a skeleton,
in which the ribs and joints are each articulated with a
painfully literal exactness, while a worm is gnawing the
vitals or protruding from the brain. Above is the Prelate
still swathed and encrusted in the accumulated honours
of high ecclesiastical position. Beneath is the man, lying
as every man sooner or later must lie, stripped of all
earthly decorations, in the nakedness and corruption of
the grave. Do you say that such a conception belongs
to the coarseness of mediæval art? Do not impair the
force, it may be, of even unwelcome truth by an adjective
conveying a narrow and unwarranted judgment. No,
that portraiture is not merely mediæval, whatever hands
may first have fashioned it; it is Christian, it is human,
it is true now, it will be to the end of time, it proclaims
the eternal contrast between the honour which may surround us in life, deservedly or undeservedly, and the for-
feiture of all honour that cometh not from God only,[1] which
surely awaits us all in death. It is a vivid exhibition
of one aspect of the truth, that "a man's life consisteth
not in the abundance of the things which he possesseth."

And there are others, nobler souls, surely, than these,
whom honour charms not, still less wealth, but who are
the devotees of knowledge. If they said out their whole
heart they would say that a man's true life does consist
in the knowledge which he possesseth. And they might
be right if they meant, by the act of knowing, something
more than apprehension by the understanding and reten-
tion by the memory; and if the Object of their knowledge
were the Infinite and Everlasting God. For "this is life
eternal, to know Thee the only true God, and Jesus Christ

[1] St. John v. 44.

XVII] *The true life of man.* 269

Whom Thou hast sent."[1] But then this knowledge which is Eternal life is something different from that to which I referred just now; it is, according to the original Bible language, an adhesion of the whole being,—of will and affections, no less than of the understanding,—to its Object. In our ordinary language, knowledge, we know, means much less than this; it means the apprehension by the understanding and reason of man, of those facts about himself and about the world around him which can be verified by observation, and which are practically useful in the conduct of life. This knowledge is sometimes called, I do not say with what reason, positive; it is triumphantly contrasted with the science of mind, and even with Divine Revelation; it is presented as solid, certain, practical; and an increasing number of minds in our day devote themselves to it with fresh enthusiasm. But it too is external to man. He apprehends it; he retains it for years; he carries it about with him; he dispenses it to others; it seems for a while to have made a home at the very centre of his being, and his memory fondles it, and his reason watches and dissects it, and his imagination decorates and dresses it up; but for all that it is not himself—it is outside his real self, and he will, one day, part company with it. Necessary truth, indeed, once ours, is, if we will, ours for ever. Such is the true knowledge of the Infinite and Eternal God; such, too, the knowledge, it may be, of truths which the constitution of our minds obliges us to recognise as necessary—as, for instance, the axioms and conclusions of mathematics, or first principles in morals—and which, as they never can have been other than true, cannot have been something eternally independent of Him Who alone is Eternal Truth, and must therefore represent, in ways which we may be allowed to understand hereafter, elements of His

[1] St. John xvii. 3.

Eternal Being. But the greater part of what we call knowledge is very different: it is as variable, contingent, evanescent, as are its objects; and this knowledge, as the Apostle says, shall vanish away;[1] we shall put it off as the mere dressing-gown of the soul when we lie down to die.

Nay, of this we have warnings, before we reach the end, in the change and decay of the mental powers. Some of us have perhaps known what it is to witness that solemn and mysterious judgment or dispensation of God, when a mind, richly endowed with faculties and resources, and stored with the accumulated knowledge of a lifetime, suddenly breaks down; discovers, as in a moment, that its well-tried machinery is not entirely at command; suspects that it no longer sees everything as it is, and that all is somehow distorted and awry, and so passes through painful alternations of reason and unreason,—just enough of the one to take the measure of the tragic presence of the other. And then, little by little, the internal survey of mental wealth, and the power of marshalling and administering it, becomes less and less distinct, and the inner chasms open more widely, and the darkness thickens around until, as far as this world is concerned, all has closed in night.

No, brethren, a man's life consisteth not in that which he possesseth. "Whether there be prophecies, they shall fail; whether there be tongues, they shall cease; whether there be knowledge, it shall vanish away."[2] Knowledge, honour, wealth, these pass: and man's truest life consists not in what he has but in what he is, in the relation or attitude of his will towards the Being who is the Author and the Last End of his existence. This relation, be assured, does not change, either for good or evil, as we pass through the gate of death. If the will be self-warped, turned away from the Face of Eternal Righteousness,

[1] 1 Cor. xiii. 8. [2] Ib.

what it is, it will remain enduringly, and no store of material wealth, or earthly honour, or mental accomplishments can relieve this central and fatal deficiency. If, through the Redemption and Grace of our Lord Jesus Christ, Who has bought the inmost self of man back from slavery by His Precious Blood, and has given it directness and vigour by acting on it through His Spirit and His Sacraments,—if man's will has been made thus true in its aim, and free, and pliant, and vigorous in its upward movement; be sure that this, too, is a thing which lasts : this is life.

Five years before he left us, one who has since his death been much in men's minds, especially within these walls, had an illness which was of a very critical character.[1] For some days he said nothing, and he was supposed to be quite unconscious. After his recovery he referred, one day, to this, the presumably unconscious, part of his illness. "People thought," he said, "that I was unconscious, but the fact was, that although I could not speak I heard all that went on in the room, and I was well occupied." To the question, "What were you doing?" he answered, "By God's mercy, I could remember the Epistle for the fourth Sunday in Advent, out of the Philippians, which begins, 'Rejoice in the Lord alway.' This I made a framework for prayer; saying the Lord's Prayer two or three times between each clause, and so dwelling on the several relations of each clause to each petition in the Lord's Prayer." How he did this he explained at some length, and then added, "It lasted me, I should think, four or five hours." To the question, "What did you do after that?" he answered, "I began it over again. I was very happy: and, had it been God's will, did not wish to get better."

[1] The Rev. E. B. Pusey, D.D., Regius Professor of Hebrew, and Canon of Christ Church, Oxford (where this sermon was preached).

Yes, assuredly, a man's life does not consist in the outward things which he possesseth. Let us, in conclusion, endeavour to apply this truth to one or two parts in detail.

1. Surely it should shape and control our notions of progress, civilisation, improvement. What do men really mean, nine times out of ten, when they employ these fascinating and attractive terms? Do they not too often mean only something that takes place in that which is outside man, instead of in man's real self, the seat and centre of his life? Take an instance. I happen to go down into a country neighbourhood and meet a person who says that everything is looking up: that the progress and improvement are quite astonishing. I ask for an explanation, and he proceeds to say that a new railway has just been opened; that they are now only six hours from London; that there are now two posts in the day; that the farms are well let; that the squire has been rebuilding his cottages on an improved model; that it is a great advantage to have the telegraph, and a Post-office Savings-bank. Do I say that these things are without their value, or other than great blessings which God, in His Providence, has bestowed? Certainly not: but the question is whether they are the decisive tests of real improvement, in the life of a being like man. If man be what the Christian Revelation tells us he is,—a spirit with a material form attached to him, a spirit on probation here for a short space of years, and with an eternity before him,—how can that be any true improvement in a town or country neighbourhood which does not take account of this fundamental fact in his existence?

Surely there are many other questions to be asked and answered before our Lord Jesus Christ would have said that that neighbourhood was improved. What are the statistics of crime? what the relations of masters and servants, of parents and children? how many people say any prayers? what is the condition of the schools? what is taught in them about another life, and how, and by whom? what is the public honour paid to God in His Church or in the use of His Sacraments? what, so far as we can know, are the average dispositions of the dying? These questions go more to the root of the matter; they prove the claim to real improvement; since the true life of a neighbourhood, as of a man, consists in something else than the abundance of its material advantages, however considerable they may be.

2. Again, look at our too common way of estimating the prosperity of a Church. We count up its sacred buildings; we calculate the amount of its fixed or variable income; we survey and value the social consideration, or political weight accorded to its ministers; we regard them as members of a "profession," to be measured by the same standards of failure or success as any other,—as officers in the army or members of the bar. For us, too often, the Church is of the earth earthy, because we see in it nothing else; we are so engrossed in the study of its outer husk that we have no eye for realities within. Yet a Church is nothing, if it be not a congregation or home of souls; and the condition of these souls, their faith, their hope, their love, their repentance, their power over the insurgent forces within and the assailing forces without them, their ability to maintain true communion with the Invisible Source of life, is the point really worth thinking of. The Church, whose life, in the judgment of her members, consisteth in the abundance of outward things which she possesseth, is in fair way to lose them. It was not so when Peter said, "Silver and gold have I none, but such as I have give I thee;"[1] it will not be so when the Bride of the Immaculate Lamb is finally summoned to the Eternal Presence-Chamber.

[1] Acts iii. 6.

3. Once more, what is the view we individually take, of whatever God may have intrusted us with, for a few brief years, in the way of capital and income? Do we let our heart go out into it, thinking only or chiefly of how we can increase its amount? or do we bear in mind that it is utterly outside our real selves, that we dispose of it for a very short time, and shall have to answer for our way of doing so? In the Sermon on the Mount, our Lord insists on the unselfish and sincere discharge of the three leading duties of Almsgiving, Prayer, and Fasting;[1] and of these, assuredly, the first is not the least. Only when we remember that a man's life consisteth not in the things which he possesseth, shall we know how to sit easily to property and to handle it conscientiously. There are, perhaps, some young men among my hearers who a few years hence will dispose of considerable fortunes. Depend on it, brethren, that much even here depends— nothing, perhaps, less than the safety of the social structure in this country—on the way in which you will understand your responsibilities. The strength of communistic theories, here and everywhere else, consists, not in any solid truth on which they rest, since generally they do but cover a singular background of tangled fallacies, but in the failure of so many among the wealthier classes to understand the true relations of property to life. Lent is a time for getting rid of illusions, and of this master-illusion among the rest, that there is any value whatever in property apart from the good use which we can make of it. The communism of the younger brother in the Gospel, and the resolute selfishness of the elder are equally persistent and equally deplorable. The real question for all of us is, What shall we hereafter desire to have felt about that which God has withheld? what shall we desire to have done with that which by His gift

[1] St. Matt. vi. 1-18.

we have, be it much or little? what shall we desire ourselves to be, when we know that the end of life is close upon us? Most assuredly that question is vital: it cannot be pondered too often or too carefully; and in answering it let us never forget that man's life—that in him which will not perish at death—"consisteth not in the abundance of the things which he possesseth."

# SERMON XVIII.

THE DEATH OF THE SOUL.

PSALM vi. 5.

For in death no man remembereth Thee: and who will give Thee thanks in the pit?

THE sixth is the first of those seven Psalms which the Church of Christ has chosen as most fully expressing the true and deep feelings and resolves of a sincerely penitent soul. The other Penitential Psalms are Psalms xxxii., xxxviii., li., cii., cxxx., cxliii. There are many Psalms with aspirations too lofty and thoughts too wide and deep for many of us to enter at all fully into them. But if we are not men with high powers of contemplation and insight, we are all of us sinners; and, if it is to be well with us hereafter, we must all, while in this life, learn the lesson and utter the sincere and heartfelt language of Christian repentance. And therefore these seven penitential Psalms are especially deserving of being committed to memory: that we may say them to God, when we are walking alone by day, or lying awake at night, and so may learn to think and feel as true penitents should; that hereafter, through the Merits and Death of Our Saviour Jesus Christ, we may be accepted, notwithstanding our sins, in the last great Day.

Now of these seven, the sixth Psalm will be easily understood by any one who has passed sleepless nights in which temporal anxieties, dangers, or misfortunes have brought before him, as such things do, the reality and pressure of his personal sins. The Psalmist sees that God is judging him; he prays that the judgment may be remedial and not merely penal; that God will not rebuke him in His indignation nor chasten him in His sore displeasure.[1] Earthly troubles and personal sins are blended in his view; they go hand in hand as cause with its swift-following effect. God has turned away from him, as it seems: he prays God to turn towards him again and to rescue him, and he grounds this prayer on his strong yearning to praise God in the time to come, as he could no longer praise Him if he should die, for his troubles are such as to threaten death; and "in death no man remembereth Thee: and who will give Thee thanks in the pit?" Why is this? Why is God remembered by no man in death? What is this "pit" in which no man gives God thanks?

It is clear, when we look to the words which David used, that he means by death bodily death, and by the "pit" that place of the departed which the Jews called Sheol, just as it is conceived of and described in the Jewish Scriptures, and especially in the Psalms. As the writers of the Psalms think over the destiny of man, they constantly have in their minds that yawning abyss into which all that is mortal in the end finds its way—that great underground meeting-place and abode of all the dead, to which every earthly grave was, as it were, a gate, in which all was still and silent, from which were shut out alike the light of the sun and the Light of God's Presence. Here no prayers were uttered: hence no praise would ascend to God: here man still lived; but it was a maimed and imperfect and half-paralysed life, in which all the higher energies of the soul had ceased to work. This it was to be "among the dead, like unto them that

[1] Ps. vi. 1.

are wounded and lie in the grave, who are out of remembrance and are cut away from Thy Hand."[1] "For the dead praise not Thee, O Lord: neither all they that go down into silence."[2]

The Psalmist, however, knew of a blessed life beyond Sheol. Thus David, speaking in the Person of Christ, exclaims: "Thou wilt not leave my soul in Sheol, neither wilt Thou suffer thine Holy One to see corruption: Thou shalt show me the Path of Life: in Thy Presence is the fulness of Joy, and at Thy Right Hand there are pleasures for evermore."[3] Again: "As for me, I shall behold Thy Presence in Righteousness, and when I wake up after Thy likeness, I shall be satisfied with it!"[4] On the other hand, it is said of men who in this life are in honour and have no understanding, that they lie in the hell like sheep, and death gnaweth upon them.[5]

Here, of course, we must remind ourselves that God's Revelation is gradual. As He did not tell the world all at once what is His true Nature and what His Attributes: so He did not tell men all at once, all that He has since told them, about the destiny which awaits us after death. Christ our Lord has carried the light of His own Presence into that dark underworld; and we Christians know more of its real character than did our Jewish ancestors in faith. We know that those who die in a state of grace enter not heaven as yet, but Paradise—an intermediate state in which they are gradually becoming more and more ready for the fully unveiled Beauty of the Most Holy. We know that just as the lost enter upon a fearful looking-for of judgment and fiery indignation,[6] which is 1.)t yet the place of punishment: so the saved are in an antechamber of heaven, the door of which will open for tl ·m at the last great day. Of this truth the supreme

[1] Ps. lxxxviii. 4.   [2] Ib. cxv. 17.   [3] Ib. xvi. 11, 12.
Ps. xvii. 16.   [5] Ib. xlix. 12, 14, 20.   [6] Heb. x. 27.

XVIII] *The death of the soul.*

Revelation was made by our Lord upon the Cross. "To-day" (He said to the penitent thief), "to-day shalt thou be with Me in Paradise;"[1] and the Paradise of which He spoke was certainly neither heaven nor yet the place of punishment. Is it conceivable that the enfranchised and pardoned soul of the penitent thief was so paralysed by death as to be unable to praise his Deliverer, or to pray for others who might yet share in his deliverance? No; the Christian dead, saved and believing, live, we may be sure, no sterile life in that world of waiting and preparation: they too cry, "How long?"[2] they pray and they give praise. They join already in the Eternal Song that rises uninterruptedly within the Sanctuary of Heaven, though as yet its echoes only reach them through the chinks of the golden gates. Of them it cannot be said, that in death they do not remember God, and that in their place of waiting they cannot give Him thanks for the mercies of Redeeming Love.

When then we Christians use David's words we must think less of that death of the body with which this life closes than of the death of the soul, which may take place while the body is still alive. David's words do not obtrude this latter sense, but they do not exclude it: and of the two senses which, like so much in Holy Scripture, they bear, it is the deeper and more spiritual one. Worse far than the death of the body is the death of the soul by sin. Darker and more noisome far than the pit of Sheol, as the Hebrews thought of it in their twilight of faith, is the prison-house which even in this life may be tenanted by a fallen soul,—a prison-house from which, humanly speaking, a perverse will, and the tyranny of habit, and repeated violations of the known Law of God, seem to forbid escape. Certainly, in this moral death, no man remembereth God; God is, for a soul thus dead, as though

[1] St. Luke xxiii. 43.   [2] Rev. vi. 9, 10.

He did not exist; His Power and His Justice, His Tenderness and His Beauty are alike nothing to it. Certainly in this pit of corruption a soul has not the heart and nerve to praise the All-Holy; it would think of Him, if at all, with sulky and indolent aversion, as of a Being whose very Perfections are to it but a grievance and a reproach.

And yet there are times—while life lasts—when even such a soul as this may be touched by the Voice and Hand of the All-Merciful. One look like that which He turned upon Peter in the Judgment Hall;[1] one word like that which Paul heard as he lay in the dust on the road to Damascus,[2] may be the starting-point of the change. The first act of the awakening soul is to pray, "Turn Thee, O Lord, and deliver my soul: O save me for Thy mercy's sake. For in death no man remembereth Thee, and who will give Thee thanks in the pit? O Christ Jesus, Who camest into the world to save sinners, stretch forth Thy pierced Hand in power and compassion; and save—even me."

At all times of the year, at all times of life, the great change by which a soul, lost in sin, may, through God's power, turn and give itself to God, is possible. May He make this Lent a blessed time, perhaps to some of us here, perhaps, through our prayers or efforts, to others whom we know; that thus we may understand the Easter Song,—ancient, but always new:

> "O Jesu, from the death of sin
> Save us, we pray; so shalt Thou be
> The everlasting perfect Joy
> Of all the souls new born to Thee."

---

[1] St. Luke xxii. 61.   [2] Acts ix. 4.

SERMON XIX.

GUIDANCE OF THE PENITENT.

PSALM xxxii. 9.

I will inform thee and teach thee in the way wherein thou shalt go; and I will guide thee with Mine Eye.—(PRAYER-BOOK VERSION.)

THIS promise occurs in the second of the seven Penitential Psalms. The Psalm was written by David soon after his great sin. The fifty-first Psalm belongs to the first period of his repentance: in this thirty-second Psalm David has had time enough to think more fully over his guilt in the past, and to understand the happiness of being indeed forgiven. And on this account, perhaps, the Psalm is chosen by the Jews to be used at the close of the service on the Day of Atonement; and you would all remember how, in the Epistle to the Romans, St. Paul connects its first verse with that faith in our Lord Jesus Christ, by which Jew and Gentile alike are justified, because it brings us into true contact with Him Who is the Propitiation for our sins.[1]

Now the words before us are not the Psalmist's words, they are the immediate words of God, which the Psalmist hears, as he prays before the Oracle. Up to this eighth verse, the Psalmist is engaged in reviewing the past. "Blessed is he whose transgression is forgiven, whose sin is covered: blessed is the man unto whom the Lord imputeth not iniquity."[2] He knows the blessedness of the pardoned soul. He knows, (it is impossible to convey by transla-

[1] Rom. iv. 7, 8.   [2] Ps. xxxii. 1, 2.

tion the exact sense of the Divine original,) he knows the threefold misery of doing wrong. It is an offence against God, or "transgression:" it is an inward defilement or degradation,—"sin:" it is an "iniquity" which clings to the soul, perhaps through life. Yet the transgression is lifted from the soul, as though it were a heavy load; the inward defilement or sin is covered; the iniquity, even though it be not entirely expelled while life lasts, is not imputed. And how has the Psalmist attained to this happiness? He has confessed his sins. There was a long interval between the sin with Bathsheba and the visit of Nathan the prophet, an interval which was spent in bitter anguish of soul that had not been without its effects upon the bodily health of David. "While I held my tongue, my bones consumed away through my complaining all the day. For Thy Hand was heavy upon me, by day and by night; my vital moisture was turned into the arid drought of summer."[1] Then came the resolution to own his sin in its threefold aspect. "I acknowledged my sin unto Thee, and mine iniquity have I not hid: I said, I will confess my transgressions unto the Lord, and so Thou forgavest the iniquity of my sin."[2] The same three words in their deep unchanging meaning are repeated: his wrong-doing was owned before God, as a transgression of God's law; as an inward depravation and defilement; as an iniquity which clings to the soul for long years. But to confess was to be pardoned.

For this happiness of pardon, David exclaims, "Every one that is godly shall pray to Thee while the day of acceptance lasts, in a time when Thou mayest be found;"[3] but in the time of great water-floods, of those troubles of life which overwhelm so many souls, those troubles shall not really come nigh the true penitent. They may sweep over his outward life; they will not touch that which, as St.

[1] Ps. xxxii. 3, 4. [2] Ib. 5, 6. [3] Ib. 7.

XIX] *Guidance of the Penitent.*   283

Paul has said,—speaking of Christians—is "hid with Christ in God."[1] And the Psalmist knows this. "Thou," he cries, "O God, art a place to hide me in: Thou shalt preserve me from trouble: Thou shalt compass me about with songs of deliverance."[2]

Songs of deliverance! The Psalmist would be thinking of Miriam's Song after the escape of Israel from Egypt;[3] of Deborah's song after the deliverance of Israel from the power of Jabin.[4] The soul, too, has its escapes and its deliverances; and the hymns which celebrate these great events in the history of Israel are echoed by the Angels, among whom, we know, on the highest authority, "there is joy in heaven over one sinner that repenteth."[5]

Here there is a pause in the poem, and presently other words follow; not words which David himself utters, but words which David hears from within the Oracle before which he is praying. No mere man could well utter such words; they are the gracious and reassuring words of God. "I will inform thee, and teach thee in the way wherein thou shalt go: and I will guide thee with Mine eye." They form an answer, these words, to the secret anxiety which is so natural to all true penitents. "How shall I know," the penitent asks, "that I may not fall again?" Life is so full of pitfalls, the flesh is so weak, the devil so strong, the way so often doubtful, that it seems impossible after penitence to start again with a good hope of persevering. Sin may have been pardoned as sin, but it remains as weakness; it remains as impaired spiritual sight; it remains, if not as a habit, yet as a propensity, which must be watched, checked, resisted. "How hard," the penitent soul murmurs, "this continued, weary, uphill struggle; this unending anxiety, conflict, suspense!"

[1] Col. iii. 3.   [2] Ps. xxxii. 8.   [3] Exod. xv. 1-21.
[4] Judg. v. 1-31.   [5] St. Luke xv. 7, 10.

No; He Who pardons sin does not desert the penitent sinner. As to David before the Oracle, so to Christians in the Church's Sanctuary, or in the closet at home, He whispers:—"I will inform thee and teach thee in the way wherein thou shalt go: and I will guide thee with Mine Eye."

Now, why should this promise of Divine Instruction and Guidance thus follow on the sincere confession of sin? The answer is, Because guidance is given where it will be followed; instruction where it will be listened to. Unless man has a hunger and thirst for righteousness he will not be filled;[1] unless he has an appetite for truth, truth would seem to him unwelcome and repulsive. And the acknowledgment of sin, painful and irksome as it is to flesh and blood, proves the existence of the appetite for righteousness which is so necessary. The acknowledgment of sin is the way in which this appetite expresses itself: it is an effort to be, at anyrate, true. And this effort is met more than half-way by the God of Truth. "I will inform thee," He says, "and teach thee in the way wherein thou shalt go: and I will guide thee with Mine Eye." In souls which are distracted by a double purpose, by the insincerities which in the end deceive conscience itself, by the subterfuges and disguises which obscure and overlie the true facts of life and conscience,—in these God's Voice is not heard. Other voices there are; but they are the voices of self-love, of self-delusion—voices sometimes loud and shrill, sometimes soft and persuasive, but not such as to bring lasting peace and joy to the troubled spirit. It is when a man has turned a deaf ear to these voices; it is when he has stripped off the disguises which hide him from himself, though they cannot hide him from God; it is when he had taken his resolution, "I will acknowledge my sin

[1] St. Matt. v. 6.

XIX]   *Guidance of the Penitent.*   285

unto Thee, and mine unrighteousness have I not hid,"[1] that God, Who is Truth, and Who loves truth, blesses this effort to be true with the encouraging promise:—" Fear not; I will inform thee and teach thee in the way wherein thou shalt go: and I will guide thee with Mine Eye." Through outward events, and inward thoughts, and the voice of friends, and a secret control which we feel and cannot analyse, God does guide His servants.

We will not pursue the Psalm further, through the lines in which the penitent king warns and encourages his countrymen in the light of his own bitter and yet joyous experience. But perhaps we too, if we have been trying to turn this season of repentance to some account, must also look a little forward, and ask ourselves whether we shall be able to keep what we have won; whether we can hope to escape the fate of the man whom our Lord describes in the Gospel, into whose soul the evil spirit, that had been cast out, returned, and with seven other spirits more wicked than himself.[2] Against this unspeakable calamity there is no provision save a humble, constant dependence on God; a dependence which is grounded on a sincere sense of our weakness, and of His Love and Power; a dependence which surely will be met by the gracious promise: "I will inform thee and teach thee in the way wherein thou shalt go: and I will guide thee with Mine Eye." Most of God's Servants have been helped on their road to heaven by particular passages of Holy Scripture; and this verse was constantly repeated, both in his public ministrations and in private conversation on religious subjects, by Keble, the author of the *Christian Year*. And there is reason to think, too, that it was much in the thoughts of a greater than Keble, St. Augustine. His biographer, Posidius, who was with him during the last forty years of his life, tells us that during

[1] Ps. xxxii. 5.   [2] St. Matt. xii. 43-45.

the last ten days before he died he would not allow any to come near him except the physician who visited him and those who brought him his food, and that he caused to be written upon the wall opposite his bed in very large letters, so that his dying eyes might easily read them, the Seven Penitential Psalms. Can we doubt that in that last hour the gracious words were a support and encouragement to him : "I will inform thee and will teach thee in the way wherein thou shalt go: and I will guide thee with Mine Eye"? May God grant that these words may help us also through life's journey, and at its close, for the sake of our only Saviour and Redeemer, Jesus Christ, to Whom, with the Father and the Holy Ghost, be all power and glory!

ND# SERMON XX.

DISAPPROVAL OF FRIENDS.

PSALM xxxviii. 11.

My lovers and my neighbours did stand looking upon my trouble : and my kinsmen stood afar off.—(PRAYER-BOOK VERSION.)

THE thirty-eighth, the third of the seven Penitential Psalms, belongs to those months of David's life which preceded the outbreak of Absalom's revolt. David's conscience had then become fully alive to the deadly nature of his sin with Bathsheba, involving as it did the treacherous and cruel plan for the destruction of her injured husband Uriah the Hittite, when this had also been followed by the crimes of incest and murder on the part of David's own children, Amnon and Absalom. David must have reflected that a parent, of all people, cannot hope to sin alone: that his example has an unequalled power,—as for good, so certainly for evil. It would seem from this Psalm that the remorse which David felt preyed on his spirits, and even on his bodily health. "There is no health in my flesh, because of Thy displeasure : neither is there any rest in my bones, by reason of my sin. I am brought into so great trouble and misery, that I go mourning all the day long. For my loins are filled with a sore disease: and there is no whole part in my body. I am feeble, and sore smitten; . . . my heart panteth, my strength hath failed me : and the sight of mine eyes is gone from me."[1] This is a description of extreme nervous depression, which rapidly passes into active disease, and which, while it lasts, makes a man unable to hold up his head and address himself to the business of daily life. Such depression, whatever its cause, is a heavy punishment, especially to men, like David, of ardent temperaments. It is hard to bear when it stands alone, and when everything round a man, the kind and reassuring words of friends, the stability and prosperity of outward circumstances, help him to endeavour to shake it off, or at least to make the best of it. But in David's case these alleviations were wanting. David had known what it was to be popular, to be the object of the enthusiasm of multitudes, and of the devoted affection of a circle of trusted friends; and his character was such as to make him crave for and lean upon these tokens of general and private attachment. He had been loved and respected ; but now—he could not mistake it—he was so no longer. The crimes which he had himself committed, and the crimes of which his court had been the scene, had sunk into the minds of his people, even of those among his subjects who would be naturally well-affected towards his person and his throne. They could not understand how the sweet Psalmist of Israel[2] in the days of Saul, how the man after God's own heart,[3] how the favoured shepherd-boy, who had been taken by God from following the ewes that he might feed Jacob His people and Israel His inheritance,[4] could stand forth in the fierce light which beats upon an Eastern throne as a vulgar adulterer and murderer: and so, we may be sure, with misgiving, and reluctance, and pain, and shame, they kept aloof from

[1] Ps. xxxviii. 3, 6-8, 10.   [2] 2 Sam. xxiii. 1.
[3] 1 Sam. xiii. 14.   [4] Ps. lxxii. 78.

him. In no case, probably, would they have joined an unfilial adventurer like Absalom, or have exchanged distance and coldness for any more distinctly hostile attitude; but with David they could not be on their old terms of intimate and effusive loyalty; king though David was, they kept at a distance from his court, and David knew and felt what their estrangement meant. "My lovers and my neighbours did stand looking upon my trouble; and my kinsmen stood afar off." If they who were nearest to him were thus minded, could he wonder that others went further? Could he fail to hear the mutterings of the rising storm which was to shake his throne to its foundations, and drive him into temporary exile, and put him in peril of his life,—the storm which ever breaks, sooner or later, on kings, and states, as well as on individual men, when the moral supports of human life have been shattered by wrong-doing? "They also that sought after my life laid snares for me. And they that went about to do me evil talked of wickedness, and imagined deceit all the day long."[1]

This alienation of David's friends suggests practical reflections in connection with the season of the year.

1. Why, you may ask, should David have cared so much about it? After all, it may be urged, if a man declines our intimacy, we may regret it, but there is no more to be said. Friends are a blessing, no doubt: but it is possible to exaggerate the value of friendship, and a sensitive and sympathetic temper is very likely, indeed, to do so.

My brethren, you must admit, on reflection, that this is not the whole account of the matter. If a friend represents nothing but a certain measure of personal goodwill towards us, if he does not represent anything that we instinctively respect, such as high character, or a holy

[1] Ps. xxxviii. 12.

and consistent life, we may not feel keenly about the loss of his good-will. But if he is a man whom we respect as well as love, and whom we love because we respect him: if he is a man who invites our confidence by his tenderness, his truthfulness, his simplicity, his courage: if we are as sure of him as we can be of any man that his intercourse with us is regulated, not by the wish to get something from us, nor yet by the desire to give us pleasure, but by a higher principle of duty, which rules him throughout and consistently: then the withdrawal of his friendship must be felt to be a serious blow,—nay, a punishment. For we reflect that such a man as I have described does not merely represent himself; that he is a representative upon earth of a higher Mind and Presence; and that when he stands aloof from us, and renounces intercourse with us, we may already hear, though afar off, the voice of the Judgment of God.

It is, of course, possible that a good man may withdraw his friendship in consequence of a mistake. He may have heard some report about his friend which is a malicious slander, but the true character of which he has at the time no means of discovering; or he may err through an infirmity of judgment, to which the best men are from time to time liable. There have been instances in our own days, as in former generations, of good men, renouncing a friendship for utterly insufficient or indeed baseless reasons on account of an imagined wrong or a trivial difference of opinion. When this is the case the object of the alienation or coldness may fall back on his conscience and on God. If he really finds nothing within to justify the withdrawal of the friendship, he may make up his mind to bear what he cannot help. His true Friend, of Whose enduring tenderness all earthly friendships are but poor and faint shadows, is still with him. A psalmist could even say, "When my father and my mother forsake me, the Lord taketh me up."[1]

But in David's present case this was impossible. David's conscience told him that the friends of his person and his throne who stood aloof from him were right; that God was with them, and not with himself; that their action was a reflection of God's judgment. Conscience makes cowards at any rate of those sinners who cannot succeed in silencing its voice; and the events of the day, and the words and actions of men around, even when directed by no distinct purpose, appear, to its sensitive anxiety, to echo the Divine judgment. David may have even seen in the estrangement of his friends more than some of them meant; his unquiet sense of guilt may have read into their actions a purpose of which they were very imperfectly conscious. But the result was the same: David was miserable. "My lovers and my neighbours did stand looking upon my trouble: and my kinsmen stood afar off."

2. He Who was of the house and lineage of David[2]— David's Son, and yet David's Lord,[3]—knew in His bitter Passion what it was to be utterly deserted by human friends. When kind words and reassuring looks would have been welcome to His Human Soul, all His disciples forsook Him and fled.[4] But what a contrast between His case and that of David! If He suffered on this score, so that David's words have a prophetic reference to Him, He suffered only from wounded affections, without any misgiving or distress of conscience. If He was deserted by His friends in His hour of darkness, the shame was not His, but theirs. Their desertion of Him expressed not God's judgment on sin, but the world's opposition to sanctity; and Jesus could only think of them with com-

[1] Ps. xxvii. 12.
[2] St. Luke ii. 4.
[3] St. Mark xii. 35-37.
[4] St. Matt. xxvi. 56.

passion—never for a moment, as David thought of the friends who kept aloof from him, with a secret though mortified reverence, based on a conviction that they were right.

My brethren, if any one of us has to put up with coldness and aversion, for which he knows there is no real reason, he may think of and unite himself in spirit to our Lord Jesus Christ; praying Him to bless this note of likeness to that which He Himself condescended to endure in His bitter Passion, and to vouchsafe to sanctify this light affliction by the awful mental Pain which He condescended for our sakes to endure.

Human friends may be parted from, though not without a heartache, when the Friend of friends is still on the same terms as ever with the conscience and the will. But if any of us, like David, have lost friends for what conscience tells us are good reasons, let us be sure that it is well for us that we should have lost them. It is better that all wrong-doing should be punished in this world rather than in the next, and punished in a manner which will lead us most surely and swiftly to return to God. To be far from Him in truth, yet surrounded by kind treatment, which implies that all is with us as it should be, is to be in danger of living and dying in a perilous illusion.

A rude awakening here on earth is doubtless trying to flesh and blood; but anything is better than an awakening deferred until the time when probation shall be over, and the door of repentance shall be shut. David's bitter solitariness prompted the prayer: "I will confess my wickedness, and be sorry for my sin. Forsake me not, O Lord, my God; be not Thou far from me."[1] And we Christians know that if God leaves us in His mercy to ourselves, to our

[1] Ps. xxxviii. 18, 21.

own thoughts of shame and sorrow for acts and words which He must condemn, and the condemnation of which we seem to trace in the altered bearing of those among His servants whom we respect and love; yet that, "if we confess our sins, God is faithful and just to forgive us our sins," because "the Blood of Jesus Christ His Son cleanseth from all sin."[1]

[1] 1 St. John i. 7, 8.

SERMON XXI.

THE IDEA OF SIN.

PSALM li. 4.

Against Thee, Thee only, have I sinned, and done this evil in Thy sight; that Thou mightest be justified when Thou speakest, and be clear when Thou judgest.

NO one but David could have written this fifty-first Psalm. The language is David's: the temper is David's: the circumstances are David's. He must have written it just after the visit of the prophet Nathan, which had at once brought him to see the real character of his sin with Bathsheba, and of his murder of Uriah, and had left him penitent and forgiven. For in this Psalm David prays not only or chiefly for cleansing and forgiveness, but for a restoration of the graces which had been lost by his sin; and it is this feature of the Psalm especially which has made it in all later ages the favourite of all true penitents. Not only does David exclaim and pray—

"Turn Thy face from my sins,
And blot out all mine iniquities."[1]

But he adds—

"Make me a clean heart, O God:
And renew a right spirit within me.
Cast me not away from Thy presence:
And take not Thy Holy Spirit from me.
O give me the comfort of Thy help again:
And stablish me with Thy princely Spirit."[2]

---

[1] Ps. li. 9.   [2] *Ib.* 10-12.

The Idea of Sin. 295

And these prayers presuppose the confession of the text: "Against Thee only have I sinned."

This confession teaches us several truths; but there is one truth in particular which it teaches very plainly: it teaches how to think of sin.

We employ many words to express the idea of wrong-doing; some of them describe it gently, some energetically, but none of them so vividly and so truly as the word Sin. When we speak of a mistake, we imply that something has been done in consequence of a pardonable ignorance; when of a fault, we are thinking of what a man owes to himself, his own standard of right action, which he has failed to achieve; when of a crime, we have more or less distinctly before our minds the law of the land, the acts by which it is violated, and its methods of asserting its supremacy. But when we speak of sin—do what we may—our thoughts turn away from self, away from human standards of goodness, human law; and we think of God. Sin is more than a mistake, more than a fault, more than a crime, although each of these words may be labels which we have placed on acts that really deserve the name of sin. Sin is an act of hostility to God; and the sense of sin is that altogether solitary and unique impression upon the soul which results from the commission of such an act.

"Against Thee only have I sinned." David, in his own Hebrew language, uses these words to describe his wrong-doing; but they all enter into what we mean by Sin. "According to the multitude of Thy mercies, blot out my transgressions:" here he thinks of sin as an act which traverses the known law or will of God. "Wash me throughly from my wickedness"—more literally, my perversity: here he thinks of sin as a malign force which has twisted his moral being from the right way. And "Cleanse me from my sin:" here he uses a distinct word from the other two, a word which includes and goes beyond them, and which describes an act whereby a man misses the one true aim of action—namely, conformity to the Perfect Will. All of these three words enter into and are expressed by one word, "sin," which means an act or movement of the will freely directed against God, and which, as such, transgresses His Will, perverts man's nature, and misses the true aim and purpose of man's life.

"Against Thee only have I sinned." This is what every true penitent says in his heart of hearts when he knows that he has offended God. His act may have wronged his fellow-creatures, it may have injured himself. David's did. David murdered a faithful servant; degraded a weak woman; forfeited the old love and loyalty of his subjects, and prepared the way for Absalom's rebellion. But in his penitence these aspects and results of his act, real as they were, are shut out from view. He sees before him God, only God : God, Whose Power had saved him from so many dangers: God, Whose Wisdom had guided him through so many difficulties: God, Whose Goodness had sustained and brightened his life in innumerable ways. He had singled out his strongest, wisest, kindest Friend to treat Him as an enemy. For sin, as I have said, considered as an act of the will directed against God, is an act of hostility; it is an act which would, if possible, annihilate God. This is not a rhetorical exaggeration, it is a plain statement of fact. For consider. Sin violates and defies the Moral Law of God: and what is God's Moral Law? Is it a law which, like the laws of nature, as we call them, might conceivably have been other than it is? Certainly not. We can conceive much in nature being very different from what it is—suns and stars moving in larger or smaller cycles, men and animals of different shapes; the chemistry, the geology, the governing rules of

The Idea of Sin.

the material universe, quite unlike what they actually are. God's liberty in creating physical beings was in no way shackled by His own laws, whether of force or matter. But can we, if we believe in a Moral God, conceive Him saying, "Thou mayest lie"? "Thou mayest do murder"? We cannot, any more than we can conceive His denying that things that are equal to the same are equal to one another. The very mind and soul which He has given us bears indelibly impressed on it His Moral Truth, just as much as the first truths of mathematics. But then these truths must have been always true; and if always true, then truths co-eternal with God; and if co-eternal with Him, not things outside Him, not independent of Him, for in that case He would not be the Alone Eternal, but they must have been essential laws or integral parts of His Eternal Nature. The Moral Law is not a code which He might have made other than it is; it is His own Moral Nature thrown into a shape which makes it applicable and intelligible to us His creatures; and therefore in violating it we are opposing, not something which He has made, but might have made otherwise, like the laws of nature,—but Himself. Sin, if it could, would destroy God; and it is this, its malignant character, which underlies David's passionate exclamation, " Against Thee only have I sinned."

And this conviction explains the words that follow. I make this confession, this protestation, the Psalmist says, " that Thou mightest be justified when Thou speakest, and be clear when Thou judgest." Whatever sentence God may pronounce must, David sees, be just. Man must justify God, must admit and acknowledge His Righteousness, however He may punish man's sin. For the gravity of sin, when it is disentangled from the lower conceptions of wrong-doing—mistake, fault, crime—and seen to be an act of hostility directed against the Being of God, warrants any penalty that God may impose. Nothing is due to man but punishment; nothing can be hoped for from God but free forgiveness.

One of the most necessary concerns, then, of a serious Christian at all times should be to accustom himself to think of his sins in this way; to free himself from the false opinions and standards which lead him, in his self-love, to make little of it. And this is the proper work of Lent. Think over any offences which you would least wish those whom you most love and respect on earth to know you to have been guilty of, and then place them in the Light of His Countenance, Who has known and knows all about them, and Who is much more deeply wronged by them than any of His creatures. Think of the violent gusts of anger, which would perhaps have taken the life of its object if it could; of the pride which has ruled the mind and will, it may be for long periods of time; of the envy which has darkened every relation with others with the shadow of malignant passion; of the lies which have gone far to shatter the fundamental sense of rectitude; of the sloth, the gluttony, the lust, which have left the mark of degradation deeply imprinted on the body, more deeply still upon the immaterial spirit; and then reflect that each and all of these were wrongs aimed at the Author of your life, the Author of all the happiness with which it has been accompanied from youth until now, the Being to Whom you are indebted for all the blessings of these many years, for the means of grace and for the hope of glory; your Creator, your Redeemer, your Sanctifier.

And if this be done, David's words, like the old Jewish law, will prove a schoolmaster to bring your soul really to Christ;[1] closer to Him perhaps than ever before; for the sense of sin discovers a want which He, and He alone,

[1] Gal. iii. 24.

can relieve. On the Cross of shame He was made to be sin for us, Who knew no sin;[1] He blotted out the handwriting that was against us, nailing it to His Cross:[2] He is the Propitiation for our sins.[3] These words of the Apostles do not lose their virtue with the lapse of years; they are as true now as eighteen centuries ago. Now, as then, guilty man has nothing that He can plead before the Sanctity of God, save the free Self-sacrifice of the All-merciful Redeemer, in looking on Whom the Eternal Father pardons the sin of the penitent.

> "Thou shalt purge me, O my Saviour, with hyssop, and I shall be clean;
> Thou shalt wash me, and I shall be whiter than snow.
> Thou shalt make me hear of joy and gladness,
> That the bones which Thou hast broken may rejoice." [4]

---

[1] 2 Cor. v. 21.   [2] Col. ii. 14.
[3] 1 St. John ii. 2.   [4] Ps. li. 7, 8.

A Catalogue of Works

IN

THEOLOGICAL LITERATURE

PUBLISHED BY

MESSRS. LONGMANS, GREEN, & CO.

39 PATERNOSTER ROW, LONDON, E.C.

Abbey and Overton.—THE ENGLISH CHURCH IN THE EIGHTEENTH CENTURY. By CHARLES J. ABBEY, M.A., Rector of Checkendon, Reading, and JOHN H. OVERTON, M.A., Rector of Epworth, Doncaster, Rural Dean of Isle of Axholme. *Cr. 8vo. 7s. 6d.*

Adams.—SACRED ALLEGORIES. The Shadow of the Cross—The Distant Hills—The Old Man's Home—The King's Messengers. By the Rev. WILLIAM ADAMS, M.A. *Crown 8vo. 5s.*

The Four Allegories may be had separately, with Illustrations. 16mo. 1s. each. *Also the Miniature Edition. Four Vols.* 32mo. 1s. each; in a box, 5s.

Aids to the Inner Life.

Edited by the Rev. W. H. HUTCHINGS, M.A., Rector of Kirkby Misperton, Yorkshire. *Five Vols.* 32mo, cloth limp, 6d. each; or cloth extra, 1s. each. *Sold separately.*
Also an Edition *with red borders,* 2s. each.

OF THE IMITATION OF CHRIST. By THOMAS À KEMPIS. In Four Books.

THE CHRISTIAN YEAR: Thoughts in Verse for the Sundays and Holy Days throughout the Year.

THE DEVOUT LIFE. By ST. FRANCIS DE SALES.

THE HIDDEN LIFE OF THE SOUL. From the French of JEAN NICOLAS GROU.

THE SPIRITUAL COMBAT. Together with the Supplement and the Path of Paradise. By LAURENCE SCUPOLI.

Andrewes.—A MANUAL FOR THE SICK; with other Devotions. By LANCELOT ANDREWES, D.D., sometime Bishop of Winchester. With Preface by H. P. LIDDON, D.D. *24mo. 2s. 6d.*

Augustine.—THE CONFESSIONS OF ST. AUGUSTINE. In Ten Books. Translated and Edited by the Rev. W. H. HUTCHINGS, M.A. *Small 8vo. 5s. Cheap Edition. 16mo. 2s. 6d.*

Bathe.—Works by the Rev. ANTHONY BATHE, M.A.
A LENT WITH JESUS. A Plain Guide for Churchmen. Containing Readings for Lent and Easter Week, and on the Holy Eucharist. *32mo, 1s.*; or in paper cover, *6d.*
WHAT I SHOULD BELIEVE. A Simple Manual of Self-Instruction for Church People. *Crown 8vo. 3s. 6d.*

Bickersteth.—Works by EDWARD HENRY BICKERSTETH, D.D., Bishop of Exeter.
THE LORD'S TABLE; or, Meditations on the Holy Communion Office in the Book of Common Prayer. *16mo. 1s.*; or cloth extra, *2s.*
YESTERDAY, TO-DAY, AND FOR EVER: a Poem in Twelve Books. *One Shilling Edition, 18mo. With red borders, 16mo, 2s. 6d. The Crown 8vo Edition (5s.) may still be had.*

Blunt.—Works by the late Rev. JOHN HENRY BLUNT, D.D.
DICTIONARY OF DOCTRINAL AND HISTORICAL THEOLOGY. By various Writers. Edited by the Rev. JOHN HENRY BLUNT, D.D. *Imperial 8vo. 21s.*
DICTIONARY OF SECTS, HERESIES, ECCLESIASTICAL PARTIES AND SCHOOLS OF RELIGIOUS THOUGHT. By various Writers. Edited by the Rev. JOHN HENRY BLUNT, D.D. *Imperial 8vo. 21s.*
THE BOOK OF CHURCH LAW. Being an Exposition of the Legal Rights and Duties of the Parochial Clergy and the Laity of the Church of England. Revised by Sir WALTER G. F. PHILLIMORE, Bart., D.C.L. *Crown 8vo. 7s. 6d.*
A COMPANION TO THE BIBLE: Being a Plain Commentary on Scripture History, to the end of the Apostolic Age. *Two vols. small 8vo. Sold separately.*
THE OLD TESTAMENT. *3s. 6d.* THE NEW TESTAMENT. *3s. 6d.*
HOUSEHOLD THEOLOGY: a Handbook of Religious Information respecting the Holy Bible, the Prayer Book, the Church, the Ministry, Divine Worship, the Creeds, etc. etc. *Paper cover, 16mo. 1s.* Also the Larger Edition, *3s. 6d.*

Body.—Works by the Rev. GEORGE BODY, D.D., Canon of Durham.
THE SCHOOL OF CALVARY; or, Laws of Christian Life revealed from the Cross. A Course of Lectures delivered in substance at All Saints', Margaret Street. *Crown 8vo.*
THE LIFE OF JUSTIFICATION: a Series of Lectures delivered in substance at All Saints', Margaret Street. *16mo. 2s. 6d.*
THE LIFE OF TEMPTATION: a Course of Lectures delivered in substance at St. Peter's, Eaton Square; also at All Saints', Margaret Street. *16mo. 2s. 6d.*

IN THEOLOGICAL LITERATURE. 3

Boultbee.—A COMMENTARY ON THE THIRTY-NINE ARTICLES OF THE CHURCH OF ENGLAND. By the Rev. T. P. BOULTBEE, formerly Principal of the London College of Divinity, St. John's Hall, Highbury. *Crown 8vo.* 6s.

Bright.—Works by WILLIAM BRIGHT, D.D., Canon of Christ Church.
LESSONS FROM THE LIVES OF THREE GREAT FATHERS: St. Athanasius, St. Chrysostom, and St. Augustine. *Crown 8vo.* 6s.
THE INCARNATION AS A MOTIVE POWER. *Crown 8vo.* 6s.
IONA AND OTHER VERSES. *Small 8vo.* 4s. 6d.
HYMNS AND OTHER VERSES. *Small 8vo.* 5s.
FAITH AND LIFE: Readings for the greater Holy Days, and the Sundays from Advent to Trinity. Compiled from Ancient Writers. *Small 8vo.* 5s.

Bright and Medd.—LIBER PRECUM PUBLICARUM ECCLESIÆ ANGLICANÆ. A GULIELMO BRIGHT, S.T.P., et PETRO GOLDSMITH MEDD, A.M., Latine redditus. [In hac Editione continentur Versiones Latinæ—1. Libri Precum Publicarum Ecclesiæ Anglicanæ; 2. Liturgiæ Primæ Reformatæ; 3. Liturgiæ Scoticanæ; 4. Liturgiæ Americanæ.] *Small 8vo.* 7s. 6d.

Browne.—AN EXPOSITION OF THE THIRTY-NINE ARTICLES, Historical and Doctrinal. By E. H. BROWNE, D.D., formerly Bishop of Winchester. *8vo.* 16s.

Campion and Beamont.—THE PRAYER BOOK INTERLEAVED. With Historical Illustrations and Explanatory Notes arranged parallel to the Text. By W. M. CAMPION, D.D., and W. J. BEAMONT, M.A. *Small 8vo.* 7s. 6d.

Carter.—Works edited by the Rev. T. T. CARTER, M.A., Hon. Canon of Christ Church, Oxford.
THE TREASURY OF DEVOTION: a Manual of Prayer for General and Daily Use. Compiled by a Priest. *18mo.* 2s. 6d.; *cloth limp*, 2s.; *or bound with the Book of Common Prayer*, 3s. 6d. *Large-Type Edition. Crown 8vo.* 5s.
THE WAY OF LIFE: A Book of Prayers and Instruction for the Young at School, with a Preparation for Confirmation. Compiled by a Priest. *18mo.* 1s. 6d.
THE PATH OF HOLINESS: a First Book of Prayers, with the Service of the Holy Communion, for the Young. Compiled by a Priest. With Illustrations. *16mo.* 1s. 6d.; *cloth limp*, 1s.
THE GUIDE TO HEAVEN: a Book of Prayers for every Want. (For the Working Classes.) Compiled by a Priest. *18mo.* 1s. 6d.; *cloth limp*, 1s. *Large-Type Edition. Crown 8vo.* 1s. 6d.; *cloth limp*, 1s.

[*continued.*

A CATALOGUE OF WORKS

Carter.—Works edited by the Rev. T. T. CARTER, M.A., Hon. Canon of Christ Church, Oxford—*continued.*
SELF-RENUNCIATION. From the French. 16mo. 2s. 6d. Also the *Larger Edition. Small 8vo.* 3s. 6d.
THE STAR OF CHILDHOOD; a First Book of Prayers and Instruction for Children. Compiled by a Priest. With Illustrations. 16mo. 2s. 6d.

Carter.—MAXIMS AND GLEANINGS FROM THE WRITINGS OF T. T. CARTER, M.A. Selected and arranged for Daily Use. Crown 16mo. 2s.

Compton.—THE ARMOURY OF PRAYER. A Book of Devotion. Compiled by the Rev. BERDMORE COMPTON, M.A. 18mo. 3s. 6d.

Conybeare and Howson.—THE LIFE AND EPISTLES OF ST. PAUL. By the Rev. W. J. CONYBEARE, M.A., and the Very Rev. J. S. HOWSON, D.D. With numerous Maps and Illustrations.
LIBRARY EDITION. Two Vols. 8vo. 21s.
STUDENT'S EDITION. One Vol. Crown 8vo. 6s.

Crake.—HISTORY OF THE CHURCH UNDER THE ROMAN EMPIRE, A.D. 30-476. By the Rev. A. D. CRAKE, B.A. Crown 8vo. 7s. 6d.

Creighton.—HISTORY OF THE PAPACY DURING THE REFORMATION. By the Rev. CANON CREIGHTON, M.A., LL.D. 8vo. Vols. I. and II., 1378-1464, 32s. Vols. III. and IV., 1464-1518, 24s.

Devotional Series, 16mo, Red Borders. *Each* 2s. 6d.
BICKERSTETH'S YESTERDAY, TO-DAY, AND FOR EVER.
CHILCOT'S EVIL THOUGHTS.
CHRISTIAN YEAR.
DEVOTIONAL BIRTHDAY BOOK.
HERBERT'S POEMS AND PROVERBS.
KEMPIS' (À) OF THE IMITATION OF CHRIST.
ST. FRANCIS DE SALES' THE DEVOUT LIFE.
WILSON'S THE LORD'S SUPPER. *Large type.*
*TAYLOR'S (JEREMY) HOLY LIVING.
*———   ———   HOLY DYING.
**These two in one Volume.* 5s.

Devotional Series, 18mo, without Red Borders. *Each* 1s.
BICKERSTETH'S YESTERDAY, TO-DAY, AND FOR EVER.
CHRISTIAN YEAR.
KEMPIS' (À) OF THE IMITATION OF CHRIST.
WILSON'S THE LORD'S SUPPER. *Large type.*
*TAYLOR'S (JEREMY) HOLY LIVING.
*———   ———   HOLY DYING.
**These two in one Volume.* 2s. 6d.

IN THEOLOGICAL LITERATURE. 5

Edersheim.—Works by ALFRED EDERSHEIM, M.A., D.D., Ph.D., sometime Grinfield Lecturer on the Septuagint, Oxford.

THE LIFE AND TIMES OF JESUS THE MESSIAH. *Two Vols.* 8*vo.* 24*s.*

JESUS THE MESSIAH : being an Abridged Edition of 'The Life and Times of Jesus the Messiah.' *Crown* 8*vo.* 7*s.* 6*d.*

PROPHECY AND HISTORY IN RELATION TO THE MESSIAH : The Warburton Lectures, 1880-1884. 8*vo.* 12*s.*

TOHU-VA-VOHU ('Without Form and Void') : being a collection of Fragmentary Thoughts and Criticism. *Crown* 8*vo.* 6*s.*

Ellicott.—Works by C. J. ELLICOTT, D.D., Bishop of Gloucester and Bristol.

A CRITICAL AND GRAMMATICAL COMMENTARY ON ST. PAUL'S EPISTLES. Greek Text, with a Critical and Grammatical Commentary, and a Revised English Translation. 8*vo.*

1 CORINTHIANS. 16*s.*	PHILIPPIANS, COLOSSIANS, AND PHILEMON. 10*s.* 6*d.*
GALATIANS. 8*s.* 6*d.*	
EPHESIANS. 8*s.* 6*d.*	THESSALONIANS. 7*s.* 6*d.*
PASTORAL EPISTLES. 10*s.* 6*d.*	

HISTORICAL LECTURES ON THE LIFE OF OUR LORD JESUS CHRIST. 8*vo.* 12*s.*

Epochs of Church History. Edited by the Rev. CANON CREIGHTON, M.A., LL.D. *Fcap.* 8*vo.* 2*s.* 6*d. each.*

THE ENGLISH CHURCH IN OTHER LANDS. By the Rev. H. W. TUCKER, M.A.

THE HISTORY OF THE REFORMATION IN ENGLAND. By the Rev. GEO. G. PERRY, M.A.

THE CHURCH OF THE EARLY FATHERS. By the Rev. ALFRED PLUMMER, D.D.

THE EVANGELICAL REVIVAL IN THE EIGHTEENTH CENTURY. By the Rev. J. H. OVERTON, M.A.

THE UNIVERSITY OF OXFORD. By the Hon. G. C. BRODRICK, D.C.L.

THE UNIVERSITY OF CAMBRIDGE. By J. BASS MULLINGER M.A.

THE ENGLISH CHURCH IN THE MIDDLE AGES. By the Rev. W. HUNT, M.A.

THE CHURCH AND THE EASTERN EMPIRE. By the Rev. H. F. TOZER, M.A.

THE CHURCH AND THE ROMAN EMPIRE. By the Rev. A. CARR.

THE CHURCH AND THE PURITANS, 1570-1660. By HENRY OFFLEY WAKEMAN, M.A.

HILDEBRAND AND HIS TIMES. By the Rev. W. R. W. STEPHENS, M.A.

THE POPES AND THE HOHENSTAUFEN. By UGO BALZANI.

THE COUNTER-REFORMATION. By ADOLPHUS WILLIAM WARD, Litt. D

WYCLIFFE AND MOVEMENTS FOR REFORM. By REGINALD L. POOLE, M.A.

THE ARIAN CONTROVERSY. By H. M. GWATKIN, M.A.

Fosbery.—Works edited by the Rev. THOMAS VINCENT FOSBERY, M.A., sometime Vicar of St. Giles's, Reading.
VOICES OF COMFORT. *Cheap Edition. Small 8vo.* 3s. 6d.
The Larger Edition (7s. 6d.) may still be had.
HYMNS AND POEMS FOR THE SICK AND SUFFERING. In connection with the Service for the Visitation of the Sick. Selected from Various Authors. *Small 8vo.* 3s. 6d.

Garland.—THE PRACTICAL TEACHING OF THE APOCALYPSE. By the Rev. G. V. GARLAND, M.A. 8vo. 16s.

Gore.—Works by the Rev. CHARLES GORE, M.A., Principal of the Pusey House ; Fellow of Trinity College, Oxford.
THE MINISTRY OF THE CHRISTIAN CHURCH. 8vo. 10s. 6d.
ROMAN CATHOLIC CLAIMS. *Crown 8vo.* 3s. 6d.

Goulburn.—Works by EDWARD MEYRICK GOULBURN, D.D., D.C.L., sometime Dean of Norwich.
THOUGHTS ON PERSONAL RELIGION. *Small 8vo,* 6s. 6d. ; *Cheap Edition,* 3s. 6d.; *Presentation Edition,* 2 vols. *small 8vo,* 10s. 6d.
THE PURSUIT OF HOLINESS : a Sequel to 'Thoughts on Personal Religion.' *Small 8vo.* 5s. *Cheap Edition,* 3s. 6d.
THE CHILD SAMUEL : a Practical and Devotional Commentary on the Birth and Childhood of the Prophet Samuel, as recorded in 1 Sam. i., ii. 1-27, iii. *Small 8vo.* 2s. 6d.
THE GOSPEL OF THE CHILDHOOD : a Practical and Devotional Commentary on the Single Incident of our Blessed Lord's Childhood (St. Luke ii. 41 to the end). *Crown 8vo.* 2s. 6d.
THE COLLECTS OF THE DAY: an Exposition, Critical and Devotional, of the Collects appointed at the Communion. With Preliminary Essays on their Structure, Sources, etc. 2 *vols. Crown 8vo.* 8s. *each.*
THOUGHTS UPON THE LITURGICAL GOSPELS for the Sundays, one for each day in the year. With an Introduction on their Origin, History, the Modifications made in them by the Reformers and by the Revisers of the Prayer Book. 2 *vols. Crown 8vo.* 16s.
MEDITATIONS UPON THE LITURGICAL GOSPELS for the Minor Festivals of Christ, the two first Week-days of the Easter and Whitsun Festivals, and the Red-letter Saints' Days. *Crown 8vo.* 8s. 6d.
FAMILY PRAYERS compiled from various sources (chiefly from Bishop Hamilton's Manual), and arranged on the Liturgical Principle. *Crown 8vo.* 3s. 6d. *Cheap Edition.* 16mo. 1s.

Haddan.—APOSTOLICAL SUCCESSION IN THE CHURCH OF ENGLAND. By the Rev. ARTHUR W. HADDAN, B.D., late Rector of Barton-on-the-Heath. 8vo. 12s.

IN THEOLOGICAL LITERATURE. 7

Hatch.—THE ORGANIZATION OF THE EARLY CHRISTIAN CHURCHES. Being the Bampton Lectures for 1880. By EDWIN HATCH, M.A., D.D. 8vo. 5s.

Hernaman.—LYRA CONSOLATIONIS. From the Poets of the Seventeenth, Eighteenth, and Nineteenth Centuries. Selected and arranged by CLAUDIA FRANCES HERNAMAN. Small 8vo. 6s.

Holland.—Works by the Rev. HENRY SCOTT HOLLAND, M.A., Canon and Precentor of St. Paul's.

CREED AND CHARACTER: Sermons. Crown 8vo. 7s. 6d.

ON BEHALF OF BELIEF. Sermons preached in St. Paul's Cathedral. Crown 8vo. 6s.

CHRIST OR ECCLESIASTES. Sermons preached in St. Paul's Cathedral. Crown 8vo. 3s. 6d.

GOOD FRIDAY. Being Addresses on the Seven Last Words, delivered at St. Paul's Cathedral on Good Friday. Small 8vo. 2s.

LOGIC AND LIFE, with other Sermons. Crown 8vo. 7s. 6d.

Hopkins.—CHRIST THE CONSOLER. A Book of Comfort for the Sick. By ELLICE HOPKINS. Small 8vo. 2s. 6d.

James.—COMMENT UPON THE COLLECTS appointed to be used in the Church of England on Sundays and Holy Days throughout the Year. By JOHN JAMES, D.D., sometime Canon of Peterborough. Small 8vo. 3s. 6d.

Jameson.—Works by Mrs. JAMESON.

SACRED AND LEGENDARY ART, containing Legends of the Angels and Archangels, the Evangelists, the Apostles, the Doctors of the Church, St. Mary Magdalene, the Patron Saints, the Martyrs, the Early Bishops, the Hermits, and the Warrior-Saints of Christendom, as represented in the Fine Arts. With 19 etchings on Copper and Steel, and 187 Woodcuts. Two Vols. Cloth, gilt top, 20s. net.

LEGENDS OF THE MONASTIC ORDERS, as represented in the Fine Arts, comprising the Benedictines and Augustines, and Orders derived from their Rules, the Mendicant Orders, the Jesuits, and the Order of the Visitation of S. Mary. With 11 etchings by the Author, and 88 Woodcuts. One Vol. Cloth, gilt top, 10s. net.

LEGENDS OF THE MADONNA, OR BLESSED VIRGIN MARY. Devotional with and without the Infant Jesus, Historical from the Annunciation to the Assumption, as represented in Sacred and Legendary Christian Art. With 27 Etchings and 165 Woodcuts. One Vol. Cloth, gilt top, 10s. net.

THE HISTORY OF OUR LORD, as exemplified in Works of Art, with that of His Types, St. John the Baptist, and other Persons of the Old and New Testaments. Commenced by the late Mrs. JAMESON; continued and completed by LADY EASTLAKE. With 31 etchings and 281 Woodcuts. Two Vols. 8vo. 20s. net.

Jennings.—ECCLESIA ANGLICANA. A History of the Church of Christ in England from the Earliest to the Present Times. By the Rev. ARTHUR CHARLES JENNINGS, M.A. *Crown 8vo.* 7*s.* 6*d.*

Jukes.—Works by ANDREW JUKES.
THE NEW MAN AND THE ETERNAL LIFE. Notes on the Reiterated Amens of the Son of God. *Crown 8vo.* 6*s.*
THE NAMES OF GOD IN HOLY SCRIPTURE: a Revelation of His Nature and Relationships. *Crown 8vo.* 4*s.* 6*d.*
THE TYPES OF GENESIS. *Crown 8vo.* 7*s.* 6*d.*
THE SECOND DEATH AND THE RESTITUTION OF ALL THINGS. *Crown 8vo.* 3*s.* 6*d.*
THE MYSTERY OF THE KINGDOM. *Crown 8vo.* 2*s.* 6*d.*

Keble.—MAXIMS AND GLEANINGS FROM THE WRITINGS OF JOHN KEBLE, M.A. Selected and Arranged for Daily Use. By C. M. S. *Crown 16mo.* 2*s.*
SELECTIONS FROM THE WRITINGS OF JOHN KEBLE, M.A. *Crown 8vo.* 3*s.* 6*d.*

Kennaway.—CONSOLATIO; OR, COMFORT FOR THE AFFLICTED. Edited by the late Rev. C. E. KENNAWAY. *16mo.* 2*s.* 6*d.*

Knox Little.—Works by W. J. KNOX LITTLE, M.A., Canon Residentiary of Worcester, and Vicar of Hoar Cross.
THE CHRISTIAN HOME. *Crown 8vo.*
THE HOPES AND DECISIONS OF THE PASSION OF OUR MOST HOLY REDEEMER. *Crown 8vo.* 3*s.* 6*d.*
THE THREE HOURS' AGONY OF OUR BLESSED REDEEMER. Being Addresses in the form of Meditations delivered in St. Alban's Church, Manchester, on Good Friday, 1877. *Small 8vo.* 2*s.*; or in *Paper Cover,* 1*s.*
CHARACTERISTICS AND MOTIVES OF THE CHRISTIAN LIFE. Ten Sermons preached in Manchester Cathedral, in Lent and Advent 1877. *Crown 8vo.* 3*s.* 6*d.*
SERMONS PREACHED FOR THE MOST PART IN MANCHESTER. *Crown 8vo.* 7*s.* 6*d.*
THE MYSTERY OF THE PASSION OF OUR MOST HOLY REDEEMER. *Crown 8vo.* 3*s.* 6*d.*
THE WITNESS OF THE PASSION OF OUR MOST HOLY REDEEMER. *Crown 8vo.* 3*s.* 6*d.*
THE LIGHT OF LIFE. Sermons preached on Various Occasions. *Crown 8vo.* 7*s.* 6*d.*
SUNLIGHT AND SHADOW IN THE CHRISTIAN LIFE. Sermons preached for the most part in America. *Crown 8vo.* 7*s.* 6*d*

IN THEOLOGICAL LITERATURE. 9

Lear.—Works by, and Edited by, H. L. SIDNEY LEAR.

CHRISTIAN BIOGRAPHIES. *Crown 8vo.* 3s. 6d. *each.*
MADAME LOUISE DE FRANCE, Daughter of Louis XV., known also as the Mother Térèse de St. Augustin.
FOR DAYS AND YEARS. A Book containing a Text, Short Reading, and Hymn for Every Day in the Church's Year. 16mo. 2s. 6d. *Also a Cheap Edition,* 32mo. 1s.; *or cloth gilt,* 1s. 6d.
FIVE MINUTES. Daily Readings of Poetry. 16mo. 3s. 6d. *Also a Cheap Edition.* 32mo. 1s.; *or cloth gilt,* 1s. 6d.
WEARINESS. A Book for the Languid and Lonely. *Large Type. Small 8vo.* 5s.
THE LIGHT OF THE CONSCIENCE. 16mo. 2s. 6d. *Also the Larger Edition. Crown 8vo.* 5s.

A DOMINICAN ARTIST: a Sketch of the Life of the Rev. Père Besson, of the Order of St. Dominic.
HENRI PERREYVE. By A. GRATRY.
ST. FRANCIS DE SALES, Bishop and Prince of Geneva.
THE REVIVAL OF PRIESTLY LIFE IN THE SEVENTEENTH CENTURY IN FRANCE.

A CHRISTIAN PAINTER OF THE NINETEENTH CENTURY.
BOSSUET AND HIS CONTEMPORARIES.
FÉNELON, ARCHBISHOP OF CAMBRAI.
HENRI DOMINIQUE LACORDAIRE.

DEVOTIONAL WORKS. Edited by H. L. SIDNEY LEAR. *New and Uniform Editions. Nine Vols.* 16mo. 2s. 6d. *each.*

FÉNELON'S SPIRITUAL LETTERS TO MEN.
FÉNELON'S SPIRITUAL LETTERS TO WOMEN.
A SELECTION FROM THE SPIRITUAL LETTERS OF ST. FRANCIS DE SALES.
THE SPIRIT OF ST. FRANCIS DE SALES.

THE HIDDEN LIFE OF THE SOUL.
THE LIGHT OF THE CONSCIENCE.
SELF-RENUNCIATION. From the French.
ST. FRANCIS DE SALES' OF THE LOVE OF GOD.
SELECTIONS FROM PASCAL'S THOUGHTS.

Library of Spiritual Works for English Catholics. *Original Edition. With Red Borders. Small 8vo.* 5s. *each. New and Cheaper Editions.* 16mo. 2s. 6d. *each.*

OF THE IMITATION OF CHRIST.
THE SPIRITUAL COMBAT. By LAURENCE SCUPOLI.
THE DEVOUT LIFE. By ST. FRANCIS DE SALES.
OF THE LOVE OF GOD. By ST. FRANCIS DE SALES.
THE CONFESSIONS OF ST. AUGUSTINE. *In Ten Books.*
THE CHRISTIAN YEAR. 5s. *Edition only.*

Liddon.—Works by HENRY PARRY LIDDON, D.D., D.C.L., LL.D., late Canon Residentiary and Chancellor of St. Paul's.

THE DIVINITY OF OUR LORD AND SAVIOUR JESUS CHRIST. Being the Bampton Lectures for 1866. *Crown 8vo. 5s.*

ADVENT IN ST. PAUL'S. Sermons bearing chiefly on the Two Comings of our Lord. *Two Vols. Crown 8vo. 5s. each. Cheap edition in one Volume. Crown 8vo. 5s.*

CHRISTMASTIDE IN ST. PAUL'S. Sermons bearing chiefly on the Birth of our Lord and the End of the Year. *Crown 8vo. 5s.*

PASSIONTIDE IN ST. PAUL'S. Sermons bearing chiefly on the Passion of our Lord. *Crown 8vo. 5s.*

EASTER IN ST. PAUL'S. Sermons bearing chiefly on the Resurrection of our Lord. *Two Vols. Crown 8vo. 5s. each. Cheap Edition in one Volume. Crown 8vo. 5s.*

SERMONS PREACHED BEFORE THE UNIVERSITY OF OXFORD. *Two Vols. Crown 8vo. 5s. each. Cheap Edition in one Volume. Crown 8vo. 5s.*

THE MAGNIFICAT. Sermons in St. Paul's. *Crown 8vo. 2s. 6d.*

SOME ELEMENTS OF RELIGION. Lent Lectures. *Small 8vo. 2s. 6d.; or in Paper Cover, 1s. 6d.*
The Crown 8vo Edition (5s.) may still be had.

SELECTIONS FROM THE WRITINGS OF H. P. LIDDON, D.D. *Crown 8vo. 3s. 6d.*

MAXIMS AND GLEANINGS FROM THE WRITINGS OF H. P. LIDDON, D.D. Selected and arranged by C. M. S. *Crown 16mo. 2s.*

Littlehales.—Works Edited by HENRY LTTLEHALES.

A FOURTEENTH CENTURY PRAYER BOOK: being Pages in Facsimile from a Layman's Prayer Book in English about 1400 A.D. *4to. 3s. 6d.*

THE PRYMER OR PRAYER-BOOK OF THE LAY PEOPLE IN THE MIDDLE AGES. In English, dating about 1400 A.D. Part I. Text. *Royal 8vo. 5s.*

Luckock.—Works by HERBERT MORTIMER LUCKOCK, D.D., Canon of Ely.

AFTER DEATH. An Examination of the Testimony of Primitive Times respecting the State of the Faithful Dead, and their Relationship to the Living. *Crown 8vo. 6s.*

THE INTERMEDIATE STATE BETWEEN DEATH AND JUDGMENT. Being a Sequel to *After Death*. *Crown 8vo. 6s.*

FOOTPRINTS OF THE SON OF MAN, as traced by St. Mark. Being Eighty Portions for Private Study, Family Reading, and Instructions in Church. *Two Vols. Crown 8vo. 12s. Cheap Edition in one Vol. Crown 8vo. 5s.*

[*continued.*

Luckock.—Works by HERBERT MORTIMER LUCKOCK, D.D., Canon of Ely—*continued.*

THE DIVINE LITURGY. Being the Order for Holy Communion, Historically, Doctrinally, and Devotionally set forth, in Fifty Portions. *Crown 8vo. 6s.*

STUDIES IN THE HISTORY OF THE BOOK OF COMMON PRAYER. The Anglican Reform—The Puritan Innovations—The Elizabethan Reaction—The Caroline Settlement. With Appendices. *Crown 8vo. 6s.*

THE BISHOPS IN THE TOWER. A Record of Stirring Events affecting the Church and Nonconformists from the Restoration to the Revolution. *Crown 8vo. 6s.*

LYRA APOSTOLICA. Poems by J. W. BOWDEN, R. H. FROUDE, J. KEBLE, J. H. NEWMAN, R. I. WILBERFORCE, and I. WILLIAMS; and New Preface by CARDINAL NEWMAN. 16mo. *2s. 6d.*

LYRA GERMANICA. Hymns translated from the German by CATHERINE WINKWORTH. *Small 8vo. 5s.*

MacColl.—CHRISTIANITY IN RELATION TO SCIENCE AND MORALS. By the Rev. MALCOLM MACCOLL, M.A., Canon Residentiary of Ripon. *Crown 8vo. 6s.*

Mason.—Works by A. J. MASON, D.D., formerly Fellow of Trinity College, Cambridge.

THE FAITH OF THE GOSPEL. A Manual of Christian Doctrine. *Crown 8vo. 7s. 6d. Large-Paper Edition for Marginal Notes. 4to. 12s. 6d.*

THE RELATION OF CONFIRMATION TO BAPTISM. As taught by the Western Fathers. A Study in the History of Doctrine. *Crown 8vo.*

Mercier.—Works by Mrs. JEROME MERCIER.

OUR MOTHER CHURCH: being Simple Talk on High Topics. *Small 8vo. 3s. 6d.*

THE STORY OF SALVATION: or, Thoughts on the Historic Study of the Bible. *Small 8vo. 3s. 6d.*

Moberly.—Works by GEORGE MOBERLY, D.C.L., late Bishop of Salisbury.

PLAIN SERMONS. Preached at Brighstone. *Crown 8vo. 5s.*

THE SAYINGS OF THE GREAT FORTY DAYS, between the Resurrection and Ascension, regarded as the Outlines of the Kingdom of God. In Five Discourses. *Crown 8vo. 5s.*

PAROCHIAL SERMONS. Mostly preached at Brighstone. *Crown 8vo. 7s. 6d.*

SERMONS PREACHED AT WINCHESTER COLLEGE. *Two Vols. Small 8vo. 6s. 6d. each.*

Mozley.—Works by J. B. MOZLEY, D.D., late Canon of Christ Church, and Regius Professor of Divinity at Oxford.

ESSAYS, HISTORICAL AND THEOLOGICAL. *Two Vols.* 8vo. 24s.

EIGHT LECTURES ON MIRACLES. Being the Bampton Lectures for 1865. *Crown 8vo.* 7s. 6d.

RULING IDEAS IN EARLY AGES AND THEIR RELATION TO OLD TESTAMENT FAITH. Lectures delivered to Graduates of the University of Oxford. 8vo. 10s. 6d.

SERMONS PREACHED BEFORE THE UNIVERSITY OF OXFORD, and on Various Occasions. *Crown 8vo.* 7s. 6d.

SERMONS, PAROCHIAL AND OCCASIONAL. *Crown 8vo.* 7s. 6d.

Mozley.—Works by the Rev. T. MOZLEY, M.A., Author of 'Reminiscences of Oriel College and the Oxford Movement.'

THE WORD. *Crown 8vo.* 7s. 6d.

LETTERS FROM ROME ON THE OCCASION OF THE ŒCUMENICAL COUNCIL 1869-1870. *Two Vols.* Cr. 8vo. 18s.

Newbolt.—Works by the Rev. W. C. E. NEWBOLT, Canon Residentiary of St. Paul's.

THE FRUIT OF THE SPIRIT. Being Ten Addresses bearing on the Spiritual Life. *Crown 8vo.* 2s. 6d.

THE MAN OF GOD. Being Six Addresses delivered during Lent 1886, at the Primary Ordination of the Right Rev. the Lord Alwyne Compton, Bishop of Ely. *Small 8vo.* 1s. 6d.

COUNSELS OF FAITH AND PRACTICE. Being Sermons preached on Various Occasions. 8vo. 7s. 6d.

THE VOICE OF THE PRAYER BOOK. Being Spiritual Addresses bearing on the Book of Common Prayer. *Crown 8vo.* 2s. 6d.

Newnham.—THE ALL-FATHER : Sermons preached in a Village Church. By the Rev. H. P. NEWNHAM. With Preface by EDNA LYALL. *Crown 8vo.* 4s. 6d.

Newman.—Works by JOHN HENRY NEWMAN, B.D. (Cardinal Newman), formerly Vicar of St. Mary's, Oxford.

PAROCHIAL AND PLAIN SERMONS. *Eight Vols. Cabinet Edition. Crown 8vo.* 5s. *each. Popular Edition. Eight Vols. Crown 8vo.* 3s. 6d. *each.*

[*continued.*

IN THEOLOGICAL LITERATURE. 13

Newman.—Works by JOHN HENRY NEWMAN, B.D. (Cardinal Newman), formerly Vicar of St. Mary's, Oxford—*continued.*

SELECTION, ADAPTED TO THE SEASONS OF THE ECCLE-SIASTICAL YEAR, from the 'Parochial and Plain Sermons.' *Crown 8vo. 5s.*

FIFTEEN SERMONS PREACHED BEFORE THE UNIVERSITY OF OXFORD, between A.D. 1826 and 1843. *Crown 8vo. 5s.*

SERMONS BEARING UPON SUBJECTS OF THE DAY. *Crown 8vo. 5s.*

LECTURES ON THE DOCTRINE OF JUSTIFICATION. *Crown 8vo. 5s.*

** For the Catholic Works of Cardinal Newman, see Messrs. Longmans & Co.'s Catalogue of Works in General Literature.

THE LETTERS AND CORRESPONDENCE OF JOHN HENRY NEWMAN DURING HIS LIFE IN THE ENGLISH CHURCH. With a Brief Autobiographical Memoir. Arranged and Edited by ANNE MOZLEY. *Two Vols. 8vo. 30s. net.*

Osborne.—Works by EDWARD OSBORNE, Mission Priest of the Society of St. John the Evangelist, Cowley, Oxford.

THE CHILDREN'S SAVIOUR. Instructions to Children on the Life of our Lord and Saviour Jesus Christ. *Illustrated. 16mo. 3s. 6d.*

THE SAVIOUR-KING. Instructions to Children on Old Testament Types and Illustrations of the Life of Christ. *Illustrated. 16mo. 3s. 6d.*

THE CHILDREN'S FAITH. Instructions to Children on the Apostles' Creed. *With Illustrations. 16mo. 3s. 6d.*

Oxenden.—Works by the Right Rev. ASHTON OXENDEN, formerly Bishop of Montreal.

THE PATHWAY OF SAFETY; or, Counsel to the Awakened. *Fcap. 8vo, large type. 2s. 6d. Cheap Edition. Small type, limp. 1s.*

THE EARNEST COMMUNICANT. Common Edition. *32mo. 1s.* New Red Rubric Edition. *32mo. 2s.*

OUR CHURCH AND HER SERVICES. *Fcap. 8vo. 2s. 6d.*

FAMILY PRAYERS FOR FOUR WEEKS. First Series. *Fcap. 8vo. 2s. 6d.* Second Series. *Fcap. 8vo. 2s. 6d.*

LARGE TYPE EDITION. Two Series in one Volume. *Crown 8vo. 6s.*

COTTAGE SERMONS; or, Plain Words to the Poor. *Fcap. 8vo. 2s. 6d.*

THOUGHTS FOR HOLY WEEK. *16mo. 1s. 6d.*

DECISION. *18mo. 1s. 6d.*

[*continued.*

Oxenden.—Works by the Right Rev. ASHTON OXENDEN, formerly Bishop of Montreal—*continued.*

THE HOME BEYOND; or, A Happy Old Age. *Fcap. 8vo.* 1s. 6d.

THE LABOURING MAN'S BOOK. 18mo, *large type, cloth.* 1s. 6d.

CONFIRMATION. 18mo, *cloth.* 9d.; sewed, 3d.; or 2s. 6d. *per dozen.*

COUNSELS TO THOSE WHO HAVE BEEN CONFIRMED; or, Now is the Time to serve Christ. 18mo, *cloth.* 1s.

THE LORD'S SUPPER SIMPLY EXPLAINED. 18mo, *cloth.* 1s. Cheap Edition. Paper. 6d.

PRAYERS FOR PRIVATE USE. 32mo, *cloth.* 1s.

WORDS OF PEACE; or, The Blessings of Sickness. 16mo, *cloth.* 1s.

Paget.—Works by the Rev. FRANCIS PAGET, D.D., Canon of Christ Church, and Regius Professor of Pastoral Theology.

THE SPIRIT OF DISCIPLINE: Sermons. *Crown 8vo.*

FACULTIES AND DIFFICULTIES FOR BELIEF AND DISBELIEF. *Crown 8vo.* 6s. 6d.

THE HALLOWING OF WORK. Addresses given at Eton, January 16-18, 1888. *Small 8vo.* 2s.

PRACTICAL REFLECTIONS. By a CLERGYMAN. With Prefaces by H. P. LIDDON, D.D., D.C.L. *Crown 8vo.*

    Vol. I.—THE HOLY GOSPELS. 4s. 6d.
    Vol. II.—ACTS TO REVELATION. 6s.
    THE PSALMS. 5s.

PRIEST (THE) TO THE ALTAR; Or, Aids to the Devout Celebration of Holy Communion, chiefly after the Ancient English Use of Sarum. *Royal 8vo.* 12s.

Pusey.—Works by the late Rev. E. B. PUSEY, D.D.

MAXIMS AND GLEANINGS FROM THE WRITINGS OF EDWARD BOUVERIE PUSEY, D.D. Selected and Arranged for Daily Use. By C. M. S. *Crown 16mo.* 2s.

PRIVATE PRAYERS. With Preface by H. P. LIDDON, D.D. 32mo. 2s. 6d.

PRAYERS FOR A YOUNG SCHOOLBOY. Edited, with a Preface, by H. P. LIDDON, D.D. 24mo. 1s.

SELECTIONS FROM THE WRITINGS OF EDWARD BOUVERIE PUSEY, D.D. *Crown 8vo.* 3s. 6d.

IN THEOLOGICAL LITERATURE. 15

Richmond.—CHRISTIAN ECONOMICS. By the Rev. WILFRID RICHMOND, M.A., sometime Warden of Trinity College, Glenalmond. *Crown 8vo. 6s.*

Sanday.—THE ORACLES OF GOD: Nine Lectures on the Nature and Extent of Biblical Inspiration and the Special Significance of the Old Testament Scriptures at the Present Time. By W. SANDAY, M.A., D.D., LL.D. *Crown 8vo. 4s.*

Seebohm.—THE OXFORD REFORMERS—JOHN COLET, ERASMUS, AND THOMAS MORE: A History of their Fellow-Work. By FREDERICK SEEBOHM. *8vo. 14s.*

Stephen.—ESSAYS IN ECCLESIASTICAL BIOGRAPHY. By the Right Hon. Sir J. STEPHEN. *Crown 8vo. 7s. 6d.*

Swayne.—THE BLESSED DEAD IN PARADISE. Four All Saints' Day Sermons, preached in Salisbury Cathedral. By ROBERT G. SWAYNE, M.A. *Crown 8vo. 3s. 6d.*

Tweddell.—THE SOUL IN CONFLICT. A Practical Examination of some Difficulties and Duties of the Spiritual Life. By MARSHALL TWEDDELL, M.A., Vicar of St. Saviour, Paddington. *Crown 8vo. 6s.*

Twells.—COLLOQUIES ON PREACHING. By HENRY TWELLS, M.A., Honorary Canon of Peterborough *Crown 8vo. 5s.*

Wakeman.—THE HISTORY OF RELIGION IN ENGLAND. By HENRY OFFLEY WAKEMAN, M.A. *Small 8vo. 1s. 6d.*

Welldon. — THE FUTURE AND THE PAST. Sermons preached to Harrow Boys. (*First Series*, 1885 *and* 1886.) By the Rev. J. E. C. WELLDON, M.A., Head Master of Harrow School. *Crown 8vo. 7s. 6d.*

Williams.—Works by the Rev. ISAAC WILLIAMS, B.D., formerly Fellow of Trinity College, Oxford.

A DEVOTIONAL COMMENTARY ON THE GOSPEL NARRATIVE. *Eight Vols. Crown 8vo. 5s. each. Sold separately.*

THOUGHTS ON THE STUDY OF THE HOLY GOSPELS.
A HARMONY OF THE FOUR GOSPELS.
OUR LORD'S NATIVITY.
OUR LORD'S MINISTRY (Second Year).

OUR LORD'S MINISTRY (Third Year).
THE HOLY WEEK.
OUR LORD'S PASSION.
OUR LORD'S RESURRECTION.

[continued.

Williams.—Works by the Rev. ISAAC WILLIAMS, B.D., formerly Fellow of Trinity College, Oxford—*continued.*

FEMALE CHARACTERS OF HOLY SCRIPTURE. A Series of Sermons. *Crown 8vo.* 5s.

THE CHARACTERS OF THE OLD TESTAMENT. A Series of Sermons. *Crown 8vo.* 5s.

THE APOCALYPSE. With Notes and Reflections. *Crown 8vo.* 5s.

SERMONS ON THE EPISTLES AND GOSPELS FOR THE SUNDAYS AND HOLY DAYS THROUGHOUT THE YEAR. *Two Vols. Crown 8vo.* 5s. *each.*

PLAIN SERMONS ON THE CATECHISM. *Two Vols. Crown 8vo.* 5s. *each.*

SELECTIONS FROM THE WRITINGS OF ISAAC WILLIAMS, B.D. *Crown 8vo.* 3s. 6d.

Woodford.—Works by JAMES RUSSELL WOODFORD, D.D., sometime Lord Bishop of Ely.

THE GREAT COMMISSION. Twelve Addresses on the Ordinal. Edited, with an Introduction on the Ordinations of his Episcopate, by HERBERT MORTIMER LUCKOCK, D.D. *Crown 8vo.* 5s.

SERMONS ON OLD AND NEW TESTAMENT SUBJECTS. Edited by HERBERT MORTIMER LUCKOCK, D.D. *Two Vols. Crown 8vo.* 5s. *each.*

Wordsworth.—Works by ELIZABETH WORDSWORTH, Principal of Lady Margaret Hall, Oxford.

ILLUSTRATIONS OF THE CREED. *Crown 8vo.* 5s.

ELIZABETH AND OTHER POEMS. *Crown 8vo.* 6s.

Younghusband.—Works by FRANCES YOUNGHUSBAND.

THE STORY OF OUR LORD, told in Simple Language for Children. With 25 Illustrations on Wood from Pictures by the Old Masters, and numerous Ornamental Borders, Initial Letters, etc., from Longmans' New Testament. *Crown 8vo.* 2s. 6d.

THE STORY OF GENESIS, told in Simple Language for Children. *Crown 8vo.* 2s. 6d.

Printed by T. and A. CONSTABLE, Printers to Her Majesty, at the Edinburgh University Press.

www.ingramcontent.com/pod-product-compliance
Lightning Source LLC
Chambersburg PA
CBHW030737230426
43667CB00007B/743